Empire and Inequality

Cultural Politics & the Promise of Democracy
Henry A. Giroux, Series Editor

Empire and Inequality: America and the World Since 9/11
    by Paul Street

The Terror of Neoliberalism
    by Henry A. Giroux

Forthcoming
Reading and Writing for Civic Literacy: The Critical Citizen's Guide to Argumentative Rhetoric
    by Donald Lazere

Schooling and the Struggle for Public Life, Second Edition
    by Henry A. Giroux

Kids in the Crossfire
    by Lawrence Grossberg

Reading French Feminism
    by Michael Payne

Listening Beyond the Echoes: Agency and Ethics in a Mediated World
    by Nick Couldry

EMPIRE AND INEQUALITY
America and the World
Since 9/11

PAUL STREET

Paradigm Publishers
Boulder • London

Copyright © 2004 by Paul Street

Published in the United States by Paradigm Publishers, 3360 Mitchell Lane Suite C, Boulder, Colorado 80301 USA.

Paradigm Publishers is the trade name of Birkenkamp & Company, LLC, Dean Birkenkamp, President and Publisher.
ISBN 1-59451-059-8 (pbk)
ISBN 1-59451-058-X (cloth)

Library of Congress Cataloging-in-Publication Data
has been applied for.

Printed and bound in the United States of America on acid-free paper that meets the standards of the American National Standard for Permanence of Paper for Printed Library Materials.

Designed and Typeset by Straight Creek Bookmakers.

09   08   07   06   05   04
5   4   3   2   1

Contents

Contents

Contents

Prologue

The left-democratic and antiwar essays collected in this volume find their most immediate origin in the horrific events of September 11, 2001, or, more accurately, in the American "power elite's" response to those events. Within a week of the terrible jetliner attacks, I was invited to speak about their meaning and implications at a teach-in coordinated by a student peace and justice organization at Northern Illinois University. In a talk titled "On 'Waking Up' and 'Losing Our Innocence' in the Wake of the September 11th Terror Attacks," I claimed that the terrible events were "a great gift to the right wing in this country." Unless checked by a determined citizenry, I argued, the in-power American right, which has been falsely labeled "conservative" (it seeks to *radically* exacerbate inequality, repression, and concentration of wealth power at home and abroad), was going to use 9/11 to divert massive public resources from meeting social needs to the expansion of the already overfed and bloated military-industrial complex. In the process, I argued, those in power would roll back civil liberties and advance policies intended to increase the already-grotesque overconcentration of wealth and power in the United States, the industrialized world's most economically unequal nation. Nine-eleven, I argued, was a great opportunity for concentrated economic and political power to advance intimately related projects of empire and war abroad and inequality and repression at home. In the end, the tragedy would serve to legitimize a dangerous and illegitimate president who was captive to multinational petroleum and military corporations whose policies were largely to blame for the Middle Eastern quagmire that gave rise to 9/11. It is "the structurally encoded role of the mainstream corporate media," I added, "to discourage Americans from really thinking about these and other things. These media are owned by a small number of gigantic corporations with all kinds of links to those petroleum and defense firms. One of those corporate-media-military giants (Brokaw's NBC) is in fact owned by the world's largest defense contractor—General Electric. On the basis less of some sort of 'conspiracy' than of basic authoritarian structural and institutional self-interest, it is the job of our media-military-industrial complex to whip us into a war fever." When "war machines move into gear," I concluded, "ordinary people die en masse, rich folks get richer, and politicians restrict civil liberties."[1]

The warnings I offered were not particularly original. Nonetheless, they have proved all-too accurate in the two and one-half years since 9/11. In fact, those warnings have provided essential background for many of the numerous articles and commentaries I've written since 9/11, a portion of which appear with small editorial changes and new annotations in this volume.[2]

The essays collected as individual chapters in this book were written between September 11, 2001, and September of 2003. Most of them originally appeared on *ZNet*, a left site to which I still contribute on a regular basis. They reflect one US citizen's horrified reflections on the in-power US right wing's determination and ability to use the terrible jetliner attacks of 9/11 as a windfall opportunity to advance intimately interrelated projects of empire and inequality at home and abroad. They were written before a number of significant developments of great relevance to those projects:

The grisly murder in April 2004 of four American mercenaries in Fallujah, Iraq, followed by a significant uprising of Sunni Muslims in Iraq, which caused the death of eighty US Marines and led to a bloody US repression that killed hundreds of Iraqis.

The April 2004 anti-occupation rebellion of Iraqi Shiites, under the banner of the young Shiite cleric Moktada al-Sadr, which combined with the Sunni insurgency to make April 2004 the bloodiest month for US troops since the initial invasion of Iraq.

The monumental scandal that emerged in May 2004 over US abuse and torture of Iraqi prisoners in Abu Ghraib and other US detention facilities in Iraq.

The removal in February 2004 of Haiti's democratically elected President Jean Baptiste Aristide, flown to Africa in a US military plane and replaced by brutal and authoritarian forces considered more sympathetic to "US interests."

The December 2003 U.S. capture and subsequent public disappearance of former US client Saddam Hussein.

The Islamic-terrorist train bombing in Madrid, Spain in March 2004 followed by the electoral defeat of Spain's Prime Minister José Maria Anzar and the decision of his Socialist successor to remove Spanish troops from occupied Iraq.

The mainstream US media's general acknowledgment that the Bush administration made false claims about Saddam Hussein's possession of weapons of mass destruction (WMD).

The emergence in March 2004 of former Bush II counterterrorism czar Richard A. Clarke as a leading critic of the Bush administration's decision to give priority to the imperial war on Iraq over the protection of Americans from al-Qaeda and other extremist Islamic terror networks.

The publication in March 2004 of Clarke's stinging anti-Bush exposé *Against All Enemies* and the publication in April 2004 of Bob Woodward's *Plan of Attack*, both of which detailed key aspects of Bush's leap from the war on al Qaeda to the war on Iraq.

The publication of of CIA analyst "Anonymous'" heretical *Imperial Hubris: Why the West is Losing the War on Terror* (Washington, DC, 0204), which argued that al Quaeda and others Islamist terror networks attack Americans and the US for "what we [Americans and the US] do" in the Middle East (project empire by "Anonymous'" account rather than "for what we are and what we think." The emergence of open acknowledgment within the United States that the occupation of Iraq had turned into a fiasco, significantly analogous to Vietnam.

The initially promising rise of Howard Dean's maverick anti-war primary campaign and the subsequent selection of the distinctly imperial and non-populist John F. Kerry as the Democratic presidential candidate for 2004.

The issuance in June 2004 of the report of the National Commission on Terrorist Attacks upon the United States, which contravened White House propaganda by finding that there was no "collaborative relationship" between Iraq and al Qaeda before or during 9/11.

The US State Department's acknowledgment in June 2004 that acts of terror worldwide increased in number during the year of America's invasion of Iraq.

The United States release in late June 2004 of Michael Moore's anti-Bush movie, *Fahrenheit 9/11*, which ridiculed the Bush administration's march to war on Iraq and included at least some key themes that strongly match the argument presented in my political writing.

The handing over of merely nominal national "sovereignty" from the US-dominated Coalition Provisional Authority to interim Iraq Prime Minister Iyad Allawi on June 28, 2004.

I find these developments richly consistent with the analysis presented in the writings collected in *Empire and Inequality*. Readers who wish to see some of my reflections on events after the summer of 2003 are encouraged to visit *ZNet's* running record of my *ZNet* publications at: *http://www.zmag.* org/Zbios.htm (search author by name).

* * *

Looking back on the writings included in this volume, I see six basic if interrelated themes. Although these are connected in essential and obvious ways, I consider each distinct enough to provide a unique vantage point from which to scrutinize the overarching issue of 9/11 and its impact on US and global power structures. The first theme, already suggested, might be called "Our Tears, Their Opportunity." Essays working with this idea show various ways in which the Bush administration and its allies seized on 9/11 to exacerbate preexisting tendencies toward global and domestic US hierarchy, inequality, and repression.

A second theme might be called "Empire Abroad, Inequality and Repression at Home." It could also be called, to use the title of an article I published on racial discrimination in the job market, "How You Gonna Export Something You Ain't Even Got at Home?" or, to use another recent title, "The Repair of 'Broken Societies' Begins at Home."[3] Essays working with this notion hold America's domestic society up to an unflattering mirror, questioning our "leaders' " qualifications to lecture the rest of the world about "democracy," "freedom," and general societal health either before or after 9/11. Noting such disturbing facts as America's astoundingly high criminal incarceration rates—which are unmatched anywhere else in the world— these essays mock and deconstruct Texas Senator Kay Bailey Hutchison's claim, made in October 2002, that the United States is a special, God- and/ or History-ordained "beacon to the world of the way life should be."[4]

However, the point of these writings is not merely to discredit the tendentious propositions of those who justify the US global empire by conjuring distorted and embarrassingly false visions of democracy at home. If the writings collected in this volume possess a master motif, it is the intimate interconnection between empire abroad and inequality (and repression) at home. If nothing else, I consider it essential to highlight the relationship, inseparable and self-reinforcing, between American domestic inequality and "homeland" repression, on the one hand, and American imperialism, on the other.

A third theme might be called "The Respectable Right and the Real Threat to Liberal Democracy." It frames post–September 11 developments in terms of a thesis advanced by the late Australian social critic and leftist political analyst Alex Carey. In his aptly titled book *Taking the Risk Out of Democracy* (1986), Carey argued that the most relevant long-term threat to liberal democracy in the West has never come from external state totalitarians of either the Stalinist "left" or the fascist right. It has come instead from the homegrown, business-connected "Respectable Right" that arose within the liberal-democratic West—most dramatically and powerfully in the US—to protect corporate power from its natural homeland antagonist: the popular democratic tradition.[5] I find Carey's argument exceedingly relevant to recent US policy and history.

A fourth theme might be called "Straw Dogs." Through it I criticize various fabricated threats and false enemies created and exploited primarily (though not exclusively) by the American right in the wake of 9/11. The concocted Evil Others include Islamic extremists who "hate America" because of its "freedom and democracy"; "moral-relativist" liberal-left academics and intellectuals who teach hatred of America and promote support for terrorism; and a supposedly "ungrateful" nation called France, which has been singled out for "sabotaging" America's supposedly noble war on terrorism. (This bizarre obsession with French "anti-Americanism" took center stage even as governments across the globe registered protests and criticisms of US policy not qualitatively different from those made by Chirac and his ministers.) The most classic and historically significant invocations of the Evil Others motif came, of course, with the rush to "war" on Iraq, when the Bush team dramatically accelerated the assembly lines of mass deception, creating ludicrous levels of officially sanctioned nonsense about the horrible threats supposedly posed by Saddam Hussein and his degraded regime. The Bush party sought domestic political dividends from all this claptrap, using the "war on terror" as cover for plutocratic and authoritarian assaults on homeland society, security, and civil liberties. Developments in post–September 11 America have given rich testimony to the wisdom of a comment made by James Madison, who in 1799 noted that the "the fetters imposed on liberty at home have ever been forged out of the weapons provided for defense against real, pretended, or imaginary dangers abroad."[6]

A fifth theme finds its inspiration in the second chapter, titled "Worthy and Unworthy Victims," from Noam Chomsky and Ed Herman's path-breaking *Manufacturing Consent: The Political Economy of the Mass Media*, published as the Cold War was nearing its partial conclusion with the collapse of the Soviet deterrent to American globalism. "A propaganda system," the authors note, "will consistently portray people abused in enemy states as worthy victims, whereas those treated with equal or greater severity by its own government or clients will be unworthy."[7] Many essays in the present volume maintain that this key distinction between "worthy" and "unworthy" victims—and the analytical "propaganda model" that informs it—continues to hold relevance in the "post–Cold War" and post–September 11 eras. It applies to American as well as overseas victims.

A sixth theme might be called "The Myth of the Powerless State." Is it true that, as many observers claim, the American public sector lacks the resources and wherewithal to carry out key objectives? No, I answer, pointing out that the American state remains powerful and capable when it comes to serving the needs of wealth, racial disparity, corporate globalization, and empire. Government is inadequate and cash-poor only when it comes to addressing the social and democratic needs of the nonaffluent majority. Under the pressure of a relentless campaign of top-down class, racial, and ideological warfare, I argue, the public sector is being stripped of its positive social and democratic functions. It is increasingly reduced to its policing and repressive functions, which are expanding in ways that are more than merely coincidental to the assault on social supports and programs. To use the terminology of the late French intellectual Pierre Bourdieu, the left (social, egalitarian, peaceful, and democratic) hand of the state is wilting, but the right (repressive, militaristic, authoritarian, and regressive) hand is growing stronger by the day, a preexisting trend deeply reinforced by 9/11.[8]

* * *

Not surprisingly, the main targets of these essays are located at the center and right of the ideological spectrum. In a few cases, however, my critical aim falls more to the left. One major article reproduced in part I ("Toward a 'Decent Left'?") is directed at pundits of the so-called liberal left (recently termed the "cruise-missile left" by Edward S. Herman), who saw 9/11 as an opportunity to advance beyond their own marginal status by tarring the "hard left" with scandalously false charges. The article defends consistently democratic leftists like Chomsky, Howard Zinn, Mike Albert, and John Pilger against unsupportable and frankly thuggish accusations made against them in the wake of 9/11 by well-placed "progressives" like Michael Walzer, Jeffrey Issacs, and Todd Gitlin, among others. In a separate essay ("Misunderstanding Power," also in part I), I address another group that has exploited the 9/11 tragedy to promote a chimerical rendition of reality: the crackpot conspiracy theorists who claim allegiance to a radical agenda. Here, I attempt to demonstrate how they read post–September 11 history backward and miss the structural and institutional bases of power. In perhaps a related vein, another essay ("It's the Empire, Stupid," in part II) engages those generally kindred left spirits who felt or at least worried that organizing against the war on Iraq was an unwelcome diversion from the important task of expanding the "antiglobalization" (really global justice) movement. Consistent with the sixth core theme mentioned above, this essay criticizes leftists who see the state as having become irrelevant in the face of hegemonic market forces and corporate globalization. Like Chomsky, John Pilger, and others on the radical-democratic left, I see state power and related global militarism as centrally relevant to the operation of the capitalist system at home and abroad. Despite the myriad changes that have restructured aspects of the US and global economic order since the 1970s, the underlying structure remains *state capitalism*, replete with the standard complement of imperial militarism. At the end of the day, capitalist "economic globalization" is "a project as old as gunboats," as Pilger once noted.[9]

* * *

Much of the writing collected here took place in a social policy research office in Chicago's South Side black ghetto. In the neighborhood surrounding this office and in many other predominantly black communities on the city's South and West Sides, a large number of teen and younger adult males are completely disconnected from both school and the job market.[10] Many of them are active members of gang organizations and engaged in the narcotics trade. Many have already served—or will soon serve—as raw material for the city, state, and nation's burgeoning prison-industrial complex.[11]

Older unemployed males, many unrecorded in the nation's official unemployment statistics (their "discouraged" status means they are no longer actively participating in the labor force), congregate around liquor stores and missions. The endemic stress, disappointment, and danger of inner-city life are etched on their faces. Equally evident is the relative absence of retail facilities, services, and institutions that are standard in richer, whiter neighborhoods: full-service modern grocery stores, drugstores, bookstores, restaurants, doctors, dentists, lawyers, dry-cleaners, banks, personal investment and family insurance stores, boutiques, coffee shops, and many others. Businesses and homes are visibly dilapidated, with many business owners relying on hand-painted signs to advertise their wares. Local business owners, many of whom are Arab, protect their enterprises from burglary with bars and gated shutters. Pawnshops and austere storefront churches are widely visible, as are liquor stores and currency exchanges advertising super-exploitative payday loans. Taxicabs are scarce, and those that do serve the neighborhoods are generally with low-budget, fly-by-night "jitney" firms.

The few whites seen in these neighborhoods are males working in traditional working-class jobs, such as street and sewer repair, construction trades, fire fighting, and the like. These are jobs that appear to be unavailable and off-limits to the African Americans who call these barren landscapes home. Police cars cruise warily, their urban gendarme occupants donning bulletproof vests deemed necessary in waging the war on drugs in neighborhoods where people with felony records outnumber those with legitimate (i.e., legal) jobs. Along with the parole agent and the correctional officer, these representatives of the state's right hand are increasingly the most recognizable faces of the public sector encountered by the younger residents of the inner city.

This is pretty much how these neighborhoods looked and felt before 9/11, when, according to a great national myth propagated by the in-power respectable right wing, "everything changed." Since 9/11, the core continuities of human suffering and hopelessness here have been accelerated and intensified. Things have gotten worse at a quickened pace, thanks in large part to the racially disparate joblessness of the current economic "recovery." Also part of the unpleasant equation is 9/11 itself, or, more accurately, the official, right-led public and media response to the terror attacks. Nine-eleven gave the Bush junta—falsely labeled conservative—a precious chance to divert public attention from the causes and consequences of urban inequality and to starve, cripple, and preempt programs that might alleviate the suffering caused by racism and related socioeconomic inequality. In large measure, they have been successful at promoting this agenda because they have been able to equate dissent with treason. America's masters of war and empire at home and abroad seized on this opening with all deliberate speed, consistent with the timeworn conduct of concentrated power since long before "everything" supposedly (according to standard American conventional wisdom) "changed" on 9/11. Empire abroad has always been both a reflection and an agent of inequality and repression at home. The rhetoric of 9/11 notwithstanding, this reality has not changed.

The widespread poverty, repression, and misery that have been relentlessly visible to me outside my office (not to mention the disturbing socioeconomic data that have regularly crossed my desk before and after 9/11) provide a curiously ironic setting from which to observe the architects of American policy and opinion proclaim their special God- and/or History-ordained capacity, prerogative, and duty to right the world's wrongs.[12]

* * *

If I have any regret about these writings, it is that they do not say more about solutions and alternatives. The main obstacle to a progressive movement for peace, democracy, and social justice, I increasingly suspect, is not mass loyalty to the dominant institutions and their rulers. It is instead traceable to the neo-liberal, corporate-imposed erosion of the social-democratic public spaces that once served as the forums in which communities and peoples debated, analyzed, and participated in political life. Indeed, we have witnessed in recent decades an unprecedented decline in popular engagement, the process by which common people asserted their interests and took responsibility for their common destiny. The result has been the privatization (consumerization) of American life, with its concomitant sense that social action and responsibility are futile propositions, stillborn by their very nature. There is a broad, deep, skeptical, even cynical sense that nothing much can be done about existing social problems—"The Wheel in the Sky Keeps on Turning"—and that the only reasonable solutions to societal difficulties are to be found in private realms, matters of purely personal correction. The world has grown too complex—too ossified—to be subject to meaningful collective agency. This sense—which I worry may be reinforced by my criticism of existing social institutions—masks despair as "realism" and retreat from democracy and social responsibility as mature personal "adjustment."

To counter it, we need a vision of the future that is both idealistic and pragmatic in its design—idealistic in the sense that it offers the promise of greater democracy and equality to all peoples, and pragmatic in the sense that it is attainable and worth struggling for. We need to restore hope and possibility by devising a political and institutional road map for positive (and possible) societal transformation. Please, therefore, do not read these essays as excuses for retreat from the great public works of social justice and democracy that need to be undertaken if humanity is to survive this new century in a desirable and recognizable form. "There are many here among us," as Bob Dylan once wrote, "who feel that life is but a joke. But ... we've been through that and this is not our fate. Let us not talk falsely now," because "the hour is getting late."

These writings are relentlessly harsh in their criticism of existing dominant American institutions and the special, structurally rooted power of the privileged few. They are animated, however, by the belief that no worthy, desirable alternative to the current dispensation can be constructed except on the basis of the most ruthlessly honest analysis of current social reality. They are animated as well by the conviction that human beings are capable of mastering the social and political forces that have for so long mastered them.

Notes

1. "On 'Waking Up' and 'Losing Our Innocence' in the Wake of the September 11 Terror Attacks," posted September 19, 2001, at www.Zmag.org/ZNET.htm.

2. Most of the essays assembled in this collection were posted by ZNet (www.zmag.org), an excellent and truly global and left-democratic website created and managed by the prolific left intellectual and activist Mike Albert and handled also by their excellent site manager, Timberly Allen. Many of these essays were linked and some even translated by countless other websites (I gave up trying to keep track) around the world, eliciting hundreds of responses from across the planet. I am grateful to ZNet for publishing so much of my work and for generously permitting me to reproduce some of those writings in this volume.

3. Paul Street, "'How You Gonna Export Something You Ain't Even Got at Home?' Notes from Chicago," originally posted April 26, 2003, at *The Black Commentator* at www.blackcommentator.com; "The Repair of 'Broken Societies' Begins at Home," *ZNet Magazine* (July 18, 2003), available online at http://www.zmag.org/content/showarticle.cfm?SectionID=40&ItemID=3928.

4. Paul Street, "Beacon to the World," *ZNet Magazine* (October 18, 2002), available online at www.zmag.org and http://www.outlookindia.com/scriptur11w2.asp?act=sign&url=/full.asp?fodname=20021023&fname=paulstreet&sid=1.

5. Alex Carey, *Taking the Risk Out of Democracy: Corporate Propaganda Versus Freedom and Liberty* (Urbana and Chicago: University of Illinois, 1997), pp. 11–17, 109–139.

6. James Madison, "Political Reflections" February 23, 1799, quoted in John Samples, "James Madison's Vision of Liberty," *CATO Policy Report* (March/April 2001), p. 12, available online at www.cato.org/pubs/policy_report/v23n.2/madison.pdf.

7. Noam Chomsky and Ed Herman, *Manufacturing Consent: The Political Economy of the Mass Media* (New York: Pantheon, 1988), p. 37.

8. Pierre Bourdieu, *Acts of Resistance* (New York: Free Press, 1998), p. 2. Variations on this theme can also be found in John Pilger, *The New Rulers of the World* (London: Verso, 2002), pp. 5, 116; and Boris Kargalitsky, "Facing the Crisis," *Links,* No. 1 (September–December 2001). See also Bourdieu's marvelous essay, "The 'Globalisation Myth' and the Welfare State," pp. 24–44 in *Acts of Resistance.*

9. John Pilger, "'Humanitarian Intervention' Is the Latest Brand Name of Imperialism," *The New Statesman* (June 28, 1999). For elaboration on this topic in the context of the American occupation of Iraq, see Paul Street, "Globalization from the Top Down," *ZNet Daily Commentaries* (September 21, 2003), available online at http://www.zmag.org/sustainers/content/2003-09/15street.cfm.

10. According to the Center for Labor Market Studies at Northeastern University, there were more than 97,000 "disconnected" youth (unattached youth out of school and the job market) in Chicago in early 2001. The number is surely well into six figures at present. See *Out of School, Out of Work: Jobless Youth in America* (Chicago: Alternative Schools Network, 2002); and *Giving Up the Race: Jobless Youth in Chicago* (Chicago: Alternative Schools Network, 2002).

11. Paul Street, *The Vicious Circle: Race, Prison, Jobs, and Community in Chicago, Illinois, and the Nation* (Chicago: Chicago Urban League, 2002), available online at www.cul-chicago.org (click on "Research Reports Available Online"); Paul Street, "Color Bind: Prisons and the New American Racism," *Dissent* (Summer 2001): 69–75; Paul Street, "Starve the Racist Prison Beast, *ZNet Magazine* (November 8, 2003), available online at http://www.zmag.org/content/showarticle.cfm?SectionID=43&ItemID=4471, reprinted in *Black Commentator,* Issue 65 (November 20, 2003), available online at www.blackcommentator.com; Paul Street, "Marriage as the Solution to Poverty: Bush's Proposal for Welfare Moms and the Real White House Agenda," *Z Magazine* (April 2002): 33–39.

12. The last five paragraphs draw heavily on Paul Street, "'Everything Changed?' Hidden Continuities of Urban Racial Inequality Before and After 9/11," *The Black Commentator,* Issue 55 (September 11, 2003), available online at http://www.blackcommentator.com/55/55_think_street.html.

PART I
Our Tears, Their Opportunity

The fetters imposed on liberty at home have ever been forged out of the weapons provided for defense against real, pretended, or imaginary dangers abroad.

—James Madison, 1799[1]

The process of transformation is likely to be a long one, absent some catastrophic and catalyzing event—like a new Pearl Harbor.

—Project for a New American Century, September 2000[2]

Today's terror attacks were major atrocities. . . . [T]hat this was a horrendous crime is not in doubt. The primary victims, as usual, were working people: janitors, secretaries, firemen, etc. It is likely to be a crushing blow to Palestinians and other poor and oppressed people. It is also likely to lead to harsh security controls, with many ramifications for undermining civil liberties and internal freedom. . . . In short, the crime is a gift to the hard jingoist right, those who hope to use force to control their domains. . . . The prospects ahead are even more ominous than they appeared to be before the latest atrocities.

—Noam Chomsky, September 12, 2001[3]

Think about "how do you capitalize on these opportunities?"
—Condoleezza Rice, White House National Security Adviser to the US National Security Council, September 12, 2001[4]

Through the tears of sadness, I see an opportunity.
—George W. Bush, September 14, 2001[5]

Introduction to Part I

My initial response to 9/11 combined shock, cynicism, and naiveté. *Shock:* at the sheer carnage, the horrifying audacity of zealots ready to die and kill en masse and the grisly spectacle of jetliners full of human beings exploding into flames; the twin towers disintegrating. *Cynicism:* in response to government and media authorities' claim of surprise at the occurrence of a major terror attack on the United States from the Arab world and especially at official claims that the attacks were motivated by hatred of the supposedly freedom-loving "American way of life." *Naiveté:* in believing that the tragedy could spawn either honest debate on the causes of such acts or policies to prevent them in the future.[6]

Though the shock is perhaps self-explanatory, a detailed exploration of my other responses to 9/11, and how those sentiments influenced my subsequent writings, might serve some purpose.

Within ten days of the attacks, President Bush told the US Congress that the enemies of the US were the "enemies of freedom." He amplified his point by posing a rhetorical question. "Americans are asking," Bush asserted, "'why do they hate us?'" In answering his own question, the president offered reassuring platitudes, leavened with a liberal dose of deception: "They hate our freedoms, our freedom of religion, our freedom to vote, and assemble and disagree with each other." To appreciate the level of dissimulation at work here, one need only consider the tens of thousands of African Americans in Florida who were illegally disenfranchised in the pivotal 2000 presidential election, more than enough to swing the outcome to favor Bush.[7]

But Bush was not the only one offering up platitudes and dissimulation to explain the unthinkable acts of 9/11. His explanations were echoed in myriad forms across the mainstream media. To cite but one example, *Chicago Tribune* columnist Stephen Chapman, writing one day after the attacks, opined that "America" had "become a target" because foreign tyrants and terrorists were threatened by and jealous of our superior, democratic "way of life." By Chapman's estimation, the core ingredients of that glorious American way were "prosperity," "happiness," "openness," "individualism," and "love of freedom" for "ordinary people."[8] Chapman, of course, was far from alone in asserting that the root cause of 9/11 was irrational hatred of American core values. His voice merged seamlessly into a nationwide chorus. Unfortunately, the facile explanations offered by Bush, Chapman, and countless others were intended not so much to elucidate causes as to reassure an arrogant nation that suddenly felt itself threatened by an "inexplicably" hostile world.

Actually, there was nothing surprising about an attack by zealots of Arab background on Washington, DC, and New York City. The motives behind the attack had little if anything to do with the terrorists' feeling about the nature of America's internal society. What most bothered them about America was its external policy in and around the chief area of the perpetrators' concern and ambition—the Middle East. In this the terrorists were not alone—Arabs of all political persuasions have found much to criticize in American policy vis-à-vis the Middle East. If bin-Laden and his followers and supporters were driven by hatred of American freedom and democracy, why were they firmly on the side of the US in the late 1980s, when America enjoyed at least as much domestic freedom and democracy as in the summer of 2001, if not more? And if bin-Laden and the rest were so angry at the internal freedom and democracy of "infidel" Western nations, why were Canada, Denmark, Holland, Sweden, New Zealand, and Switzerland (to name a few non-Islamic democratic states) right to be much less worried about major attacks from al Qaeda?

The answer, of course, is to be found in American foreign policy. The US government in the Reagan era funded extremist Islam as part of its late–Cold War campaign against the "evil" Soviet Union. The extremists were in some fashion American allies. There is no evidence to suggest that bin-Laden's attitude toward democratic institutions changed during the intervening years (he hated them back then as much as he does now), which leads to the conclusion that the source of extremist Islam's current antipathy toward America has nothing to do with Western-style political structures. Moreover, the other "infidel" nations—those spared the terrorists' vicious onslaught—were hardly lacking in the democratic institutions of the sort presumably being extolled by Bush and Chapman. In fact, in many respects their "democratic" institutions were (and are) healthier and more developed than their American counterparts. What these nations did lack, however, was America's terrorist record of destructive intervention in the Middle East and elsewhere.[9]

All this led to more cynicism on my part, particularly in response to the ease, rapidity, and confidence with which Bush, his collaborators, and his enablers in the government and media identified "us" (Americans) with "good" and "them" with "evil." In reality, the terror attacks were all too morally consistent with a long and bloody record of US behavior and policy. Arundhati Roy provides a useful synopsis:[10]

The U.S. empire rests on a grisly foundation: the massacre of millions of indig-enous people, the stealing of their lands, and following this, the kidnapping and enslavement of millions of black people from Africa to work that land. Thousands died on the seas while they were being shipped like caged cattle. . . . In the best-selling version of popular myth as history, U.S. "goodness" peaked during World War II. Lost in the din of trumpet sound and angel song is the fact that when fascism was in full stride in Europe, the U.S. government actually looked away. . . . Drowned out by the noisy hosannas is [America's] most barbaric, in fact the single most savage act the world has ever witnessed: the dropping of the atomic bomb on the civilian populations in Hiroshima and Nagasaki. The war was nearly over. The hundreds of thousands of Japanese people who were killed, the countless others who were crippled by cancers for generations to come were not a threat to world peace. They were civilians. Just as the victims of the World Trade Center bombings were civilians. Just as the hundreds of thousands of people dying in Iraq because of U.S.-led sanctions are civilians. . . . Since the Second World War, the United States has been at war with or attacked, among other countries, Korea, Guatemala, Cuba, Laos, Viet-nam, Cambodia, Grenada, Libya, El Salvador, Nicaragua, Panama, Iraq, Soma-lia, Sudan, Yugoslavia, and Afghanistan. This list should also include the U.S. government's covert operations in Africa, Asia, and Latin America, the coups it has engineered, and the dictators it has armed and supported. It should in-clude Israel's U.S.-backed war on Lebanon, in which thousands were killed. It should include the key role America has played in the conflict in the Middle East, in which thousands have died fighting Israel's occupation of Palestinian territory. It should include America's role in the civil war in Afghanistan in the 1980s, in which over one million people were killed. It should include the embargoes and sanctions that have led directly and indirectly to the death of hundreds of thousands of people, most visibly in Iraq. Put it all together, and it sounds very much as though there has been a World War III, and that the U.S. government was (or is) one of its chief protagonists.

At the risk of being redundant, it is worth repeating that the US quite happily supported Osama bin-Laden and his murderous ilk when both were pursuing anti-Soviet objectives during the 1980s; it was during this time that Uncle Sam was also supporting Saddam Hussein, in the hope that his secular, if autocratic, regime could stem the tide of the Iranian revolution.[11]

Back in the imperial "homeland," Chapman's (not to mention Bush's) outraged formulation ignored rampant poverty, authoritarianism, class rule, powerlessness, racial inequality, mass incarceration, depression, oppression, and misery. It evaded the epidemic negation of freedom and democracy in a savagely unequal and plutocratic land, where the top 1 percent owns more than 40 percent of the wealth and possibly an even higher percentage of its politicians and policymakers. It equally ignored related connections between the suffering experienced by people outside America thanks to American policies and America's hyperconsumerist, ultimately ecocidal "way of life."[12]

My cynicism was complemented by a certain naiveté, which came in the form of an initial hope that the September 11th terror attacks would provide an opportunity for Americans to honestly confront our domestic and related foreign policy records. A chance, perhaps, to stand down our entrenched psychic and ideological defenses—to understand how and why we cause ourselves and others pain, why millions across the world resent us (many to the point where they could applaud 9/11), and how we might stop the vicious circle of injury at home and abroad. Nine-eleven, I wanted to believe, might initiate a process by which we jettisoned our manufactured ignorance and innocence about how much harm our policymakers and our "democratic American System, capitalism" (as Tom Brokaw described the dominant authoritarian US system of socioeconomic management and hierarchy on 9/11) have been causing others. Perhaps, I hoped, the tragedy would convince us to reevaluate our long-standing sense of special historical superiority to the rest of the world. Maybe the national drama would jolt Americans out of their hyperprivatized, commodified, and fragmented daily experience, replacing neo-liberal societal disintegration with a new sense of civic duty and public engagement.

Well, 9/11 was an opportunity all right, but it was seized primarily by the in-power Respectable Right, falsely termed "conservative," to exacerbate existing tendencies of inequality, repression, empire, and thought control. It was a windfall for Bush and his authoritarian allies to increase the already outrageous overconcentration of wealth and power at home and abroad and to tar all who opposed this aristocratic agenda as "enemies of freedom" and allies of terrorism. It was used to divert attention and concern away from stunning socioeconomic and racial disparities, spiritual crisis, ecological collapse, declining societal health, chronic overwork, mass civic disengagement, soulless consumerism, and countless other problems that arise from the increasingly unchecked operation of the American System. It was used to privilege the right (repressive and militaristic) hand of the state over the left (social and democratic)—the police officer, prosecutor, and prison warden over the librarian, welfare worker, teacher, and lifeguard. It was exploited to help the White House assault the relevance of international law and the sanctity of America's own justly prized commitment to civil liberties. It was used to shift the subject away from the need for true democracy, peace, and social justice, and to enable the ascendancy of a "belligerent nationalism" that constructs community on the basis of fear and mindless conformity rather than democratic possibility. It was used by "elites" to speed up the American public sector's ongoing transformation into a repressive, neo-liberal "garrison state."

This weak-left/strong-right state increasingly acts as little more than the authoritarian agent of capital's dictates. It replaces compassion with repression and criminalizes and militarizes social problems that result from the deepening of socioeconomic and related racial inequalities at home and abroad.[13] It conducts a massive transfer of wealth and power from social programs to the military, even as rising poverty and unemployment wreak havoc on American families and neighborhoods. It utilizes massive tax cuts to further transfer wealth from embattled middle- and lower-income groups to the rich.

The renewed "war on terrorism," spawned in large measure by 9/11, has "functioned," to quote Noam Chomsky writing about the Cold War in the early 1970s, as a "device for mobilizing support . . . for ventures that carry a significant cost, economic and moral." As with the Cold War, in this new "war on terrorism" (the first one, proclaimed under Reagan, was designed and engineered by many of the same people conducting the current one), "the citizen must agree to bear the burdens of imperial wars and government-induced production of waste, a critical device of economic management." He is "whipped into line by the fear that we will be overwhelmed by an external enemy if we let down our guard."[14]

In the official public and mainstream (corporate) media version of this apparently permanent war, the virtuous, freedom-loving and benevolent United States engages in a noble effort to protect its own people—and indeed the world—from the scourge of terrorism. This is an inaccurate depiction of what is occurring and what is at stake. The reality is that the Bush administration and its superprivileged clients and allies, who control the world's leading military and incarceration state, use the threat of terrorism as a cover and a pretext for policies that deepen inequality and repression at home and expand imperial power abroad. These policies and practices assault basic domestic civil liberties and roll back social and economic protections in a nation that is already the most unequal in the industrialized world. They eviscerate existing social programs and pre-empt potential ones in order to inflate the already massive public subsidies provided to gargantuan high-tech defense corporations. They expand and camouflage US support for state terrorism conducted by nations like Israel, Russia, China, Indonesia, and other countries whose murderous actions against indigenous and occupied peoples are described in benign and supportive terms by US policymakers and the dominant US media. They directly terrorize millions in Middle East, including the people of Iraq. And they increase not just the social and economic insecurity of the American people but also their direct physical homeland insecurity.

* * *

Except for the last one, all of the chapters presented in part I were written before the United States launched "Operation Iraqi Freedom." The initial gullibility I described above had largely passed by the spring of 2002, when I argued (in the first chapter, titled "Misunderstanding Power") that the concentration of wealth and power gives "elites" the capacity to turn an event like 9/11 into a pretext for regressive and authoritarian policy. By the fall of 2002 (when I wrote the chapter, "Our Tears, Their Opportunity," that gives part I its *noir* title), this naiveté was fully replaced by a pessimistic realization that it was the right which had taken advantage of the opportunities presented by the tragic events of 9/11. The final chapter (titled "*Who* Hates America?"), written with the benefit of "wartime" hindsight, is dedicated to the proposition that the truest and most significant enemies of American "freedom" and "democracy" in the wake of 9/11 are homegrown, as Alex Carey knew.

I
Misunderstanding Power: Explaining the Popularity of 9/11 Conspiracy Theories
June 6, 2002

Thanks in part to recent disclosures that a minimally competent federal security establishment would have had reasons to know and act on intelligence predicting something like what occurred last September,[15] conspiracy theorists are having a field day with 9/11.[16] But it didn't take such disclosures, or the current congressional inquiry into what the relevant federal officers knew and when they knew it,[17] to put the great American conspiracy industry into high gear. From the beginning, really, a small army of conspiracy-thinkers offered variations on the basic theme that Washington (and, in some versions, Tel Aviv) was somehow in on the terrible September attacks.

In the mild version of 9/11 conspiracy theory, Washington merely knew about the impending attacks and chose not to act. In the hard-core version, Washington (and/or Israel) actually plotted and conducted the attacks.

The motive(s)? To provide the perfect excuse for the subversion of democracy, to serve the interests of Big Oil and the military-industrial complex, to strengthen Israel's grip on its Palestinian subjects, and to expand the reach of US military power yet further across the globe. To create, in short, a pretext for developments pretty much along the lines of main historical currents since September 2001.

Many of the conspiracy charges, it seems, come from somewhere on the "left" side of the political spectrum, where conspiracy thinking is more common than some radicals like to admit. The far right, it is becoming increasingly clear, has no monopoly on the paranoid and crackpot interpretation of historical events past and present.

September 11th conspiracy theorists advance some truly bizarre ideas, including the notions that the World Trade Center was destroyed by explosives, that the planes were commandeered by American military remote control, and that WTC Tower 2 was hit by a missile. According to one website, the Pentagon was not actually hit by an airplane.

Conspiracy theorists also make a number of accurate and uncontroversial observations that they would like to think provide circumstantial evidence for their strange interpretations. They note Washington's (Cold War) history of training and equipping al Qaeda, Bush Senior's role as former CIA chief, and the huge influence of Big Oil and the "defense" industry on the current White House. They point to the creepy circumstances of Bush Junior's 2000 "selection" by the Supreme Court, the Bush administration's initial oil-driven overtures to the Taliban, and the White House's equally petroleum-related suspension of serious investigation of the Saudi-connected bin-Laden network. They note that Bush Senior and Dick Cheney were consultants to the Carlye group, which advised the bin-Laden family and has made out quite well from the post–September 11 expansion of the Pentagon budget. They point to friendly historical relations between the US petroleum executives and the Taliban, reflecting the global oil corporations' determination to build a pipeline from Turkmenistan to Pakistan via Afghanistan. They note America's long history of secret intervention in the internal politics and policies of other nations. And they point, of course, to growing evidence that top CIA and FBI officials failed to act on abundant evidence that should have sparked them to prevent the attacks.

"Left" conspiracy theorists put special emphasis on regressive and repressive policy developments since 9/11. Look, they say, at the following examples (as if these were all you needed to know about):

- the overnight media transformation of Bush from incompetent illegitimacy to supposed grand statesman and the related suppression and distorted reportage of the real facts of the 2000 presidential "election"
- the closing of meaningful debate on the harshly regressive domestic policy agenda of the Bush administration and allies in Congress
- the restriction of civil liberties at home and abroad, in the name of a new permanent War on Terror, really a permanent war of US and US-allied state terror
- the massive new Pentagon budget, transferring an unprecedented windfall of taxpayer money to politically connected high-tech "defense" corporations, granting them a practically blank check to build massively expensive weapons and support systems that often have nothing to do with protecting the nation against terrorism
- the construction of new US military bases and the expansion of America's military presence in Southwest Asia, providing new imperial protections for US-based petrochemical interests in the region

- the US government's lockstep support for Israel's vicious and criminal assault on the Palestinian people, justified in part by the notion that 9/11 gave Americans a new appreciation for virtuous Israel's struggle with dastardly suicidal madmen!

The list goes on.

"Come on, man," one conspiracy theorist recently told me, with a sneering grin, incredulous at my inability to sign on with his dark, all-knowing interpretation of the above developments. "The Bushies and all their rich buddies have got everything they ever wanted from this thing. You *know* they cooked it up."

In one case, the suggestion of high-level US complicity has come from a progressive member of Congress—Representative Cynthia McKinney (D-Ga.). Last April, McKinney noted that "persons close to the [Bush] administration are poised to make huge profits off America's new [September 11–provoked] war." McKinney pointed especially to the Carlyle Group, a Washington-based and defense-related investment firm that employs a large number of high-ranking government officials and retains the senior George Bush as a leading adviser. McKinney noted that the Carlyle Group and other firms close to the White House "directly benefited from the increased defense spending arising from the aftermath of September 11."(D-Ga.).[18]

Space limitations prevent me from listing and refuting the various specific claims of 9/11 conspiracy theories, but three points of rebuttal should suffice. First, it is hugely unlikely that the necessary network of players and operatives would or could have undertaken such a complicated and insanely risky enterprise as conducting the attacks or, for that matter, covering up evidence of their likely occurrence. Even on the incredibly dubious assumption that the required high-level players were so uneasy in their privileged pre-September lives that they felt compelled to concoct such schemes of mass murder on American soil, the likelihood of discovery would have made it prohibitively dangerous.

Second, conspiracy theorists of the hard version forget that the likely perpetrators—the bin-Laden network—had both the independent means and (uncontroversially) the motive(s) to conduct the operation. There's something almost racist in the notion that only people of European ancestry could have carried out an act of 9/11's scale. The operation, moreover, is deeply consistent with the threats made and the targets marked by the likely culprits for quite some time.

Third, it is incredibly naive to think that the elitist consequences of 9/11 —more wealth and power for the few and less of both for the many— somehow prove that 9/11 was the product of an elite US conspiracy. Conspiracy theorists of the sort who sneered at me fail to understand that aristocratic outcomes from crises are basically written into America's economic and sociopolitical structure. Democracy is a political system in which each person has an equal vote and an equal degree of policy influence. It cannot meaningfully exist in a society structured along the lines of the contemporary US, where 1 percent of the population owns 47 percent of the nation's wealth and an even greater proportion of its politicians, policymakers, and media. It cannot exist where ordinary people who lack cohesive organization, meaningful institutions of autonomous power, popular expression, democratic organization, and even a sense of common interests must face off against highly organized and extremely class-conscious wealthy interests. It cannot exist where such people are worked, commuted, and shopped to the point of exhaustion and must rely on a highly concentrated privately owned media for basic information. It is especially absent from the making of foreign policy, which is even more insulated from popular influence than domestic policy and whose largely hidden conception and execution carry vast consequences for the entire planet without anything but the slightest input from world citizens.

The structure of media ownership is especially pivotal in the current era. The owners and managers of the highly globalized corporate media, who have strong linkages with the military and oil industries and the national security state, possess awesome, structurally encoded power to shape popular perceptions of current events. It does not serve their interests to translate the meaning of events in ways that question elite privilege and the related American imperial project. The outcome—extremely biased coverage that favors war, imperial expansion, military expenditure, and reduced civil liberties at home over critical democratic examination of US foreign policy and its role in making terror attacks on US targets predictable—is itself remarkably predictable, even without resorting to conspiracy theory.

A key consequence of this harsh structural reality is that those who possess wealth and power enjoy a remarkable capacity to exploit crises. They act on their special, structurally enabled capacity to turn terrible events and developments into alleged reasons for policies that further their wealth and power at the expense of everyone else.

Such are the traditional and consistent goals and behavior of those who sit atop society's leading institutions. As Noam Chomsky noted last February, the privileged search "relentlessly" for pretexts to advance their standard agenda, summarized in what Adam Smith called "the vile maxim of the masters—'Everything for me and nothing for everyone else.'" Chomsky went on to say that "[c]rises" "make it possible to exploit fear and concern to demand that the [people] be submissive, obedient, silent, distracted, while the powerful use the window of opportunity to pursue their own favored programs with even greater intensity." They are a means for "disciplining the population," which tends to look with disfavor at policies embodying the "vile maxim" and "shifting wealth and power even more" into "the master's" hands.[19]

The aftermath of 9/11, Chomsky further noted, is "typical" in this regard. As John Pilger recently observed in his important work, *The New Rulers of the World,* "the attacks of September 11, 2001 did not 'change everything,' but accelerated the continuity of events, providing an extraordinary pretext for destroying social democracy." Indeed, they have provided the post–Cold War era's most spectacular excuse to date for the ongoing "reduction of democracy to electoral ritual: that is, competition between indistinguishable parties for the management of a single-ideology state."[20]

As when they are applied to other events, conspiracy theories regarding 9/11 reflect two core misunderstandings of power and how it operates in the US. The first, broadly encouraged by the American educational, political, and media establishments, holds that the US is in fact a democracy. People who accept this fairy tale—quite unlike both the Founding Fathers (most of whom agreed with John Jay that "those who own the country ought to run it") and the modern American business class—cannot easily grasp policy outcomes that dramatically serve the interests of the few over the many. For them, the temptation is strong to see such outcomes as the product of a dark conspiracy operating behind the backs and against the wishes of their elected representatives and other leaders of the society's main institutions.

The second misunderstanding is of a very different nature. It wraps itself in an all-knowing sneer of cynicism, yet holds a curiously wide-eyed and fantastic view of the masters or at least some part of the ruling class. Common among those who have been disabused of democratic myths and feel especially powerless in the face of concentrated power, it holds that dastardly elites manipulate the course of history from on high, pretty much in accordance with their own wishes. Little happens in the course of human events, some conspiracy theorists think, without the approval and intervention of an all-powerful but strangely secret elite.

Real understanding of power is found outside these poles of illusion. Those who possess it know that the weight of dominant influence over sociopolitical decisionmaking and public information (mass persuasion) is rooted in historically developed structures of concentrated power— "state and private, closely inter-linked," as Chomsky describes it. They do not conclude from this that certain select members or designated operatives of the master class have been granted limitless potency to shape history from above. History, they know, is full of remarkable developments, some inspiring (e.g., the early phases of the Russian Revolution, the anti–Vietnam War movement) and others quite horrific (e.g., 9/11), that occur to the surprise and against the wishes of the "power elite."

That "elite," they are aware, possesses exceptional capacity to transform unexpected and initially unwelcome developments into pretexts for the expansion of their wealth and power. In the past, for example, it turned the initially unwelcome (for the privileged) existence of the Soviet Union into a pretext for the (welcome) historically unparalleled expansion of the military-industrial complex. It turned the antiwar movement, urban racial unrest, and antipoverty programs of the 1960s into pretexts for the expansion of a racist, authoritarian criminal justice (punishment) state and related punitive workfare regime that enforces harsh class and race inequalities in contemporary America. And now, with special assistance from an initially unwelcome and truly historic and evil terror attack last September, it has made the threat of terrorism into an excuse and rationalization for the expansion of imperialism, militarism, and class privilege.

But noting these outcomes, rooted in structurally encoded inequalities of ideological and policy power, is very different from saying that the masters "cooked up" the developments they were able to exploit. Such a judgment conclusion reads history through the rearview mirror and exaggerates the power and foresight of the current war party in power.

Ordinary people would be fortunate if the masters of war and wealth needed to work behind or otherwise undermine the United States' leading institutions to achieve regressive and repressive policy results like the ones we have seen since 9/11. At the same time, we can be thankful that those masters have not become the godlike manipulators of history and consciousness, capable of creating historical events resembling scenes from a bad *X-Files* episode. History lurches forward, in all its horror and glory, full of possibilities that continue to be chained and tragic consequences that remain predictable unless and until we develop and act upon an appropriate understanding of power and how it operates.

2
Defending Civilization and the Myth of Radical Academia
July 15, 2002

I know it is no laughing matter when America's thought-police go on patrol. Still, even if only as a defense mechanism, I couldn't help but laugh when I finally read the by-now notorious report on alleged academic anti-Americanism put out last November by the arch-reactionary American Council of Trustees and Alumni (ACTA). Bearing the melodramatic title *Defending Civilization: How Our Universities Are Failing America and What Can Be Done About It,*[21] the ACTA report lists exactly 115 examples of supposedly outrageous radical "responses" of the denizens of academe to 9/11 and the bombing of Afghanistan. Its authors claim to show that America's universities are dangerously out of step with basic American values—indeed, with the core values of Western Civilization.

The ACTA's chairman emeritus and founder is Lynne Cheney, the former head of the Reagan-era National Endowment for the Humanities, wife of the vice president, and author of patriotic children's books. Claiming to promote the understanding of American history and Western civilization, the ACTA is a Washington-based front group for Cheney's right-wing agenda, dedicated to the supremacy of rich white males and the promotion of American Manifest Destiny past and present.

Our institutions of higher learning, the ACTA claims, have fallen into the clutches of a fifth column. They are dominated, Cheney and her cohorts would like us to believe, by a cabal of excessively liberal and radical professors for whom nothing, not even "civilization" itself, is sacred. Yes, these evil academic sorcerers encourage America's impressionable youth to abandon all meaningful distinctions between "good and evil," to question the God-ordained supremacy of the United States, and to always "BLAME AMERICA FIRST." The ACTA is trying to counter that propaganda by promoting the teaching of real American and Western history, understood to mean the top-down story of the Great White Men as told to us by the Great White Men.[22]

It doesn't require much exposure to radical historical literature to see here the living ghosts of the McCarthy era.[23] It's especially chilling to witness academic McCarthyism being dusted off and taken out for a post–September 11 spin by an organization whose founder is married to the most powerful vice president in American history, who, in turn, is helping oversee and implement a horrifying Orwellian campaign of permanent terrorist war on terrorism.

Still, *Defending Civilization* elicits amusement in at least four ways. First, it is laughable how little one had to say on an academic campus after 9/11, ideologically speaking, to make it into the ACTA's little black book. Here are some of the ACTA's entries, presented verbatim as evidence for *Defending Civilization*'s thesis of rampant academic anti-Americanism:

> "Break the cycle of violence"—Pomona College faculty panel discussing US obligations in the Middle East.
>
> "We need to learn to use courage for peace instead of war"—Professor of Religious Studies, Pomona College.
>
> "We need to think about what could have produced the frustration that caused these crimes. To have that kind of hatred is a phenomenon we will have to try to understand"—Director of the Program on International Intelligence at the Woodrow Wilson School's Center for International Studies, Princeton University.
>
> "An eye for an eye leaves the world blind"—student sign at Harvard rally.
>
> "Our grief is not a call for war"—poster at New York University.
>
> "If Osama bin-Laden is confirmed to be behind the attacks, the US should bring him before an international tribunal"—Professor at Stanford.

Among all of the ACTA's 115 "response" entries, only 3 at the most are actually "anti-American." Just 1 or 2 actually justify the 9/11 attacks, and just 16 show speakers even daring to suggest (as I did on September 18 at Northern Illinois University) that understanding the attacks and thereby preventing future occurrences might entail a critical self-examination of US foreign policy.

Second, *Defending Civilization* engages in some amusing double- and even triple-entry McCarthyite bookkeeping. One unfortunate speaker, identified as a "journalist at [a] University of North Carolina teach-in," accounts for at least three separate listings (numbers 17, 82, and 90) and may account for two others (76 and 105). A "professor of linguistics at MIT" (presumably Chomsky) gets two listings, as do others.

Third, it is interesting to note that most of the 115 academic "responses" were not in fact made by academics. They came from the mouths of students and also from nonacademics like the mysterious North Carolina journalist. In the McCarthyite mentality of the report's authors, no doubt, the insufficiently patriotic responses of students reflected their brainwashing by radical professors.

Last but certainly not least, *Defending Civilization* and the ACTA promote a laughably inaccurate image of life on America's colleges and universities. Along with the truly hilarious myth of the liberal media, the notion that America's campuses are held captive by radicals is a standard right-wing nostrum, repeated so frequently as to become a self-evident article of faith between and among conservatives.

The real facts of power and ideology on American campuses are quite different, however. To be sure, academia possesses a hardy cadre of critical and independent thinkers that fulfill the elementary requirements of honest and responsible intellectual work. Those requirements include discovering and communicating the truth about things that matter to ordinary people who care and can do something positive about it in terms that such people can understand. Those who fulfill these requirements embrace the goal of acting as "public intellectuals," but not in the standard sense of the term. Rather than simply being "in the public," usually to advance agendas of private concentrated power, they interpret the role to mean writing and speaking "for the public," informing and empowering the people in the struggle against structures of concentrated power private and public. They tend to be passionately dissatisfied with the existing status quo at home and abroad. They gravitate toward radical opposition to existing policies and institutions in a national and world society that is fundamentally structured around hierarchy and empire. They do not pretend to possess a specialized monopoly on the relevant knowledge certified by a professional degree and the mastery of arcane monographs and secret seminar handshakes. They appeal to and learn from ordinary people rather than simply lecturing them, seeking to rise, as in Eugene Debs's excellent phrase, not "from" but rather "with the masses."

Tragically, such intellectuals are far and few between on the campuses of America. For every Howard Zinn, Edward S. Herman, (the late) E. P. Thompson, or Noam Chomsky, there is a large mass of academics whose research, publications, and lectures stand in a relation of self-satisfied subordination and often direct service to the forces of concentrated economic and political power. Most academics in the liberal arts and social sciences, including even a number who think themselves radicals, spend the bulk of their time on thoroughly innocuous and marginally significant topics that offer only the slightest hint of threat to the powers that be. Their reports are commonly constructed only for one another, marked by an incestuous and career-generating discourse (including various mystified forms of neo-"Marxism" and "post-modernism") that leaves nonspecialists cold and in the dark. As one radical teaching-centered history professor told me years ago, his colleagues "spend most of their time

17

writing long love letters to each other." The "love letters" referred, of course, to the academics' parade of specialized self-refereed and self-referential books and articles. These long and involved lifeworks rarely attain anything but the most select insider readership. They excel mainly at enabling their authors to gain tenure and promotions and at gathering dust on the shelves of university libraries. Meanwhile, those professors who focus on teaching, on communicating with and inspiring the thousands of students in their classrooms and lecture halls—the children of people who pay professors' salaries—are ridiculed for not knowing who the real audience is.

At the same time, the radical potential of academia is badly diluted by the profoundly anti-intellectual superspecialization and subdivision of knowledge and labor across diverse academic departments and programs. The modern university's artificial separation of thought (reflected in an academic lecture I once heard on "Marx the sociologist, Marx the political scientist, Marx the economist, Marx the historian, and Marx the anthropologist") makes it difficult for academics and students to perceive the connections essential for meaningful intellectual work and radical criticism. The few who rise above it to are often denounced for speaking outside their little assigned corner of academic expertise. On more than a few occasions, I have heard academics criticize Noam Chomsky for having the gall to write about developments outside his formal field of linguistics. Among Chomsky's many sins, in the mind of such individuals, is his propensity to step into the territory of their special field area.

Among those academics who do rise above the mass of scholastic specialization and discourse to write and speak about things that matter in a way meant to be heard outside the academy, basic truths about class, power, and the consequences of "elite" actions are nearly unmentionable. These academics tend to write and speak in alternately glowing and realistic terms about the United States as the homeland and headquarters of "freedom," "free-market (actually state) capitalism," and "democracy," all falsely conflated with one another. They speak in all-knowing terms about the "end of history," meaning the end of the historical struggle for social justice. They honor the superior "efficiency" of "market" (actually corporate and state-capitalist) forces that are raping human society and the earth on which it depends. They talk in matter-of-fact fashion about the absence of any alternatives to the existing socioeconomic, political, and world-imperial orders.

The hardy minority of genuine academic radicals who point out the falsity of these arguments and seek to rescue the campus from its stultifying subordination to power is pushed to the margins of their fields and institutions. They are written off as alienated cranks. They are not invited to the parties, conferences, foundation gatherings, and media events at which the rewards and "pleasures of academe" are passed out. They are mocked for failing to understand that giving assent to power, either directly or indirectly, is the ticket to a comfortable life of tenure, sabbaticals, summers off, and reduced teaching loads.

Yes, there is a great moral and intellectual void in America's institutions of higher learning, but it is a right- and not left-leaning nothingness that cripples US campuses. Right-wing reactionaries from the White House on down can relax when it comes to the universities and colleges of America. The situation there is very much under the control of the right people.

3
Toward a "Decent Left"?
Liberal-Left Misrepresentation and
Selective Targeting of Left Commentary on 9/11
July 1, 2002

The Liberal-Left Attack

Among the many disagreeable aspects of 9/11's aftermath we might include the intensification of internal unpleasantness within an American left that was already rather snippy with itself. This latest unpleasantness has been a fairly one-sided affair, with most of the heat coming from the more centrist liberal-left, associated with journals like *Dissent* and *American Prospect* and writers like Michael Walzer, Jeffrey Issac, and Christopher Hitchens. It has been directed at the more radical left, associated primarily with *Z Magazine*, ZNet, and—insofar as the liberal-left is willing to name names—Noam Chomsky.

The liberal-left accusations, many of which have been repeated and updated in the recently released spring issue of *Dissent* (a journal in which I have published two major articles on domestic policy), include the following:[24]

- Leftists made "relativist justifications" and "excuses" for terror inasmuch as they spoke and wrote about the pivotal role that United States foreign policy and related Middle Eastern poverty had played in creating the context for the rise of terrible and extremist terror networks in the Mideast and because they noted that the US and its clients were responsible for massive terror across the world today and for the last fifty or more years.
- Radicals excused terror as the only weapon left to the weak and powerless, forgetting that terror is a reflection of the morally flawed human agency of people who have failed to build a strong political relationship with the masses they claim to represent.

- Radicals embraced 9/11 as a proper, populist, and progressive expression of Third World anti-imperialism along the lines of, say, the Vietnamese or the Cuban revolutions.

The liberal-left charge of left apology appeared in the first post–September 11 editorial in *In These Times* (which tends, I think, to avoid easy ideological characterization and to steer something of a middle course between *Dissent* and *Z Magazine*). It claimed that certain unnamed "commentators, mostly on the left" had "excuse[d] the inexcusable attacks on the World Trade Center and the Pentagon by Islamic extremists" with the "relativist" claim that the US and its clients had often matched and gone beyond the crimes of 9/11 during recent history.[25]

This charge was more than echoed by Michael Walzer, editor of the social-democratic journal *Dissent*. In an article titled "Excusing Terror: The Politics of Ideological Apology" in the liberal-left journal *American Prospect* (October 22, 2001), Walzer accused "parts of the European and American left" of justifying the September attacks with "rationalizations" rooted in their "political culture of excuses." According to Walzer, the left excused terror as the only weapon left to the weak and powerless, forgetting that terror is the evil choice of people who have failed to build a strong political relationship with the masses they claim to represent. Walzer agreed with *The Nation*'s leading liberal-left columnist Christopher Hitchens that left critics (whom Hitchens called "the Chomsky-Zinn-Finkelstein crowd"[26]) naively saw 9/11 as some sort of virtuous anti-imperialist response to the interrelated evils of world-capitalist inequality, corporate globalization, and US hegemony. He even accused the left of thinking that the victims of 9/11 and of terror generally deserved their fate because they were beneficiaries of empire.

The liberal-left attack on the left got especially personal in an October *American Prospect* essay penned by Indiana University professor and frequent *Dissent* contributor Jeffrey Issac and bearing the pithy title "Thus Spake Noam." Issac named Chomsky as a de facto apologist for the September atrocities on the basis of a rhetorical argument made by Chomsky in *The New Military Humanism* (2000). To be morally consistent, Chomsky argued in that book, those who supported the bombing of Belgrade as punishment for Serbian actions in Kosovo should also have advocated the bombing of Jakarta (Indonesia), Washington DC, and London to punish Indonesia's US- and UK-sponsored genocidal invasion, annexation, and more recent terrorization of East Timor. This argument, Issac claimed, encouraged anti-American terrorism because it made "no policy-relevant distinctions" and implied "moral equivalency" between the behavior of the terrorist Indonesian state and the noble intentions and actions of humanitarian and democratic states like the US and England. Isaac further claimed that Chomsky himself encouraged terrorism by offering no serious alternatives to US imperialism and seeing no meaningful global "dialectic" other than that between evil American empire and quasi-virtuous anti-imperialist/anti-American terror.[27]

As is apparent from the latest *Dissent,* the liberal-left assault continues. In essays by Walzer and Issac, this issue skewers the American left for opposing the bombing of Afghanistan. The left expresses, Walzer and Issac claim, naive opposition to elementary principles of self-defense and thoughtless embrace of terrorist monsters just because they hate America. Walzer accuses the left of "failure to register the horror of the [September 11th] attack" and even of "barely concealed glee that the imperial state had finally gotten what it deserved."

For Walzer and Issac, leftists' failure to appreciate the necessity of America's imperial response to September 11th is a result of the tangled web of left pathologies. These pathological patterns include:

- a lingering "rag-tag Marxist" belief that "any group that attacks the imperial power must be a representative of the oppressed, and its agenda must be the agenda of the left"
- "guilt," "festering resentment," and "self-hatred" produced by living in the world's only superpower and "enjoying its privileges" and by "long years spent in [supposedly] fruitless opposition to the global reach of American power"
- a knee-jerk "moral-purist" attachment to "blaming America first" and a related sense that "everything that goes badly in the world goes badly because of us"
- a sense "of not being entitled to criticize anyone" outside the privileged US and a related suspension of any and all judgment about the behavior and values of non-Americans
- a naive attachment to pacifism that is in reality a morally bankrupt commitment to powerlessness and "doing nothing" in the face of manifest evil, leaving Americans defenseless in the face of future attacks

Walzer is so disgusted by radicals' "self-hating" refusal to sign up with the official explanations of and response to 9/11 that he wonders, in a question that provides the title for his *Dissent* essay, "Can There Be a Decent Left?"

Straw Dogs and Red Herrings

The liberal-left's charges against the left are serious, going to the heart of the left's moral integrity. Fortunately, however, it is easy to show that the liberal-left attack horribly misrepresents what radicals actually said and wrote about the causes and meaning of 9/11. In what follows, as part of the beginning of what I hope will be a more comprehensive response from the left, I hold up some of these charges against the record of early left commentary that is easily reviewed from the ZNet website. My focus is primarily on what leftists said and wrote regarding the origins and meaning of the September jetliner attacks. I will leave it to others to respond in detail to the liberal-left's claims regarding what the left recommended as an appropriate response to 9/11. Those claims amount to an embrace of unilateral militarism and a rejection of the left's historical preference for an approach to world tensions that relies on international law, multilateral negotiation, and, ultimately, social justice and democracy—all with portentous consequences for Americans and others at home and abroad. As will be seen, the distance between the liberal-left description of left response and the reality of what the left actually said and wrote is quite remarkable—a chasm really. One is left to wonder, indeed, whether writers like Walzer had the decency to actually read the left's readily available commentary before assaulting it.

Making Excuses, Reveling in the Attacks, and Refusing to Criticize Foreign Monsters?

The left has consistently denounced the 9/11 attacks as what Chomsky on October 18 at MIT called "a horrendous atrocity, probably the most devastating instant human toll of any crime in history, outside of war."[28] "U.S. crimes," wrote Stephen Shalom and Mike Albert on September 17, 2001, "in no way justify or excuse the attacks of September 11. Terror is an unacceptable response to U.S. crimes."[29] Here is my own comment at a September 18th forum at Northern Illinois University:[30]

> The September 11th terror attacks on the World Trade Center were hideously and horribly evil. There is no acceptable justification for the destruction of innocent lives, mostly of ordinary working people, including secretaries, firemen, janitors, food service workers, and child care workers. Whoever ordered, financed, and directed the assault is by definition a cold-blooded monster. They must be found and held accountable for their colossal crime.

Of course, these sorts of unambiguous statements are not good enough for the liberal-leftists. They seem to think the left excused and even approved of 9/11 because it had the audacity to question the official Bush line that America was targeted because of its supposed special commitment to freedom and democracy and because it discussed some of the factors that helped "create a [Middle Eastern] environment conducive to recruiting people to commit" horrible acts against the US. Those factors included the widespread and understandable feeling among Arabs that "the U.S. obstructs freedom and democracy as well as material plenty for others," US support of Israeli oppression of the Palestinians, US support for authoritarian regimes that supply US corporations with huge profits and powerful opposition to movements that oppose those profits, and U.S. promotion of a global economic system that creates massive poverty in the Middle East and elsewhere.[31]

Also reprehensible to the liberal-left was the left's insistence on seeing 9/11 in a comparative and historical context relative to terrorist US actions and those of its client states and to the general course of atrocity in the human record. Chomsky had what the liberal-left considers the unpardonable effrontery to note that 9/11's terrible human consequences have been matched and exceeded by numerous terrorist actions conducted by the US and its clients. Chomsky also had the insolence to observe that 9/11 was historic in that international terrorism during the last four centuries has been inflicted by the world's European and North American states on each other and on the Third World. September 11th marked, he noted, "a change in the direction in which the guns were pointed. That's new."[32]

The liberal-left critique of left "relativism" is based on an imbecilic conflation of explanation with rationalization and understanding with approval. It is based also on a concomitant failure to see the at-once practical and moral necessity for an explanation that goes beyond the misleading rhetoric of the political, military, and media establishment. Does a historian embrace Adolph Hitler's crimes when he or she writes about the historical circumstances that contributed to the rise of Nazism? No more than a good sociologist justifies murder by analyzing the social, economic, and/or other circumstances that tend to increase the number and frequency of homicides.

In a famous essay on historical causation, *What Is History?* (1961), the great British Soviet historian Edward Hallett Carr noted that an Institute and Chair of Criminology had recently been set up at Cambridge University. "It would not, I feel sure, occur to any of those investigating the causes of crime to suggest that this committed them to a denial of the moral responsibility of the criminal." In this brilliant work, Carr wrote with appropriate intellectual and moral disdain for those who argued that "explaining human behavior in causal terms implies a denial of human free will" and "encourages historians to evade their supposed obligation to pronounce moral condemnation on the Charlemagnes, Stalins, and Napoleans of history." He noted that few people in everyday life hold to the ridiculous idea that human actions are governed purely by free will, without relation to external and historical circumstances. Without knowledge of those circumstances, Carr knew, there can be no intelligent understanding of historical crimes to provide a reasonable basis of action to prevent replication of terrible past events.[33]

Consistent with Carr's common-sense analysis, the post–September 11 leftists talked and wrote about the historical and social context that had likely given rise to al Qaeda and its terrible deeds, not to excuse those deeds but rather to understand them and prevent their reoccurrence. At the same time, they noted American crimes, past and present, and those of other regimes, not to excuse those committed on September 11, 2001, but rather because those crimes are in fact part of the context for the 9/11 atrocities. They sought also to remind citizens that American policymakers held no moral basis to claim special virtue and a related right to launch a military response that would certainly widen the circle of human suffering, killing many innocent Afghans (as in fact occurred), and possibly provoke new attacks on Americans. And they hoped to tell their fellow Americans why most of the rest of the world, not without real sympathy for the victims, nonetheless saw 9/11 from a very different perspective—something we might want to understand if we wish to respond in a way that contributes to healing rather than to more violence.

Prevention, not rationalization, was and remains the motive behind the writings of the "left commentators." As Chomsky put it in the immediate aftermath of the attacks, "we have a choice as to how to react: . . . we can express justified horror; we can seek to understand what may have led to the crimes, which means making an effort to enter the minds of the likely perpetrators. . . . [W]e may try to understand, or refuse to do so, contributing to the likelihood that much worse lies ahead."[34]

Confusing Authoritarian Islamic Terror Networks with the Virtuous Struggle of the Poor and Weak Against Imperialism, Capitalism, and the Powerful?

Since Chomsky is the main butt of their post–September 11 attacks on the left, the liberal-leftists ought to review the following early (October 2nd) exchange between Chomsky and a questioner who communicated through an MSNBC chatroom. This exchange, which is easy to access at www.zmag.org/chatwithchom, clearly shows that Chomsky had no naive, romantic, or "Marxist"—"rag tag" or otherwise—ideas about the virtuous proletarian and/or anti-imperialist character of 9/11's likely perpetrators, the Taliban, or other extremist Muslim organizations:[35]

Chip Berlet: I agree with you that aggressive militarism is not the answer to this mess, but the Taliban and Osama bin Laden's networks seem to me to be totalitarian and apocalyptic clerical fascist movements. Isn't this a moment the left needs to just say it is against terrorism, and that groups like the Taliban and OsB's networks are not liberation struggles but reactionary or fascistic movements that we oppose?

Chomsky: As far as I'm aware, that's what the left has been saying for 20 years. I know I have ever since these groups were organized by the CIA, Pakistani and Egyptian intelligence and other US allies. They were organized recruited, trained, and armed to fight a holy war against the Russians, which they did. But they also started right away carrying out terrorist acts. 20 years ago they assassinated the president of Egypt and they've been carrying out terror ever since. The groups that the CIA organized were drawn from extremist radical Islamic groups and they have been pursuing their own agenda. They did what the CIA wanted them to, but they have been pursuing their own agenda. There is no doubt that from the start they were murderous terrorist organizations. I don't know if the word fascist is exactly correct, they don't have that kind of ideology. But they' re extremely dangerous and have been for 20 years. It is quite obvious. That's been the position, as far as I'm aware, of any serious person on the left as far back as I can remember.

Here, further, is Chomsky's readily available, published response, given within ten days of the 9/11 attacks, to a radio journalist who wondered if bin-Laden and al Qaeda were motivated by bitterness toward US-sponsored capitalist globalization and related American cultural hegemony:[36]

As for the bin-Laden network, they have as little concern for globalization and cultural hegemony as they do for the poor and oppressed people of the Middle East who they have been severely harming for years. They tell us what their concerns are loud and clear: they are fighting a Holy War against the corrupt, repressive, and "un-Islamist" regimes of the region, and their supporters, just as they fought a Holy War against the Russians in the 1980s. . . . Bin Laden himself has probably never even heard of "globalization." Those who have interviewed him at length, like Robert Fisk, report that he knows virtually nothing of the world and doesn't care to.

Here and in numerous other pieces that could be cited, Chomsky and others on the left showed that they had leftist illusions about the character of 9/11's likely perpetrators. It was common among the post–September 11 leftists, in fact, to note that bin-Laden was an extraordinarily wealthy man, a member of the same social class as George W. Bush who couldn't care less about the Third World's poor and oppressed and owed much of his terrorist capability precisely to American empire.

It is true that the left rejected the mainstream US claim, repeated by the liberal-left, that Islamic hatred of progressive modernity and the American "way of life" (whatever the relationship between those) were the main motives behind the attacks. It is also true that the left accompanied its post–September 11 writings and speeches with some rather harsh commentary on the different ways that American global policy generates hatred of the United States within the Middle East and how that hatred provided fertile soil for the seeds of anti-American terrorism. To say this is not, however, to assert that the September 11 attacks were specifically motivated by a desire to strike a blow at American imperialism.

In fact, the left *downplayed* grievances against American empire as the motivation behind 9/11, suggesting the very different explanation fleshed out in the following readily available statement from the ZNet site:[37]

> Why [did the terrorists] commit a grotesquely provocative act against a power so large, so armed, and so dangerous as the United States? Perhaps provoking the United States was precisely the intent. By provoking a massive military assault on one or more Islamic nations, the perpetrators may hope to set off a cycle of terror and counter-terror, precipitating a holy war between the Islamic world and the west, a war that they can lead and that they may hope will result in the overthrow of all insufficiently Islamic regimes and the unraveling of the United States, just as the Afghan war contributed to the demise of the Soviet Union. Needless to say, this scenario is insane on every count one can assess.

On September 22, Chomsky argued that[38]

> [b]in Laden's prime target is Saudi Arabia and other corrupt and repressive regimes of the region, none of which are [by bin Laden's estimate] truly "Islamic." He and his network are intent on supporting Muslims intent on defending themselves against "infidels" wherever it may be: Chechnya, Bosnia, Kashmir, Western China, Southeast Asia, North Africa, maybe elsewhere. They fought and won a Holy War to drive the Russians out of Muslim Afghanistan, and they are even more intent on driving the Americans out of Saudi Arabia, a far more important country to them, as it is home to the holiest Islamic sites.

At an important October 18th talk at MIT, Chomsky made a crucial distinction "between two categories which shouldn't be run together." The first category comprised the "actual perpetrators," whom he described in no uncertain terms as monstrous criminals. The second was the significant "reservoir of [popular] support" or "at least sympathy" for attacks on the US in the Middle East, thanks to various well-known dark and deadly aspects of US policy in the region. Even in the second category, Chomsky noted, much of the most significant support came not from the poor but from Arab bankers, lawyers, and professionals—hardly the natural enemies of capitalism championed by the advocates of "rag-tag Marxism."[39]

Finally, Chomsky spoke and wrote quite clearly against the notion of terrorism as the "weapon of the weak." Indeed, he argued that terrorism is "primarily a weapon of the strong, overwhelmingly, in fact. It is held to be a weapon of the weak because the strong also control the doctrinal systems and their terror doesn't count as terror."[40]

Blaming the Victims and Choosing Terror over Democratic Resistance?

The liberal-left's suggestion that the left blamed the victims and not the terrorists for the atrocities of 9/11 was shameless unsubstantiated radical-bashing rather than serious criticism. Walzer could not and cannot find anyone outside the lunatic fringe who is saying or writing anything that comes even remotely close to holding the dead and maimed of September 11 as responsible for their fate. Also without a shred of evidence was the suggestion that anyone in the "American and European left" disagreed with the notion that sane and serious left activists choose the construction of democratic social movements over the terror used by maniacal Muslim medievalists.

It is true that the left pointed out some uncomfortable facts regarding the historical and ongoing role of US policy in the Middle East. It argued that the US had been consistently and powerfully opposed to the democratic process there, that this opposition contributed to the "reservoir" of anti-Americanism that creates space for terrorists to thrive in, and that the US has long contributed critically in various ways, some direct, to the selection of medieval extremism and terror over nonviolent resistance in the Arab world. To note these facts was not, however, to embrace or apologize for terror—unless, again, one clings to the imbecilic notion that to understand a crime is to support it.

Embracing 9/11 in Advance by Calling for the Bombing of Washington?

Issac's use of Chomsky's *New Military Humanism* also falls squarely into the cheap-shot category. Written more than a year before September 11, 2001, that book naturally never embraced the bombing of Washington, London, or Jakarta. Also contrary to Issac, it made more than a few "policy relevant distinctions" between the humanitarian crimes committed in Kosovo and East Timor. Chomsky argued that those distinctions, including the comparative sheer quantity of death and destruction inflicted by state terrorists (much greater in the case of Indonesia's US- and UK-sponsored assault on East Timor than in the case of Serbia's attack on Kosovo), made Washington more deserving of punitive bombing than Belgrade in a world where it was deemed appropriate to punish state crimes against humanity with deadly international attacks on the criminal states' civilian populations. It was clear, however, that neither Chomsky nor anyone else on the serious left even remotely embraced or embraces such a world. Chomsky's argument was merely rhetorical, meant to illustrate the inconsistency of US foreign policy and rhetoric rather than to embrace the horrible actions that would result if the argument were made consistent in policy. Issac's contention regarding Chomsky's text was hideous enough in and of itself. To insert this appalling argument into his post–September 11 smear of Chomsky was doubly lacking in basic decency, leftist or otherwise.

Advocating No Response?

The liberal-left is wrong, finally, in claiming that the left has advanced and advances no response to the terror attacks and the threat of future terrorism. Both before and since 9/11, Chomsky and others on the left have spoken and published clearly and at length on the superiority and desirability of an approach to world tensions that relies on international law, multilateral negotiation, and, ultimately, global social justice and democracy. The preference for such a path—advanced less in the name of pacifism than of violence-reduction, increased security (including that of Americans at home and abroad), and civilized decency —has been consistently evident in left commentary. By saying that the left advocates "doing nothing," the liberal-left hopes to deflect attention away from its unfortunate identification of "doing something" with bombing innocent civilians and the expansion of US state terrorism.

Selective Targeting

Reflecting deep servility to power, there was a delicious selectivity at the root of Hitchens, Walzer, and Isaac's focus on radicals in denouncing those who combined basic morally responsible notions of historical causation with honest discussion of American empire in order to understand 9/11. To be consistent across ideological lines, they should have leveled their inaccurate charges of moral-relativist excuse mongering at the *Wall Street Journal*. The *Journal* ran a candid September 18th story describing the broad basis of approval for the attacks among even affluent residents of the Middle East. Many of the latter were reported by the *Journal* as thinking "that what happened in New York is not all that different from what America has inflicted on Iraqis, Palestinians, Sudanese, and other Muslims." A related *Journal* dispatch reported that sympathy for the American victims in the Arab world was "qualified with a reflexive twinge of satisfaction that the US was at last paying a price for its strong support of Israel and its insistence on sanctions against Iraq, Libya, Syria, and other states."[41]

Newsweek would have been a yet more appropriate target for liberal-left attacks on those who have the temerity to explain Middle-Eastern anti-American terror. Under the title of "Why Do They Hate Us?" that magazine's October 15th cover story offered an extensive discussion of how imperial US policies in the Middle East—the same ones emphasized by bin-Laden et al.—create massive "raw anti-Americanism" across the region. The article was written by Fareed Zakaria, a one-time managing editor of *Foreign Affairs* with a Harvard doctorate who supported the US bombing campaign in Afghanistan. Zakaria was certainly no member of the "Chomsky-Zinn-Finkelstein crowd" or the "American and European left."[42]

An even better target would have been the establishment *Chicago Tribune*. On Sunday September 30th, that paper's Perspectives section contained a piece titled "A New World Disordered: The Seeds of Terror Thrive in Poor Ground" by international correspondent R. C. Longworth.

Longworth argued that the savage inequalities and related mass unemployment generated by US-sponsored corporate globalization created fertile soil for terrorism even while it opened Americans to easy attack. "If any region has got the worst of the global economy, but none of the best," Longworth elaborated, "it is the Middle East." Lacking some liberal-leftists' faith in the autonomous power of human moral agency, regardless of historical and material circumstances, he argued that the best way to preempt future Middle East–based terror attacks would be to reduce the region's savage social and economic inequality.

Longworth quoted a former US Commerce Department official, William Van Dusen Wishard (obviously a radical moral-relativist apologist for anti-American terror), to chilling effect. According to Wishard, "in a globalized world with instant communications, *it is impossible to have excessive opulence alongside grinding poverty without something, sometime, somewhere, exploding. We Americans have flaunted our affluence and power in the face of the world, and the world has reacted in varying degrees, terrorism being only the most extreme form of reaction.*"[43] There are many more examples, including even *USA Today*, that provided a moderately intelligent discussion of the roots of the new Arab anti-Americanism in an imperial US policy.

But the ultimate missing target in the liberal-left's attack on terrorism's supposed apologists (well, explainers) was the US policy establishment. Liberal-leftists on the hunt for the argument that terrorist attacks on American targets are a predictable result of American empire should have reviewed a report produced in 1997 by the Defense Science Board for the US Undersecretary of Defense for Acquisition and Technology. This elite study found that "historical data show a strong correlation between U.S. involvement in international situations and an increase in terrorist attacks against the United States. In addition," it continued, "*the military asymmetry that denies nation states the ability to engage in overt attacks against the United States drives the use of transnational actors* [i.e., international terrorists]."[44]

Liberal-leftists looking for dangerous people who argue that imperial chickens come home to roost in terrible ways could also have read the recent millennial vision statements of the US Space Command and the CIA. Both predict increasing terrorist threats to "US national interests and investments" resulting from US-sponsored economic "globalization," which they acknowledge—quite contrary to official US statements on the alleged universal benefits of "free trade"—to be widening the gap between the planet's "haves" and "have-nots."

There were and are many other examples of establishment candor on the dangerous backlash that empire creates. As the distinguished senior Far East scholar Chalmers Johnson has shown, the US Central Intelligence Agency has long used, internally, the phrase "blowback" to describe the unintended consequences (including terrorist attacks on American soil) of secret US foreign policies. "Blowback," writes Johnson in his chillingly prophetic *Blowback: The Costs and Consequences of American Empire*, based largely on establishment sources, "is shorthand for saying that a nation reaps what it sows, even if it does not fully know or understand what it has sown. Given its wealth and power, the United States will be a prime recipient in the foreseeable future of all of the more expectable forms of blowback, particularly terrorist attacks against Americans in and out of the armed forces anywhere on earth, including within the United States."[45] Imperial strategists and policymakers, of course, need to deal candidly with the world as it is, not with the fantasy versions sold to the people to keep the masses in line. In that world, they know and acknowledge—when speaking to each other—that events like those of September 11 are a reasonably predictable outcome of US global policy.

It was not surprising, however, that the *Wall Street Journal, Chicago Tribune, USA Today, Newsweek,* government officials, and even Johnson did not get scolded for "excusing terror" by the liberal-left watchdogs. Deeply deferential to power, the latter saw no advantage in criticizing more respectable voices for saying some of the same things, albeit from a very different perspective, as their hated rivals on the left. Like the standard schoolyard bully, they preferred to pick on the easy target at the edge of the playground, avoiding confrontation with those who own and rule the schoolyard.

Basic Decency

Certainly, thanks largely to 9/11, things are difficult enough for those who believe in social justice in the United States without the progressive community diving into an orgy of internecine warfare precipitated partly by medieval lunatics like bin-Laden. In the hope of restoring some unity on the more leftward side of American life and in the interest of its own integrity, the liberal-left should tear down some of the straw dogs it has built up to its left in the wake of 9/11's terrible events. The liberal-left's attacks on post–September 11 left commentary are based on truly extraordinary misrepresentations of what the left actually said and wrote about the historic crimes inflicted on America last summer. It is only basic decency to consult the real record of those you judge.

4

Who Is the Real Criminal: Johnny Taliban or Donny Pentagon?

October 18, 2002

Two weeks ago, the verdict came in on John Walker Lindh, the 21–year-old "American Taliban" who fought with the former government of Afghanistan. Lindh escaped life in prison on terrorism charges by pleading guilty to providing service to a terrorist organization and to carrying explosives (a rifle and two grenades) while performing that service. He faces as many as twenty years in prison, losing his young adulthood to America's massive, globally unmatched, mass incarceration state.[46]

It is not clear why Lindh converted to Islam when he was 16 or what role his family circumstances and/or community surroundings in California played in that conversion. It is not clear why his parents supported his decision to move to Yemen or whether he was trained in a terrorist camp run by al Qaeda. I suspect but do not know that he feared for his life if he tried to escape after the September 11 attacks. It is not clear, but also not likely, that he ever hoped to receive financial compensation for books, TV appearances, and/or other promotions relating to his bizarre experience—as such compensation is forbidden under the terms of the July 14 plea agreement.

What we do know, however, is that Lindh's "terrible crimes" are laughably minor compared to those committed by US policymakers before and during America's post–September 11 "war on terrorism," in which he became unwittingly trapped. Lindh, a short-term foot soldier in a distant rag-tag army, may get as many as twenty years for *carrying a rifle and two grenades, with no evidence that he ever actually hurt so much as a flea.* How many years behind bars, then, do the guardians of Western civilization propose for monumentally terrorist US decisionmakers like former Secretary of State Henry Kissinger?

Kissinger is guilty of war crimes and crimes against humanity in such far-flung locations as Cambodia, East Timor, Cyprus, Chile, and Vietnam. Among his victims are 250,000 East Timorese, murdered in a genocidal invasion approved and equipped by the United States under the direction of Kissinger and President Ford in 1975.[47]

Kissinger receives hefty fees for speaking engagements, media appearances, and books that are marketed as containing the wisdom of one of civilization's great statesmen.

How many years, then, for the US presidents and other military officials involved in the operation of the United States' notorious School of the Americas (SOA), recently renamed the "Western Hemisphere Institute for Security Cooperation" in response to humanitarian protests? "Over its decades of existence," Rahul Mahajan writes in his excellent *New Crusade: America's War on Terrorism*, the SOA "has graduated hundreds of future military dictators, death squad leaders, torturers and others who have spread misery throughout Latin America." It has spawned, to give just one among numerous examples, Efraim Rios Montt, "whose reign of terror over Guatemala in the 1980s," notes Mahajan, "saw the killing of over 100,000 Mayan Indians." The SOA's record of death and destruction makes al Qaeda look minor league by comparison, though it is worth noting that bin-Laden and his crew got their start with crucial assistance from the SOA's operator, the United States.[48]

How many years for George Bush Senior and General Norman Schwarzkopf, whose crimes during the Persian Gulf "War" include the "Highways of Death" massacre, when US bombers mercilessly attacked thousands of retreating military and civilian vehicles flying white flags? How many years for the Pentagon officials who ordered the destruction of most large water treatment plants and dams in Iraq, creating "an explosion of water-borne disease"[49] there?

How many years for Bill Clinton, who ordered an August 1998 cruise missile strike on the El Shifa pharmaceutical plant in Sudan, resulting in thousands of civilian deaths? Clinton also continued economic sanctions that claimed the lives of as many as 500,000 Iraqi children between the end of the Gulf War and 1996. How many years for Clinton's secretary of state, Madeleine Albright, who told *60 Minutes* reporter Leslie Stahl that "the price" of those US-caused juvenile fatalities was "worth it" to achieve noble US global objectives? How many for Clinton and Albright in connection with the 1999 "humanitarian bombing" of Serbia, which targeted basic civilian infrastructure, including water treatment and electricity generation?[50]

How many years for the top US policymakers who provide essential economic support and advanced US-made (Boeing and Lockheed Martin) military support for Israel's illegal, deadly, and racist occupation of Palestinian territory? The most recent example of officially unmentionable Israeli terrorism involved the use of an F-16 fighter to level an entire civilian apartment block in the Gaza Strip. The annual US taxpayers' price tag in support of Israeli apartheid is more than $5 billion.[51]

And regarding the current US war on terror to expand empire and government power while serving oil interests at home and abroad, how many years for Bush Junior, Secretary of Defense Donald Rumsfeld, and other top officials for their cavalier liquidation of thousands of innocent Afghan civilians? Victims of easily predictable and in fact widely predicted "collateral damage" that US officials and a sickeningly hypersubservient "mainstream" (actually corporate) media have worked to criminally suppress, those civilians died so that the US might maintain proper imperial credibility in the wake of the September 11 attacks.[52]

Listen to the comments of an "unidentified Pentagon official" about the deaths of ninety-three civilians in the October 22nd attack on the village of Chowkar-Karez: *"The people there are dead because we wanted them dead."*[53] That anonymous official could have said much the same about more than 600 Taliban-affiliated prisoners slaughtered, many with hands tied behind their backs, in an attack carried out by the Northern Alliance with the help of US bombers and helicopters.[54]

"Because we wanted them dead." That is the language of a Mafia Don, who wants it understood that nobody touches his operation without getting their legs broken.

It is irrelevant, apparently, that most of 9/11's culprits were Saudis. There was not a single person of Afghan ancestry on the four hijacked planes. Still, by one rigorously researched estimate, that of business professor Marc Herold, US bombs killed more than 4,000 Afghan civilians, outdoing 9/11's body count, just between October and January.[55]

There are many more examples, and we look forward to Rumsfeld's future paid speeches, reflections, and memoirs, returning us to the inspiring days when history's most powerful nation pulverized preindustrial villagers and sheepherders in one of the world's weakest and poorest states.

Who, then, is the *real criminal* these days—Johnny (Walker Lindh) Taliban or Donny (Rumsfeld) Pentagon? The latter's crimes, of course, along with those of his cohorts, are ongoing and may soon crescendo into a bloody imperialist assault on Iraq.

Merely to ask these questions, in the US at least, is to indicate one's status as a member of the lunatic fringe. It is to open oneself up to the charge of "anti-Americanism," of being on the wrong side of the all-or-nothing division of the world—"Either you are with us or you are with the terrorists"—announced by George W. Bush on September 20.[56] It is also to develop a deepened sense of why the US has worked so hard to undermine the new International Criminal Court, which other nations understandably see as a basic step toward the global rule of law.

You don't have to join the Islamic Jihad to run afoul of the new world order and the global criminal justice state proclaimed by Bush, Rumsfeld,

Rice, and the rest. You only have to question the extent to which the US government is a credible opponent and not in fact a leading practitioner of terrorism. You only have to grasp an unmentionable fact: that America's war on terrorism is mainly about "the extension and maintenance of US government power, at home and abroad. Other motives," Mahajan rightly notes, "are strictly secondary."[57]

5
Our Tears, Their Opportunity
October 21, 2002

What a Difference a Day Made

One of the nation's dirty little secrets is that 9/11 is by far and away the best thing that has happened to the George W. Bush White House. Only thirteen and a half months ago, Bush was on the defensive. His approval ratings were mediocre amidst considerable public doubt about the legitimacy of his "election," his intellectual capabilities, and the wisdom (much less the fairness) of his darkly regressive domestic agenda. His foreign policy, falsely described as "isolationist"—Bush and his advisers hardly hoped to withdraw the US from its global engagements—was commonly said to be out of touch with contemporary global requirements.

But to paraphrase the onetime American jazz singer Dinah Washington, oh what a difference a day made. The jetliner attacks of September 11 and the fear they unleashed have been a windfall for an administration whose essential mission is to deepen the nation's inequality of wealth and power (a nation that is already the most unequal in the industrialized world) and to expand its imperial power abroad (though it is already the most powerful global state in world history). This is the unmentionable truth behind Bush's revealing words, uttered just three days after the tragic events: "Through the tears of sadness," Bush told the American people, he saw "an opportunity."[58]

Opportunity, indeed! It's not just that 9/11 provided Bush and his allies an occasion to marginalize and repress those who question his domestic agenda and the legitimacy of his presidency. To the delight of the White House, the terrorists also gave the Bush team the freedom to pursue long-standing and distinctly nonisolationist objectives abroad.

The Bush Doctrine

Consider the White House's *National Security Strategy of the United States,* a document in which each presidential administration outlines its strategic plan to "defend" America. The Bush Doctrine, released last September, is the boldest and most explicitly imperial version of this document yet to be produced. To "protect the nation," it formally announces a "new" international and military doctrine for the United States. The US has decided, this doctrine proclaims, that no government or coalition will ever be permitted to challenge US supremacy.

Deterrence, the official policy of the US for more than fifty years, is irrelevant. In the new world order, vaguely defined as "free" and "democratic" by US elites, the US is determined to crush anyone who even dreams of trying to match its power. Embracing an openly aggressive foreign policy based on the idea that "the best defense is a good offense" and expressing brazen disregard for international law and opinion when such law and opinion do not suit American interests, the September 2002 Bush plan officially endorses preemptive assaults on perceived enemies. It sees America as the world's self-appointed gendarme, uniquely qualified to launch "preventative" wars of its own choosing.

The *National Security Strategy* advances America's right to attack other "sovereign" nations when foreign governments fail to meet their "sovereign responsibilities," determined by the world's super-state—the United States. It favors unilateral US action over collective global security and multilateral efforts, counseling the US to engage only in short-term and shifting coalitions appropriate to changing needs in crisis situations. It endorses the unworkable, costly, and destabilizing Star Wars missile defense system, repudiating decades of nuclear arms control and suggesting to other nuclear states that the US is positioning itself for first-strike capability. In short, it is a blueprint for total US domination through unilateral action and military superiority. A more nakedly Orwellian approach to world affairs is difficult to imagine.[59]

A "Warmed Over" Strategy for World Dominance

Three Septembers

Just as Orwellian is the White House's claim (parroted in mainstream media accounts of America's "post–September 11 foreign policy") about the document's inception, which it attributes to the *September 2001* attacks. Those who bother to look can find many of the same ideas enunciated by the White House in *September 2002* in a related *September 2000* report issued by the arch-imperialist Project for a New American Century (PNAC): *Rebuilding America's Defenses: Strategy, Forces, and Resources for a New Century.*

The PNAC document advocated explicit imperial unilateralism, rejection of US reliance on collective security and coalitions, preemptive US military action where "necessary," massive expansion of military expenditures and overseas bases, rejection of deterrence/containment doctrine, the violation (wherever and whenever necessary) of uncooperative nations' sovereign rights, and prevention of the emergence of any government or coalition of governments with the power to challenge US military supremacy. It also called for a massive ($15–$20 billion) increase in military spending, required to "transform" the American military into an imperial super-force able "to fight and decisively win multiple, simultaneous major theater wars" (p. iv). "The process of [this] transformation is likely to be a long one," PNAC actually claimed, "absent some catastrophic and catalyzing event—like a new Pearl Harbor" (p. 51).[60]

The list of people behind the organization that produced this audacious document, released three months before the judicial coup that installed Bush, reads like a "Who's Who" of the Bush foreign policy establishment. It includes noted warmonger Paul Wolfowitz (now deputy defense secretary), John Bolton (now undersecretary of state), Stephen Cambone (head of the Pentagon's Office of Program, Analysis, and Evaluation), Eliot Cohen (member of the Defense Policy Board), Devon Cross (member of the Defense Policy Board), Lewis Libby (chief of staff to Vice President Dick Cheney), and Don Zakheim (comptroller for the Defense Department). They enjoyed their much-desired "catastrophic and catalyzing event"—their "new Pearl Harbor"—on September 11, 2001.

For Condoleezza Rice, Bush's top national security adviser, it seems that the beginning of the Cold War provided the better historical analogy. Just days after the terror attacks, she called together senior members of the National Security Council and asked them to "think about how do you [the US foreign policy establishment] capitalize on these opportunities," which she likened to those of 1945–1947,[61] when the Truman administration advanced the trumped-up threat of Soviet "communist" expansionism as a cover for America's more truly global and imperialist objectives in the wake of WWII.

The Original "Post–Cold War" Blueprint

This document in turn owes an openly acknowledged debt to a still older blueprint, drafted in 1992. Nine years prior to September 2001, when, American elites disingenuously insist, "everything changed," Wolfowitz, a then-obscure strategist working for then-Defense Secretary Dick Cheney, drafted a then-shocking policy paper titled "Defense Planning Guidance." Among other things, this key strategy paper advocated total US global domination and the prevention of the emergence of any rivals to American supremacy. It made no mention of collective or multilateral action, calling only for occasional American exploitation of ad hoc coalitions that do not last beyond immediate crises in which US interests are threatened—a perfect description of the Bush administration's immediate response to 9/11. Preemptive military action was included in the list of options for the US to consider in its efforts to "prevent the re-emergence of a new [post-Soviet] rival."

Leaked to the *New York Times,* Wolfowitz's paper was withdrawn because of the widespread criticism its explicit imperial chauvinism elicited. The Pentagon dismissed it as a "low-level draft" and made the false claim that Cheney had never read it.[62]

No such withdrawals are required in the wake of 9/11. As David Armstrong of the *National Security News Service* has recently noted in *Harper's Magazine,* mainstream commentators focusing only on the supposedly defensive and "new" preemption component of the Bush Doctrine have missed the rich imperial consistency between the latest national security blueprint and the original "post–Cold War" planning of Cheney and Wolfowitz:[63]

> Reaction to the latest edition of the Plan [Doctrine] has, thus far, focused on preemption. Commentators parrot the administration's line, portraying the concept of preemptory strikes as a "new" strategy aimed at combating terrorism. . . . Preemption [however] . . . is just part of the Plan, and the Plan is hardly new. It is a warmed-over version of the strategy Cheney and his co-authors rolled out in 1992 as the answer to the end of the Cold War. Then the goal was global dominance and it met with bad reviews. Now it is the answer to terrorism. The emphasis is on preemption, and the reviews are generally enthusiastic. Through all of this, the dominance motif remains, though largely undetected.

New Tragedies on the Horizon: The Limits of Power

Nothing, however, is more blinding than imperial arrogance. The socialization process and inherent ideological codes of ruling-class membership atop an imperial state do not permit US policymakers to grasp the limits of their power and the unintended consequences of their actions. Consistent with a long record of US foreign policy failure driven by narcissistic and imperial pretense and a naive faith in the long-term effectiveness of military "fixes," the implementation of the Bush Doctrine in the case of greatest immediate significance—that of Iraq—promises, among other things, to

- squander what's left of the global goodwill that America garnered in the immediate aftermath of the terrorist attacks, thus serving as a dangerous model for others' future international behavior;
- distract American and world attention and resources away from the urgent need to diffuse the Middle Eastern tinderbox by resolving the

Israel-Palestine conflict in an equitable fashion and demilitarizing the entire region;

- distract the US and the world from appropriate actions to prevent further attacks by al Qaeda and other nonterritorial terror networks that baffle American imperialists, who seem addicted (partly for reasons of perceived US credibility) to attacking territory-specific regimes; and
- generate "catastrophic side effects," including a dangerous destabilization of the entire Middle East, a massive upsurge of virulent anti-Americanism in the Islamic world, and a new wave of terror attacks on nonpolicymaking Americans at home and abroad.

It might be possible to derive some satisfaction from the probability that the Bush Doctrine will not succeed if the playing out of the likely failures did not carry grave consequences for ordinary people not only abroad but also—in an age when technology and globalization permit previously unimaginable horrific attacks on the "homeland"—at home. As the distinguished radical historian Gabriel Kolko notes in his recent book *Another Century of War?* America's historical reliance on weapons and force has long "exacerbated or created far more problems for the United States than it has solved [Vietnam is only the classic example]. After September 11," Kolko observes, "there can be no doubt that arms have not brought security to America. It is not only in the world's interest that America adapt to the realities of the twenty-first century. *What is new is that it is now, more than ever, in the interest of the American people themselves.* It is imperative that the United States acknowledge the limits of its power—limits that are inherent in its own military illusions and in the very nature of a world that is far too big and complex for any country to even dream of managing."[64]

For this to happen, the American people must, as in the past, disrupt the normal top-down flow of policymaking in the eye of the imperial, world-systemic hurricane. They must challenge the power of an arrogant, narcissistic policymaking "elite" that values the expansion of US military and economic power more than the security of its own population. They must confront dangerous, disingenuous rulers who see opportunity in our tears and who create the context for yet more tragedy abroad and at home through the ceaseless power- and profit-mad pursuit of total global domination.

6
Who Hates America?
April 9, 2003

A Terrorist Recruiting Bonanza

As American armed forces tighten George W. Bush's bloody grip on Baghdad, some interesting answers emerge to the question of who really "hates America." Certain obvious and officially acknowledged haters come quickly to mind—Saddam Hussein and his supporters, and the members of al Qaeda and other extremist Islamic terror networks. Other "haters" are less officially recognized.

They include a significant share, probably a majority, of the "Arab Street." People in the Middle East have no special love for Saddam, a ruthless dictator whose demise is certainly a positive event in and of itself. Still, they are outraged by Bush's brazen, deadly, and illegal invasion of the Arab world and don't take seriously Bush's claim to be exporting "democracy," something that is in rather short supply in the American homeland. They know that Operation Dominate Iraq is a test run for future American attacks on Middle Eastern states. In line with Osama bin-Laden's fondest hopes, Bush's "war" on Iraq is expanding preexisting widespread Arab "anti-Americanism," fed by US sponsorship of Israel, the presence of American troops in Saudi Arabia, and US-imposed economic sanctions that have killed a half-million Iraqi children.

You won't hear very much about this broader Arab "anti-Americanism" and its sources from the official corporate-state television broadcasters at Fox News and CNN. But you can read a fair amount about it in places like the *Wall Street Journal*, where it is deemed safe and necessary to acknowledge that Bush's imperialism is generating broad Arab bitterness against America, a recruiting bonanza for bin-Laden and his ilk.

"A Tidal Wave of Hatred for the US"

Contrary, however, to the convenient American "clash of civilizations" thesis, dividing the world between Islam and Christianity (the West), Bush's "war" (massacre) is also recruiting a significant number of non-Arabs and non-Muslims into the "I hate Uncle Sam" club. "There is a tidal wave of hatred for the US," writes Indian novelist and anti-imperial activist Arundhati Roy, "rising from the ancient heart of the world. In Africa, Latin America, Asia, Europe, Australia. I encounter it everyday." Roy reports from mostly Hindu India:[65]

> Sometimes it comes from the most unlikely sources. Bankers, businessmen, yuppie students, and they bring to it all the crassness of their conservative, illiberal politics. That absurd inability to separate governments from people: America is a nation of morons, a nation of murderers, they say (with the same carelessness with which they say, "All Muslims are terrorists"). . . . Suddenly, I, who have been vilified for being "anti-American" and "anti-west," find myself in the extraordinary position of defending the people of America.

Consider an anonymous e-mail I received last November from an Australian who calls himself "Overtones." "It breaks my heart that all those people died in September 11th," Overtones writes,

> but you Americans are terrorists. I personally cannot think of anyone more heroic than the pilots of those hijacked planes carrying out their suicide missions. . . . You Americans missed the whole point of the attack. It was a cry of pain and desperation for Lord knows how much death, destruction, rape and plunder by American foreign abuse. The arrogance displayed by this policy is breathtaking in its scope and application.
>
> Must you Yanks meddle with everything? I know it's all done in the name of the almighty dollar and limitless power in the hands of the very few to rape whatever and wherever for their own profit. . . . We have a beautiful little planet here, but not for long if [the White House] is given the freedom to do as they wish. And since you Yanks elected this cretin things have rapidly progressed from pathetic to worse.
>
> The attack on the trade towers was a cry of desperation and you not only missed it but are now in the process of fucking over the entire world because of something you Yanks started in the first place. . . . Saddam and Bush are more similar than not [but] as a threat to world peace Bush takes the cake. It is the American exploitation and total disregard for the rest of the world that will plummet the world into a spiral of destruction. Stop the wholesale abuse of the world any way you can my friend because the whole world hates your government. Cooperation, not war! Doesn't it occur to [Bush et al.] that we cannot stop the world and get off? Bush does not have the capacity or simple common sense and it seems neither do your countrymen.

These angry words were sent across cyberspace five months before Bush pushed the buttons to set in motion the killing chains on America's rolling slaughterhouses of empire.

Mr. Overtones's current sentiments about "you terrorist Yanks" are probably expressed in accurate if more erudite terms by Greek composer Mikis Theodorakis. According to last Monday's *New York Times*, in an article titled "Anti-Americanism in Greece Is Re-invigorated by War," Theodorakis recently called the American people "detestable, ruthless cowards and murderers of the people of the world. From now on, I will consider as my enemies those who interact with these barbarians for whatever reason." Theodorakis is probably one of the majority of Greeks who report holding "a more positive view of Saddam Hussein than of Mr. Bush" and who think "the United States" is "as undemocratic as Iraq."[66] He has many allies across Western civilization, including a respectable German dentist who recently announced his determination to refuse service to "Americans and Britons."

September Sympathy Lost: "To Support America Is Politically Dangerous"

Bush's "war" has bred an unprecedented rift with Europe, evidenced by the growing movement there for boycotts against American goods and companies—a rift exacerbated by the Bush administration's contemptuous treatment of the United Nations in preparation for the attack. This treatment included bugging foreign UN ambassadors' phones (widely reported everywhere but in the US) and the provision of blatantly falsified information to justify the attack (from Europe's standpoint the US would have done better to avoid the pretense of interest in serious UN engagement).

European "anti-Americanism" has moved beyond the left to include much of the center-right, which traditionally supported the US in the age of the (supposed) great Soviet threat. In the post–Cold War and post–September 11 world, right-leaning *Newsweek* commentator Fareed Zakaria notes, "center-right [European] parties might still support Washington, but many do so out of inertia and without much popular support." "To support America today in much of the world," he observes, "is politically dangerous." Consistent with that judgment, opposition to US policy was a significant "vote-getter" in elections held in at least three countries during the last year—Germany, South Korea, and Pakistan. While the US "has the backing of a dozen or so governments," Zakaria further notes, it "has the support of a majority of the people in only one country in the world, Israel. If that's not isolation, then the word has no meaning."[67]

More than three out of four citizens oppose the US "war" in such purchased "coalition" states as Spain, Italy, Hungary, and Czechoslovakia. Ninety percent were opposed in Iraq's neighbor Turkey, where popular sentiment forced the parliament to deny the United States war-basing rights even as the Bush administration offered that nation billions in new assistance.[68]

It is now commonplace to observe that the people of America could not possibly expect to receive anything close to the degree of world sympathy they received after 9/11 if they were hit by another significant terror attack.

American Government versus American People—A Waning World Distinction?

America's foreign critics have long tended to follow Roy's distinction (a welcome one for antiwar Americans like myself) between America's government and its people, denouncing the policies of the former but generally exonerating the latter. But with more than 70 percent of the US population reportedly supporting the White House's butchery in Iraq, we should not be surprised if much of the world joins Mr. Overtones in blurring that great distinction. Stories and images of Iraqi civilian deaths *are* available to Americans, even though corporate and state thought-police filter out the most provocative evidence—the severed civilian bodies and charred remains shown by more responsible information sources like the independent Arab news network Al Jazeera, bombed this week by Uncle Sam. The world knows about this availability since it also gets CNN. How impressed can Americans expect others to remain over the fact that our outward support for our blood-soaked president is based on the false government- and media-generated belief that Saddam represented a serious threat to America? It's a good question when 83 percent of American "war" supporters report they will continue to support the military action "even if the [US and UK] forces don't find weapons of mass destruction."[69]

"They Hate Our Freedom"?

One wouldn't know it to listen to the White House and Fox News, but rising world sentiment against America has little to do with envy and/or resentment of America's supposed glorious internal "freedoms" and "democracy." There is much that non-Americans find disgusting about American society, including its crass commercialism—so intense you can't watch the last minute of a close basketball game without seeing at least ten advertisements. Contrary to the narcissistic American idea that the world spends significant time ruminating on America's inner life, however, what angers overseas "anti-Americans" most is not the nature of America's domestic society but what America does externally. And Europeans are not likely candidates for envying or hating supposed American "freedoms" and "democracy," since they possess greater degrees of social, economic, political, and cultural freedom and democracy themselves. Europeans, after all, enjoy stronger welfare states, socialized health insurance, more humane work schedules, more diverse and inclusive political systems, less commercialized and corporate-dominated media, and a generally more intact and decent civil society. According to the highly overrated and widely (within the US "elite") celebrated American imperialist theoretician Robert A. Kagan, this makes them dysfunctionally "postmodern," ill-suited to the harsh, "Hobbesian" realities of a brutish world that requires the firm hand of global military supervision that only the Americans can provide.[70]

Moreover, how envious or fearful can foreigners be of the "freedoms" of a severely overworked country that currently incarcerates a greater percentage of its population than any nation in modern history? As the self-described "beacon to the world of the way life should be" (these being the immortal words spoken by millionaire Texas Senator Kay Bailey Hutchison last summer),[71] America remains unique among "modern" industrial states in its refusal to provide its populace universal health coverage, something contemplated for occupied Iraq. America elevates consumption, entertainment, private experience, and spectatorship over active public citizenship; entrenches corporate plutocracy so deeply that a majority of its citizens doesn't bother to vote; falsely conflates democracy with corporate-state capitalism; and distributes wealth more unequally than any other industrialized state. It reflexively blames the victims of its harsh structural inequalities for their presence at the bottom of its steep socioeconomic hierarchies.

Homegrown Hatred from the Top Down

As this chapter may already suggest, there's another group that hates America with every bit as much passion as Mr. Overtones. But you'll never hear in the "mainstream" media about *this* group's curious and home-grown anti-Americanism, which flows down from the peaks of homeland hierarchies. For many in this group, mostly from the top hundredth (at least) of the American hierarchy and strongly represented in the current White House, the terrible jetliner attacks of September 11 have been a gift from heaven, a great "opportunity" for domestic as well as imperial conquest. In short, 9/11 has permitted them to launch a two-pronged assault on the American population under the cover of the "war on terrorism" and a greatly expanded "culture of fear."

The first prong is an elaborate campaign to redistribute American wealth and, hence, power yet further upward through massive tax cuts precisely calculated to overwhelmingly benefit the richest Americans, with devastating effects on the nation's ability to meet basic social and civic needs. Disingenuously sold as mechanisms for broad economic stimulus, these regressive measures are certain to damage the overall economy and cripple efforts to support Americans outside the exalted circles of privilege.

The second prong is an attack on American civil liberties, democracy, and public space, the worst such assault in fifty years, designed to marginalize dissent, restrict the spectrum of acceptable debate, and constrict democratic imagination. Beyond the specific measures of homeland repression, including the draconian, falsely named "Patriot Act," this attack seizes upon a sense of public emergency created in the wake of 9/11 to redefine public space in authoritarian, regressive, and state-capitalist ways. "For Bush and Ashcroft," writes the prolific left critic Henry Giroux, "the culture of fear" crafted by state and media in the post–September 11 era "provides the conditions in which Americans can be asked to spy on each other, dissent can be viewed as un-American, and dissenters can be subjected to possible internment. At the core of Bush's notion of community and hyper-patriotism," Giroux perceptively observes, "is a notion of temporality detached from a sense of public deliberation, critical citizenship, and civic engagement." Community, in the Bush–Ashcroft–Fox News view, is stripped of democratic and open-ended meanings. It is "embraced through a debased patriotism that is outraged by dissent" and focuses its "strongest appeals to civic discourse . . . on military defense, civil order, and domestic security." Under the rules of the expanded new authoritarianism, the most significant things Americans can do to support and strengthen their "democracy" besides joining the armed forces are to work hard for their boss, make money, go home and watch television, and buy commodities.[72]

The two prongs are inseparably linked. Policymakers and corporate interests seeking to increase the already extreme concentration and centralization of American wealth and power find it very useful indeed to smear their critics as "anti-Americans." A time of (apparently endless) public emergency is not an appropriate moment, we are told, to question the Leaders' noble schemes to stuff Fat Cat pockets yet fuller with cash originally marked for the most vulnerable among an increasingly insecure populace. To criticize such vile plutocracy "while we are fighting our war on terrorism"—to quote the not-yet-disgraced Trent Lott rebuking that subversive radical Tom Daschle last year[73]—is to flirt, we are told, with treason. This is a leap that would immediately be recognized as profoundly anti-American by such notable early Americans as Thomas Jefferson, for whom the right to dissent was a sine qua non of the revolutionary new nation he helped create. It directly and hauntingly confirms the early warning of no less an American than James Madison, who noted that "the fetters imposed on liberty at home have ever been forged out of the weapons provided for defense against real, pretended, or imaginary dangers from abroad."

There are a number of supplemental and related ways in which the current rightist US regime expresses its deep contempt for ordinary Americans and their weak democracy. These include the transparently racist theft of the 2000 presidential election, the White House's refusal to permit a serious investigation of 9/11, the closing off of vital public access to

White House documents, the vicious White House assault on Medicare, and Bush's cynical version of "welfare reform." The latter increases work requirements and promotes marriage as the solution to poverty even as jobs disappear and government funding for childcare and job training is slashed to pay for airline bailouts and retroactive wealth-fare tax cuts.[74] And of course 9/11 rescued Bush's initially moribund and underfunded education bill, which "offers school children more standardized testing but does not guarantee them decent health care and adequate food."[75]

The Bush administration and its supporters even possess the sheer class arrogance to slash federal expenditures on American veterans at the same time that the White House conducts another war, exposing predominantly working-class members of the armed forces to cancer-causing Depleted Uranium. It orders its military personnel to damage themselves (too) by slaughtering essentially defenseless people. Most of those soldiers are in the military because they are denied standard middle-class pathways to education and careers, much less the red-carpeted pathways enjoyed by most of the chicken-hawk war masters in the White House. This is done to protect and advance the interests of the wealthy few, under the disingenuous name of a "democracy" that is severely depleted and degraded even in the imperial "homeland."

Meanwhile, the Bush gang's priorities are suggested by White House budget submissions that elevate imperial conquest far beyond homeland security, even as the launching of a new military crusade escalates the likelihood of terror attacks that may rival and transcend the horrors of 9/11.

When many millions across the world, including more than a million Americans, took to the streets against the "war" even before it was technically launched, Bush and his "posse" dismissed this remarkable outpouring of antiwar sentiment as essentially irrelevant. Bush refused to directly answer reporters' questions about the reasons for mass opposition to his Iraq policy at home and abroad. Following standard White House doctrine, Bush, Rice, and Rumsfeld lectured us on how fortunate we are to possess the right to protest, unlike the people of Iraq. As if this had been granted to us by benevolent masters and was not a long-standing freedom to be asserted as our birthright. And as if this birthright was more seriously endangered by Saddam Hussein than by Christian fundamentalist enthusiast John Ashcroft and other sponsors of the Patriot Act (both I and II) and Total Information Awareness.

The list of plutocratic and authoritarian outrages inflicted on the US populace under the guise of the "war on terrorism" and the "leadership" of the George Orwellian Bush administration—by far the wealthiest White House in history—goes on and on. Perhaps nothing, however, epitomizes the sheer contempt in which that administration and its allies hold the American people and democracy more perfectly than the monumental propaganda campaign it has conducted since last September to convince Americans to accept the frankly—yes—moronic notion that Saddam posed a serious threat to Americans. Faced with a relentless barrage of false innuendo and pseudo-documentation, delivered by comforting faces on a glowing army of private telescreens, a critical mass of overworked Americans was convinced to support a thoroughly unjust and unnecessary "war" against a nation most Americans could not identify on a world map. It did not help that America's inadequately funded schools rarely encourage or permit the sort of instruction that would enable citizens to see through the lies of their "leaders," contrary to the mission of free public education in America (itself under attack by Republicans). Once the "war" began, of course, the original reasons became irrelevant: "Support Our Troops," no matter what.

Thanks to all this, the American people are increasingly being condemned along with their government by the rest of the world, rightly or wrongly—a development that cannot but worsen the chances for preventing the twenty-first century from descending into an orgy of bloodshed.

Ingratitude

It is interesting and instructive to compare this unmentionable home-grown "anti-Americanism" with foreign versions of the phenomenon. Unlike the overseas variants, the homeland variety is directed *without qualification* at the American people, freedom, and democracy. It is partly directed at American government, true, but only at one portion—the diminishing part that still serves the needs and protects the liberties of ordinary people. Beneath disingenuous pseudo-libertarian rhetoric about the superiority of the "free market" over the evil public sector, however, it loves another piece of American government—the massive and often underestimated part that serves wealth and empire.

Unlike the rest of the world's "anti-Americanism," the top-down domestic version is marked by extreme, ironic gratuitousness. Brutal and unattractive as many foreigners' "racist" anti-Americanism may be, their hostility to America makes a certain amount of sense in connection with tangibly brutal nasty things the US has done and is planning to do to overseas people and world order. In the case of Bush and his friends, however, the American society and people they hold in such profound contempt have permitted them to become unimaginably wealthy and powerful, something we might (naively) expect to evoke feelings of thankfulness and a sense of *noblesse oblige.* But no, the prosperity and influence that Americans have granted to these spoiled, ill-tempered, brutal, and authoritarian men, at least one of whom (Rumsfeld) openly identifies his policies with the legacy of Chicago mobster Al Capone,[76] only feed their revulsion at the hideous spectacle of their domestic populace. The more they punch away at us and our democracy, the more, it seems, they loathe us, disgusted and egged on by their sense of our weakness and division.

Their hatred of America is notable for truly stunning ingratitude. It is directed at a people and a nation that has granted them riches and power beyond their wildest dreams. It is rooted to no small extent in a sense of guilt over the fact that their possession of these assets is based on theft, deception, and subversion of the principles in whose name they claim to rule. It is also based, perhaps, on a nagging sense that the domestic hierarchy and inequality that underpin their audacious global project are the Achilles' heel of their imperial dreams.

Notes for Part I

1. James Madison, "Political Reflections" (February 23, 1799), quoted in John Samples, "James Madison's Vision of Liberty," *CATO Policy Report* (March/April 2001), p. 12, available online at www.cato.org/pubs/policy_report/v23n.2/madison.pdf.

2. Project for a New American Century, *Rebuilding America's Defenses: Strategy, Forces, and Resources for a New Century* (September 2000), p. 51.

3. Noam Chomsky, "A Quick Reaction," *Counterpunch* (September 12, 2001), available online at http://www.counterpunch.org/chomskybomb.html.

4. Quoted in Nicholas Lemman, "The Next World Order: The Hawks' Plans to Reshape the Globe," *New Yorker* (April 1, 2002), p. 44.

5. Quoted in Toby Harnden, "Father Defends Bush's Flight from Danger," *The Telegraph* (UK) (September 14, 2001), available online at http://www.telegraph.co.uk/news/main.jhtml?xml=/news/2001/09/14/wbush14.xml.

6. See Paul Street, "On 'Waking Up' and 'Losing Innocence,'" *ZNet Magazine* (September 19, 2001), available online at http://www.zmag.org/streetcalam.htm.

7. "Excerpts of President Bush's Address September 20, 2001 before a Joint Session of Congress," *Indianapolis Star* (September 21, 2001), available online at www.indystar.com/library/factfiles/crime/national/2001/sept11/transcripts/0921bush.html.

8. Stephen Chapman, "What We Have Lost, and What We Will Keep," *Chicago Tribune* (September 12, 2001).

9. See the perceptive comments of Howard Zinn in his *Terrorism and War* (New York: Seven Stories Press, 2002), pp. 12–13.

10. Arundhati Roy, Introduction to Noam Chomsky's *For Reasons of State* (New York: Pantheon, 2002 [reprint of 1970 edition]), pp. xii–xiii.

11. Tariq Ali, *The Clash of Fundamentalisms* (London: Verso, 2002), pp. 209–210.

12. Paul Street, "Mirror, Mirror," posted March 8, 2003 at www.zmag.org/content/showarticle.cfm?SectionID=51&ItemID=3203.

13. Henry A. Giroux, *The Abandoned Generation: Democracy Beyond the Culture of Fear* (New York: Palgrave, 2003), pp. 1–15.

14. Chomsky, *For Reasons of State,* p. xxxvii.

15. For a good summary of evidence, with abundant citations from numerous mainstream newspapers at home and abroad, see Patrick Martin, "Was the US Government Alerted to September 11 Attack?" *World Socialist Web Site,* available online at http://www.wsws.org/articles/2002/jan2002/sept-j16.html.

16. As of September 2003, there may be as many as 100 websites dedicated to advancing 9/11 conspiracy theories. For key links, see http://members.austar meto.com.au/~hubbca/9_11.htm; http://yama333tripod.com; and http://apfn.net/messageboard/5-01-03/discussion.cgi.55.html.

17. "Initial Scope of Joint Inquiry," *Congressional Record,* June 5, 2002 (Senate), available online at http://www.fas.org/irpcongress/2002_cr/s060502.html.

18. Juliet Eilpern, "Democrat Implies September 11 Administration Plot," *Washington Post* (April 12, 2002), p. A16.

19. Noam Chomsky, "A World Without War," *World Social Forum* 2 (Port Allegre, Brazil), Featured Talk, *ZNet Magazine* (May 29, 2002), available online at http://www.zmag.org/content/ForeignPolicy/chomwsf2t.cfm.

20. John Pilger, *The New Rulers of the World* (London: Verso, 2003), pp. 1–2.

21. American Council of Trustees and Alumni, *Defending Civilization: How Our Universities Are Failing America and What Can Be Done About It* (Washington, DC, 2001).

22. See also William J. Bennett, *Why We Fight: Moral Clarity and the War on Terrorism* (Washington, DC: Regenry, 2002), pp. 3, 16–17, 74–78. Bennett is a member of the ACTA's board. He is also a member of the Presidential National Advisory Council (PNAC), an organization that played, we shall see, a pivotal role in the design and advocacy of the Bush Doctrine of "preemptive war," put into practice against Iraq and the rest of the world in March 2003.

23. For a literally McCarthyite, Cold War antecedent, see E. Merrill Root, *Collectivism on the Campus: The Battle for the Mind in American Colleges* (New York: Devin-Adair Company, 1955).

24. Michael Walzer, "Can There Be a Decent Left?" *Dissent* (Spring 2002); Walzer, "The Politics of Ideological Apology," *The American Prospect* (October 22, 2001), available online at http://www.prospect.org/print/V12/18/walzer-m.html; Jeffrey Issac, "Ends and Means in Campus Politics," *Dissent* (Spring 2002).

25. Joel Bleiffus, "The Problem with Evil," *In These Times* (October 15, 2001), available online at http://www.inthesetimes.org/issue/25/23/edit2523.html.

26. Christopher Hitchens, "Against Rationalization," *The Nation* (October 8, 2001).

27. Jeffrey Issac, "Thus Spake Noam," *The American Prospect* (October 16, 2002), available online at http://www.prospect.org/webfeatures/2001/10/isaac-j-10–16.html; Noam Chomsky, *The New Military Humanism: Lessons from Kosovo* (Monroe, NE: Common Courage, 1999).

28. Noam Chomsky, "The New War Against Terror," talk at The Technology and Culture Forum, Massachusetts Institute of Technology (October 18, 2001), available online at http://www.counterpunch.org/chomskyterror.html.

29. Stephen Shalom and Michael Albert, "Terror Begets Terror" (September 17, 2001), available online at http://www.dawoodi-bohras.com/spotlight/terror_questions.htm.

30. Street, "On 'Waking Up' and 'Losing Our Innocence.'"

31. Michael Albert and Stephen Shalom, "Z Net's September 11 Talking Points," available online at www.zmag.org/qacalam.htm.

32. Chomsky, "On the Bombings," www.zmag.org/chomnote.htm; Chomsky, "The New War Against Terror."

33. Edward Hallett Carr, *What Is History?* (New York: Vintage, 1961), pp. 120–125.

34. Chomsky, "On the Bombings."

35. Noam Chomsky, "U.S. Foreign Policy and Relations with the Muslim World" (October 2, 2001), available online at http://www.msnbc.com/news/637155.asp.

36. Noam Chomsky, *9–11* (New York: Seven Stories Press, 2001), pp. 31–32.

37. Albert and Shalom, "Talking Points."

38. Interview by radio station B92 (September 22, 2001), available online at http://www.b92.net/intervju/eng/2001/0919–chomsky.phtml.

39. Chomsky, "The New War Against Terror."

40. Noam Chomsky, "Terrorism Works," posted November 23, 2001 at http://www.mediamonitors.net/noamchomsky3.html.

41. *Wall Street Journal* (September 18, 2001), quoted in Indymedia Center Los Angeles, "Arab States Resist," available online at http://regenerationtv.com/pipermail/imc-la/2001–September/003164.html.

42. Fareed Zakaria, "The Politics of Rage: Why Do They Hate Us?" *Newsweek* (October 15, 2001), available online at http://www.msnbc.com/news/639057.asp#BODY.

43. R. C. Longworth, "A New World Disordered: The Seeds of Terror Thrive in Poor Ground," *Chicago Tribune* (September 30, 2001); emphasis added.

44. Quoted in Chalmers Johnson, *Blowback: The Costs and Consequences of American Empire* (New York: Metropolitan Books, 2000), p. 9; emphasis added.

45. Ibid., p. 223.

46. Susan Candiotti, "Walker Sentenced to 20 Years," *CNN.Com/LawCenter* (October 4, 2002), available online at http://www.cnn.com/2002/LAW/10/04/lindh.statement/.

47. For details see Christopher Hitchens, *The Trial of Henry Kissinger* (London: Verso, 2001).

48. Rahul Mahajan, *New Crusade: America's War on Terrorism* (New York: Monthly Review Press, 2002), pp. 55–56.

49. Ibid., p. 107.

50. Mahajan, *New Crusade*, pp. 9–10, 14–15, 22, 27–28, 38, 43–46, 49, 56, 105–107, 112–115, 117–122, 139–137, 156; Mahajan, "'We Think the Price Is Worth It'"; Chomsky, "A Quick Reaction."

51. Suzanne Goldenberg, "Twelve Dead in Attack on Hammas," *The Guardian* (July 23, 2002), available online at http://www.guardian.co.uk/israel/Story/0,2763,761746,00.html; Richard H. Curtiss, "The True Cost of Israel to U.S. Taxpayers: True Lies About U.S. Aid to Israel," *Washington Report on Middle Eastern Affairs* (n.d.), available online at http://www.wrmea.com/html/us_aid_to_israel.htm.

52. Marc Herold, *A Dossier on Civilian Victims of United States' Aerial Bombing of Afghanistan: A Comprehensive Accounting* (Durham, NH: Department of Economics and Women's Studies, University of New Hampshire, December 2001).

53. Quoted in Seamus Milne, "The Innocent Dead in a Coward's War," *The*

Guardian (December 20, 2001), available online at http://www.guardian.co.uk/afghanistan/story/0,1284,622000,00.html.

54. Robert Fisk, "We Are the War Criminals Now," *The Independent* (November 29, 2001), available online at http://www.counterpunch.org/rfisk2.html; Jerry White, "After US Massacre of Taliban Prisoners, the Stench of Death and More Media Lies," *World Socialist Website* (November 29, 2001), available online at http://www.wsws.org/articles/2001/nov2001/mass-n29.shtml.

55. Herold, *A Dossier on Civilian Victims.*

56. "Text: President Bush Addresses the Nation," *Washington Post Online* (September 20, 2001), available online at http://www.washingtonpost.com/wp-srv/nation/specials/attacked/transcripts/bushaddress_092001.html.

57. Mahajan, *New Crusade*, p. 33.

58. Quoted in Harnden, "Father Defends Bush's Flight."

59. The President of the United States, *The National Security Strategy of the United States* (September 2002), available online at http://www.whitehouse.gov/nsc/nss.pdf.

60. Project for a New American Century, *Rebuilding America's Defenses: Strategy, Forces, and Resources for a New Century.* For useful discussions, see John Pilger, "The New Pearl Harbor," *The New Statesman* (December 12, 2002), available online at http://pilger.carlton.com/print/124759; and L.F.M. DeCauter, "The Key to This War: The Educational War Plans of the PNAC," URBANmag.reactiebox (n.d.), available online at http://www.urbanmag.be/dyn/servlet/artikel?artikel=688&action=show.

61. Quoted in Lemman, "The Next World Order."

62. Public Broadcasting System's *Frontline*, excerpts from "Defense Planning Guidance" (2003), available online at http://www.pbs.org/wgbh/pages/frontline/shows/iraq/etc/wolf.html; Patrick Tyler, "Lone Superpower Plan: Ammunition for Critics," *New York Times* (March 10, 1992).

63. David Armstrong, "Dick Cheney's Song of America," *Harper's* (October 2002).

64. Gabriel Kolko, *Another Century of War?* (New York: The New Press, 2002), pp. 70–71; emphasis added.

65. Arundhati Roy, "Mesopotamia. Babylon. The Tigris and the Euphrates," *The Guardian* (April 2, 2003), available online at www.guardian.co.uk/Iraq/Story/O,2763,927849,00.html.

66. "Anti-Americanism in Greece Is Re-invigorated by War, *New York Times* (April 7, 2003), p. B12.

67. Fareed Zakaria, "Arrogant Empire: The Global Debate Is Not About Saddam," *Newsweek* (March 24, 2003), available online at http://www.msnbc.com/news/885222.asp.

68. Ibid.

69. Elaine Povich, "Support Grows for Bush, War," *Newsweek* (April 6, 2003).

70. Robert A. Kagan, *Of Paradise and Power: America and Europe in the New World Order* (New York: Alfred A. Knopf, 2002).

71. United States Senator Kay Bailey Hutchison, Senate Floor Speech, *Congressional Record, Proceedings and Records of the 107th Congress, Second Session* (October 9, 2002), p. S10149, available online at http://hutchison.senate.gov/speec274.htm.

72. Giroux, *The Abandoned Generation*, pp. 1–70.

73. Public Broadcasting System, *Online News Hour, Political Wrap Background* (March 1, 2002), available online at http://www.pbs.org/newshour/bb/

political_wrap/jan-june02/wrap_3-1a.html; Matthew Rothschild, "The War Party Tolerates No Opposition," *The Progressive Web Exclusives* (March 1, 2002), available online at http://www.progressive.org/webex/wx030102b.html.

74. Paul Street, "Marriage as the Solution to Poverty: Bush's Proposal for Welfare Moms and the Real White House Agenda," *Z Magazine* (April 2002), pp. 33–39.

75. Giroux, *The Abandoned Generation,* pp. 71–102.

76. "From Pearl Harbor to the Cold War, into the twilight zone of 21st-century nuclear terrorism, if there is a core belief driving the new Pentagon chief as he attempts to overhaul US defense strategy, it is that America continues to face lethal enemies, and vulnerability is not an option. 'History teaches us that weakness is provocative,' [Donald] Rumsfeld said on the day President Bush appointed him Defense Secretary. The native Chicagoan and former wrestling champion, known as 'Rummy' to friends, views the world as a relatively ruthless, Hobbesian place where thugs flaunt—and respect—brute force. Those of us from Chicago recall Rumsfeld's remark that 'You get more with a kind word and a gun than you do with a kind word alone,' he quips." Ann Scott Tyson, "Rumsfeld's World View: A Ruthless Place," *Christian Science Monitor* (May 17, 2001).

PART II
Masters Marching to War

Come you masters of war
. . . You that hide behind walls
You that hide behind desks

—Bob Dylan, "Masters of War," 1963[1]

Why shouldn't we go after Iraq, not just al Qaeda?
—Donald Rumsfeld, September 12, 2001

Public opinion has to be prepared before a move against Iraq is possible.
—Colin Powell, September 12, 2001[2]

Introduction to Part II

For a surprising amount of time, at least in retrospect, many progressives (myself included) doubted that the White House would transform America's post–September 11 "war on terrorism" into an invasion and occupation of Iraq. We didn't really think that Bush and his War Party, which barely squeaked into office after losing the popular (and even the electoral) vote in 2000, would dare attempt so bizarre (to us) a transformation, moving from "real" threats (al Qaeda and its ilk) to such obviously (it seemed) concocted and imaginary dangers (Iraq and the Hussein regime). Thanks to the initial Gulf War and the murderous US-engineered sanctions that followed, we noted, Iraq was a terribly weakened state. It was hardly a threat to even its immediate neighbors, including Kuwait, the country it had fatefully invaded (with what it thought was US approval) in 1990. Its capacity to engage in significant military action, including the use of unconventional weapons of mass destruction (WMD), was minimal, as former US weapons inspector Scott Ritter and other knowledgeable observers reported.

Saddam Hussein may have refrained from expressing sympathy for the United States after 9/11 (hardly shocking given that the sanctions had killed at least a million of his subjects, including more than half a million children), but there was no discernible connection between the secular Baathist Iraqi regime and al Qaeda or other extremist Muslim terror networks. Osama bin-Laden and Saddam Hussein were bitter enemies, and the notion of the latter "handing off" a significant nuclear, biological, and/or chemical weapons capacity—assuming he had such capacity—to the former was preposterous.

An American attack on Iraq, we reasoned, would likely spark new terror attacks on the US, divert scarce intelligence and military resources away from the campaign against nonstate terrorism, and destabilize the Middle East yet further. It would spawn massive alienation in Europe and much of the rest of the world, where large segments of the population were already deeply troubled by a wide array of US policies (including rejection of the Kyoto treaty, insistence on pursuing missile defense, and refusal to support the International Criminal Court). More immediately, it would undo the coalition formed to track down and eliminate international terror networks. It would spark significant domestic protest. It would also violate fundamental precepts of international law, which forbid the use of war for any purpose other than defense against an imminent attack on one's own territory. Finally, once the war was over, the US would have to undertake in some fashion "nation-building," reconstructing Iraq once it had finished destroying it. No one doubted that this would be an extremely expensive endeavor, one for which the Bush administration had demonstrated little desire and/or capacity.

The best way to provoke Saddam into providing his dreaded weapons to the terrorists or using them himself (assuming they existed), we reasoned, was to threaten his existence. Only when he had nothing left to lose would Saddam likely unleash his biological and chemical materials (again, assuming they existed). There was no evidence that he was suicidal, which, we reasoned, would have been a necessary prerequisite for him to conduct a significant operation against the US.

American troops, we figured, would be put at risk by an invasion of Iraq. Many would come home in body bags, an outcome well understood by military authorities, some of who served in Vietnam. In keeping with the specious business of "nation-building," once the US did unseat Hussein—and many of us were naive about how long that would take—US forces would have to remain in Iraq for untold years, carrying out an expensive, difficult, and risky occupation.

A war against Iraq could generate catastrophic side effects for the US, we noted, including dangerously destabilizing the entire Middle East, fomenting virulent anti-Americanism in the Islamic world, and possibly even sparking war between the two nuclear powers on the subcontinent—India and Pakistan. "If the US is seen as turning its back on the Israeli-Palestinian conflict" to settle old scores with Saddam, warned Brent Scowcroft, national security adviser to Bush Senior, "there would be an explosion of rage against us. We would be seen as ignoring a key interest of the Muslim world in order to satisfy what is seen as a narrow American interest. Even without Israeli involvement, the results could well destabilize Arab regimes in the region, ironically facilitating one of Saddam's strategic objectives."[3] Scowcroft might have added that destabilizing Arab regimes was also one of Osama bin-Laden's primary goals.

The financial cost of war and occupation would be massive, according to estimates by leading Harvard economist William Nordhaus and others.

Government expenditures on such a scale seemed contrary to the Bush administration's determination to slash taxes for those most able to pay—the super-wealthy. The prospect of serious financial repercussions was one of the reasons that plenty of establishment sorts like Brent Scowcroft argued strongly against an invasion of Iraq.

As for the purported democratic and humanitarian imperatives of US policy, Iraq was only one of many states—including no small number of US clients and allies in the "war on terrorism"—deserving of humanitarian intervention (Turkey, for example, *is* an egregious violator of its Kurdish population's human rights). In contrast to the prowar line promoted by Bush and his minions, the first step in alleviating the suffering of the Iraqi people and bolstering their capacity for democratic self-rule would be to lift the horrific and curiously Saddam-enhancing sanctions that had been imposed following the first Gulf War. For all these reasons we scoffed at the notion that an invasion of Iraq was imminent.

In retrospect, we were operating under a false assumption: the existence of a rational power elite that cared about facts and possessed a reasonable sense of the limits of its own power. We underestimated the chutzpah and sheer authoritarian arrogance of Bush's fundamentalist right regime, falsely labeled conservative. We should have known better: this was the regime that attained unimaginable power with the help of racist Florida voter-list scrubbers and corrupt US Supreme Court justices, not to mention the historic gift of almost unprecedented legitimacy provided by eighteen suicidal hijackers on 9/11/2001.

According to a September 2002 CBS News report, "barely five hours after American Airline Flight 77 plowed into the Pentagon," Bush's Al Capone–admiring defense secretary Donald H. Rumsfeld was "telling his aides to come up with plans for striking Iraq—even though there was no evidence linking Saddam Hussein to the attacks." According to notes "that show exactly where the road toward war with Iraq began," taken by aides meeting with Rumsfeld inside the still-smoldering Pentagon structure on September 11, the defense secretary wanted "best info fast. Judge whether good enough [to] hit S.H. [meaning Saddam Hussein] at the same time. Not only UBL [meaning Osama bin-Laden]." Rumsfeld added: "Go massive. Sweep it up. Things related and not."[4]

According to Bob Woodward's uncritical, power-worshipping bestseller *Bush at War,* which was based on rare access to top players, Rumsfeld raised the question of attacking Iraq at the National Security Council meeting held on September 12, 2001, asking (by Woodward's unquoted paraphrase) "Why shouldn't we go after Iraq, not just al Qaeda?" "Rumsfeld was speaking," Woodward notes, "not only for himself when he raised the question. His deputy, Paul Wolfowitz, was committed to a policy that would make Iraq a principal target, the first round in the war on terrorism. Moreover, according to Woodward, "[b]efore the attack, the Pentagon had been working for months on developing a military option for Iraq . . . any serious, full-scale war against terrorism would have to make Iraq a target—eventually. Rumsfeld was raising the possibility that they could *take advantage of the opportunity afforded by the terrorist attacks* to go after Saddam immediately."[5]

On the morning of September 12, according to a series of *Washington Post* articles coauthored by Woodward, Rumsfeld called for an attack on Iraq, claiming that that nation must be "a principal target of the first round in the war against terrorism." "Iraq was temporarily spared," notes the British journalist John Pilger, relying on Woodward, "only because Colin Powell, the secretary of state, persuaded Bush that 'public opinion has to be prepared before a move against Iraq is possible.'"[6] Just five days later, according to a *Washington Post* story published in January 2003, Bush "signed a plan for war in Afghanistan that also directed the Pentagon to begin planning options for an invasion of Iraq." As Anthony Lewis notes, "The story went on to say that longtime advocates of military action against Iraq believe that Bush moved to their view 'within days, if not hours'; of the September 11 attacks."[7]

By the time of his paranoid 1950s-like State of the Union address in January 2002, Bush was preposterously identifying Iraq as the leading part of a three-state "Axis of Evil" (combining the truly strange bed partners Iraq, North Korea, and Iran) and denouncing it for weaponizing anthrax, something the US had been doing itself. The die was well cast by October 2002, when Bush made the bizarre claim that Iraq was threatening to send unmanned aerial vehicles carrying chemical and biological weapons to the US. According to the *Washington Post*, Bush had in fact "made up his mind" to attack Iraq as early as April 2002. Two months later, the State Department's director of policy planning, Richard N. Haass, asked Condoleezza Rice "whether they should talk about the pros and cons of confronting Iraq." "Don't bother," Rice told Haass, "the president has made a decision."[8]

In reality, Rumsfeld, Vice President Cheney, Deputy Defense Secretary Paul Wolfowitz, and a number of arch-imperialist, hyperconservative ideologues who became George Bush Junior's foreign policy brain trust had been agitating for an American invasion of Iraq as early as 1997. That year saw the formation of the Project for a New American Century (PNAC), an influential right-wing lobbying and policy group whose key founders included Cheney, Rumsfeld, former defense advisory board chair Richard Perle, Wolfowitz, I. Lewis Libby (Cheney's chief of staff), and William J. Bennett (education director under Reagan). In January 1998, PNAC urged President Clinton to attack and invade Iraq. Wolfowitz even outlined a plan of attack on Iraq before the House National Security Committee in September of the same year.

PNAC's goals were bigger than the overthrow of Saddam, however. Its *Rebuilding America's Defenses: Strategy, Forces, and Resources for a New Century,* issued in September 2000, outlined an ambitious program for expanded and permanent US domination of the world's natural and human resources. More important than subjugating Iraq, by PNAC's estimation, was taking control of the entire Persian Gulf, home to the world's greatest material prize in an age of global petro-capitalism—massive oil reserves. "While the unresolved conflict with Iraq provides the immediate justification," PNAC noted, "the need for a substantial American force presence in the Gulf transcends the issue of the regime of Saddam Hussein."[9]

The team of hawkish zealots in and around Bush Junior's audacious White House saw the prospects of an American attack on Iraq in very different ways than ruling-class fuddy-duddies like Scowcroft and (probably) Bush père. For Rumsfeld, Wolfowitz, Cheney, Perle, Karl Rove, Elliot Cohen, Elliot Abrams, Libby, and other delusional planners, promoters, and executors of the Bush Doctrine, dropped into the driver's seat by the 2000 Bush coup and the "catastrophic and catalyzing event[s]" of September 2001 (a "new Pearl Harbor" that was almost openly wished for in PNAC's *Rebuilding America's Defenses*), Iraq's weakness made it a welcome target. That weak and battered land was an ideal stage on which to demonstrate the administration's determination to unilaterally rule the world by sheer military force and to engage in "preemptive" wars wherever and whenever it desired, in bold defiance of international law and standard norms of responsible state behavior. The problematic fact that Saddam's undeniably ugly regime (deeply enabled by the US both before and after the first Gulf War) neither posed a credible military/WMD threat nor was linked to 9/11 and al Qaeda would be handled with systematic deception. The great Iraqi threat, in all its permutations, would be built up in the minds of the American populace through an elaborate propaganda campaign, conducted with crucial assistance from an obedient corporate media.

The likelihood of future terror attacks on Americans was a price the War Party was more than willing to pay, counseling us that such attacks were "inevitable." Its fear of such occurrences was mitigated, no doubt, by the relative safety of its members and its knowledge that such attacks would deepen yet further its capacity to repress dissent, close off debate, pursue empire, and transfer more massive sums of public money from social programs to the military. At the same time, many of Bush's Hawks appear to have convinced themselves that 9/11 provided the US with a golden opportunity to reshape the entire Middle East in a way that would ultimately spread "democracy," "free-market capitalism," and concomitant social, economic, and political progress. Such was the bourgeois-revolutionary doctrine of Wolfowitz, who saw attacking, invading, and then reconstructing Iraq as a chance both to project hard (military) power and to create a showcase demonstration of seductive American "soft" power: consumer capitalism and "democracy," falsely conflated with each other but nonetheless consistent with standard US doctrine.

The costs of reconstruction, Wolfowitz and the rest of the War Party thought, could be met by tapping Iraq's underused oil reserves, the second largest in the world after US client state Saudi Arabia. This economic windfall would be complemented by the lifting of economic sanctions after Saddam was removed, putting Iraq on the path to positive development, overseen by a benevolent Uncle Sam. With the lifting of sanctions, the removal of troops from Saudi Arabia (Iraq would provide the new foundation for the US military presence in the Middle East), and renewed efforts to calm the Israeli-Palestinian conflict, Arab terrorism's main issues would disappear. The claims of humanitarian hypocrisy would be further drowned out by inspiring images of cheering Iraqi crowds, throwing flowers at their American liberators—the soldiers of "Operation Iraqi Freedom." Insofar as "dead-end" Saddam supporters insisted on resisting the benevolent forward march of history, they would be easily handled by the unassailable military superiority of the US.

As for those irritating Europeans and other silly little world citizens who foolishly questioned Uncle Sam's limitless planetary stomping rights in the post–Cold War and now post–September 11 eras, they would come around once they realized the futility of their anger at a historically unmatched military superpower that no longer cared about or needed their approval. Confronted with the fait accompli of America's invasion, the Bush team reasoned, the Europeans would come running for their pieces of the rich petroleum and reconstruction pie. Moreover, insofar as the "Old World's" opposition came from the left, it was of little consequence anyway, since the left was being marginalized by neo-liberal global capitalism. The leftists were the reactionary "dead-enders" of "Old Europe," easily dismissed in the same manner as the "antiglobalization" protestors, who shared their obsolete notion that there might be a conflict between oligarchic corporation capitalism and the requirements of democracy and societal health. Their irrelevance would be deepened by American control of Iraqi oil, important less for immediate American profit or petroleum needs than for the power it provided US policymakers to ensure that rival core states in Europe and Asia—considerably more dependent upon Persian Gulf oil than the US—behaved in accordance with the needs of the leading segments of the American business class.

Of course, the budget-busting combination of massive regressive tax cuts and dramatically escalated "defense" (imperial) spending was part of the Bush administration's well-funded neo-Reaganite project of starving the left hand and feeding the right hand of the state. This project calls for the fiscal evisceration of public programs that serve the poor, the nonaffluent majority of ordinary working people, and the overall health of society: education, family cash assistance, health insurance, pubic transportation, job training, environmental protection, school and housing desegregation, consumer protection, trade protection, workplace safety, protections against racial and gender discrimination, voter protection and registration, accurate social fact-gathering and reporting, public media, meaningful rehabilitation services for prisoners and ex-offenders, and the like. In short, it feeds the center-right privatization campaign of delegitimizing the government's left hand by bankrupting the social-democratic functions of the public sector. It is a matter for conjecture whether the Bush team really believed (against common economic sense and the analyses of even some right-wing economists) that the need for social programs to alleviate human suffering would be mitigated by a "broadly based economic stimulus" resulting from tax cuts directed mainly to the already superwealthy privileged few. An earlier story in the history of the same project—chief Reagan economic adviser David Stockman's revelation that the real point of regressive Republican tax cuts was to bankrupt social programs for the poor—is more than a little suggestive.

What is not a subject for guesswork is the political role that Bush's team expected the attack on Iraq to play. Their "defense" spending financed a spectacular overseas military extravaganza—choreographed in Orwellian collaboration with a captive, "in-bedded" corporate media—that carried huge collateral benefit in the domestic arena. This was by design. Consistent with the teachings of Machiavelli, the warnings of Madison, and the counsel of chief Bush political adviser Karl Rove, the administration kept a critical margin of the active US electorate focused on foreign adventures rather than on issues closer to home, such as declining retirement accounts, uncertain employment prospects, dwindling leisure time, inadequate and inflated health coverage, endangered civil liberties, a bleak future for social security, and a general sense of personal and familial insecurity. The real drive to replace Osama and al Qaeda with Saddam and Iraq in the role of chief global Evil Other and terrorist threat moved into high gear in September 2002, just in time for the forthcoming midterm elections. As Rove knew quite well, Bush's party was vulnerable on domestic issues, especially "the economy" (the 2001 recession and the subsequent, and ongoing, "jobless recovery"). It needed to focus the active electorate as much as possible on Madison's "pretended or imaginary dangers abroad."

The great propaganda campaign was quite successful, at least for a time, thanks in large part to the subservient role played by the dominant media, whose owners and managers functioned as true Masters of War in the spring of 2003. Right after the invasion of Iraq, the *New York Times* released a survey indicating that 42 percent of the US public saw Saddam as directly responsible for 9/11. A CBS poll released at the same time indicated that 55 percent of the public thought that Saddam directly supported al Qaeda. There wasn't a shred of evidence in support of either belief, and obviously neither of them emerged out of thin air. As Henry Giroux and Susan Searls Giroux point out, these ideas were "ardently legitimated by President Bush, Vice President Cheney, Colin Powell, and Condoleezza Rice." Moreover, Giroux and Searls Giroux continue, "[t]hey were also allowed to circulate in the dominant press either with uncritical, jingoistic enthusiasm, as in the case of the Fox News Channel, or through the dominant media's refusal to challenge both assumptions—both positions, of course, in opposition to foreign news sources such as the BBC, which repeatedly challenged such assertions."[10]

Prior to the invasion of Iraq, the dominant media refused to meaningfully challenge the Bush team's ludicrous assertions about Saddam's ability and willingness to use unconventional weapons and the extent of his program to develop nuclear weapons. As the perceptive left media critic Norman Solomon notes, "the default position of U.S. media coverage gave the White House the benefit of doubts," in sharp contrast to the British press's "vigorous exposure" of "deceptions about Iraq." American reporters exhibited "reflexive deference toward pivotal players like Donald Rumsfeld, Colin Powell and Condoleezza Rice" and "chronic overreliance on official sources," a standard problem with corporate journalism. They "failed," Solomon further notes, "to scrutinize contradictions, false statements and leaps of illogic." When Colin Powell made his "watershed" speech at the United Nations in February 2003, presenting flimsy, trumped-up evidence of Iraq's alleged WMD capacity, journalists "swooned rather than draw on basic debunking information that was readily available at the time." They "provided stenography for top U.S. officials, while editorial writers and pundits lavished praises." The "most deferential coverage" of all was granted to Bush, whose chronic promulgations of bold falsehoods were treated as "no big deal."[11]

I say "successful, at least for a time" because opinion indicators have been moving against the war and occupation for some time now. Reflecting the steady flow of US casualties and the persistent social and political chaos in "postwar" Iraq, 43 percent of respondents told Gallup pollsters in July 2003 that things were going badly in Iraq, up from just 13 percent in early May. "In a mid-July Washington Post–ABC poll," Paul Loeb reported, "six of ten of those surveyed said the war damaged the image of the United States abroad, half said the conflict permanently damaged US relations with key allies, and 52 percent considered the level of US casualties 'unacceptable.' A Zogby poll around the same time found a one percent majority actually saying it was time for someone new in the White House." The political landscape, Loeb noted, had "shifted," becoming "far more hospitable towards dissenting views and an embrace of multinational intervention in Iraq through the United Nations." Bush's numbers have fallen since July.[12]

The reasons for this sharp reversal are not difficult to find. As widely predicted, the WMDs have not been found and US occupation forces are facing regular guerilla resistance, supported by no small part of Iraq's population. Demoralized GIs have been using the Internet to send out depressing stories of misery from this terrible desert front, even while Bush dared Iraqi militants to attack "our boys" ("Bring 'em on," said the president, a former National Guard deserter in the Vietnam era). The Israel-Palestine conflict is in full escalation, hardly tamed and possibly worsened, as predicted, by the American "war." The White House has been forced to admit that it failed to plan adequately for the postwar pacification and "reconstruction" of Iraq.

Beyond all this, it has become apparent that the administration can't pay for Iraq, thanks at least in part to savagely regressive US tax cuts, imposed by the Bush team under the cover of the "war on terrorism." The Bush administration's pathetic recent efforts to obtain foreign financial and military assistance to maintain an occupation in Iraq—an occupation opposed by much of the world—have done little to improve international opinion of the United States, let alone generate sympathy for the suffering caused by 9/11. As a front-page story in a recent edition of the *New York Times* reports, "in the two years since Sept. 11, 2001, the view of the United States as a victim of terrorism that deserved the world's sympathy and support has given way to a widespread vision of America as an imperial power that has defied world opinion through unjustified and unilateral use of military force." The greatest single factor in that transformation, the *Times* finds, was—surprise—"the war in Iraq."[13]

Meanwhile, Osama bin-Laden celebrated 9/11's second anniversary with an appearance on Al Jazeera, cheerfully exhorting (in a video filmed in the spring of 2003) Iraqi resistance fighters to "bury" Americans in Iraq. Bring-'em-on Bush and Bring-'em-on bin-Laden seem united in shared ruling-class hatred for the predominantly working-class troops who serve in the US military. (If large sectors of the US economy have reeled under the weight of Bush's recession and "jobless recovery," the military has in contrast fared quite well, attracting countless dispossessed youths facing bleak futures. In a barren economic landscape, Uncle Sam's promises of tuition assistance and job training can look very attractive. Unfortunately, those benefits come at a price.)

Meanwhile, as of this writing, the American population is increasingly impatient with the failing US labor market and the starvation of public programs and social services that naturally follow from the combination of massive "defense" expenditures and even larger plutocratic tax cuts. What the hell, many Americans rightly wonder, is the point of a "jobless recovery"? How in hell can we make massive expenditures to "reconstruct" Iraq when our own schools, job structure, transportation infrastructure, and healthcare system—not to mention race relations and civil liberties— are under attack and in terrible disrepair, the product of the conscious and deliberate starvation of the nonrepressive functions of the public sector in the imperial homeland? The progressives' predictions are being borne out. Our original criticisms of the war planners are being validated in spades, and the "optimistic" postwar assumptions of the Wolfowitz-Rumsfeld-Perle crowd are being revealed as scandalously irresponsible. The arch-imperialists have no clothes.

* * *

The chapters in part II alternate between disgust and inspiration. *Disgust:* at the relentless determination of War Party Bush to "lie and deceive" in order to "play with [our] world like it's [their] little toy" (Bob Dylan in "Masters of War" [1963]) and "prepare public opinion" to make "possible" "a move against Iraq" (Colin Powell on September 12, 2001). It was a real-life performance fit for George Orwell's fictional *Nineteen Eighty-Four,* replete with politically mandated twisting of the past and present and a rich vocabulary of absurdist "doublespeak." *More disgust,* even revulsion, at the willingness of dominant media to uncritically transmit these pivotal, historic, and fateful deceptions, reflected in reporting and commentary that have read like something straight out of Chomsky and Herman's *Manufacturing Consent.*

Inspiration: at the extraordinary outpouring of popular protest against US war plans, including the millions who marched for peace in the imperial homeland, part of the greatest wave of preemptive war resistance in human history. The depth, breadth, and scale of the domestic and overseas resistance to Bush's war were truly remarkable—unprecedented for such an early stage in an American military campaign. Despite the best jingoistic efforts of the White House and corporate-state media, popular antiwar activism reached a level that peace organizers did not attain until many years into the Vietnam War. It saved Iraqi lives by contributing significantly to the creation of a political climate in which policymakers feared mass civilian casualties would translate into a public relations disaster for Washington.

This is reason for hope, as indicated in a front-page article in the *New York Times* two days after the remarkable popular peace protests that took place at home and abroad on February 15, 2003. "The fracturing of the Western alliance over Iraq and the huge antiwar demonstrations around the world this weekend," noted *Times* reporter Patrick E. Tyler, "are reminders that there may still be two superpowers on the planet: the United States and world public opinion."[14] The majority of humankind has very different values and priorities than America's Masters of War and Empire. This is a source of hope, despite those in power who give a militaristic middle finger to the world's people.

7
Big Brother Bush, "Suicidal" Saddam, and the Homegrown Threat to Liberal Democracy
January 22, 2003

Beyond Democratic Constraint?

It is hard to avoid the chilling conclusion that the corporate plutocrats and arch-imperialists in and around the Bush administration do not think they are required to speak or act with even moderate respect for the political intelligence and/or relevance of the citizenry. They believe that basic rules of evidence and democracy, which require justifications and debate rather than simply edicts from policymakers, offer little if any constraint on their actions and pronouncements. They think they have achieved something like the status of Big Brother in George Orwell's *Nineteen Eighty-Four.* Big Brother never had to make real sense to his population, which was in no position to respond to the absurdity of his nonsensical pronouncements—War Is Peace, Love Is Hate, and so on—or to his constant manipulation of history to fit the current party line.

How else would you explain the veritable flood of preposterous pronouncements and contradictory policies flowing with regularity out of the Bush administration? A few examples follow:

- The claim that it is in the interest of the American people to enact massive tax cuts for the rich that not only will do nothing to stimulate a sluggish wealth-top-heavy economy but also will combine with massive "defense" expenditures to deepen the federal deficit and undercut desperately needed social expenditures.
- The claim that jetliner attacks carried out with box cutters illustrate the need to spend untold billions on an outlandish and unworkable high-tech missile defense shield.

- The claim that there exists a global "Axis of Evil" comprising Iraq, Iran, and North Korea—three states with little basis (beyond common demonization by Uncle Sam) for mutual alliance and considerable difference and enmity among them.
- The truly fantastic contention that the Iraqi regime is threatening to send unmanned airplanes carrying chemical and biological weapons to the US.
- The claim to be seriously concerned about the human rights of Iraqi and other world citizens while the White House aggressively supports governments that inflict massive terror on subject and occupied peoples, including Colombia, Israel, Turkey, China, and many others.
- The claim to be concerned for "democracy" and "freedom" around the world while deepening relationships with numerous authoritarian states in the name of the "war on terrorism" and using 9/11 as a pretext to roll back cherished civil liberties at home.
- The claim to champion democracy while openly embracing the short-lived oligarchic *coup* conducted last April against the popular elected and constitutional Chavez government of Venezuela—a state too friendly to the poor for the White House's tastes.
- The claim to be grievously offended by the use of "special preferences" in college admissions (i.e., race-based affirmative action at the University of Michigan) even while Bush refuses to criticize the aristocratic legacy system that provided the only possible basis for his admission to Yale.

The list of Bush absurdities goes on and on.

Spinning Divergent Responses to "Evil Axis" Others

Perhaps the most relevant Big Lie currently rolling out of the White House spin factory relates to the nature and objectives of the Iraqi government. Here we have the neo-Stalinist North Korean regime of Kim Jong Il announcing its determination to significantly expand an already-existing stock of nuclear weapons. A million North Korean troops have been placed on alert, ready to do battle with jackbooted enemies from what North Korean state television calls "the citadels of imperialism." And here we have Iraq, still reeling from the first Persian Gulf "war" (a one-sided assault by world history's most powerful military state) and a subsequent decade of deadly US-led sanctions. The second nation poses no serious military threat to its own neighbors, much less to the West. UN inspectors under Bush's glare are hard-pressed to find significant evidence that significant "weapons of mass destruction" are being manufactured and/or stored in the land of Saddam Hussein. They are reduced to reporting the discovery of empty containers, hardly a refutation of former chief UN weapons inspector

Scott Ritter, a former American military intelligence officer, who insists that Iraq has been effectively disarmed.

Bush's response to the first threat is to put it on the back burner, promising diplomacy and negotiation, oiled by reassuring words that American does not seek to attack or invade. The White House response to the second situation is a full front-burner preparation of its awesome air-, land-, sea-, and space-based military machine for another bloody assault on Iraq, followed by occupation and "reconstruction."

How does the Bush administration explain such divergent responses to "Evil Axis" perfidy, especially when the threat posed by North Korea would appear to be so much greater? Kim Jong Il, the Bush administration tells us, is a "rational actor," subject to constraint and deterrence. He can be argued with and persuaded. He is possessed of common sense and realism, a special instinct for survival and a sense of limits.

But Saddam, the White House insists, is no such animal. He is hopelessly reckless, driven, and brutal. He simply cannot be deterred from acting on his bizarre and sinister determination to use weapons of mass destruction. If we let a lunatic like Saddam get nuclear weapons, the argument runs, it is certain that he will use them against us and our allies, either directly or by "handing them off" to al Qaeda or some other like-minded group. The likelihood that such an action would lead to his total annihilation is irrelevant, we are told. The failure to launch a preemptive war against this madman, we are informed, will be written in mushroom clouds over our cities.

The proof for this judgment, the White House argues, is found in the record of Saddam's thoroughly irrational, even "insane" past behavior. That historical record includes his attacks on Iran (1980) and Kuwait (1990), resulting in millions of Iraqi deaths, as well as the use of chemical weapons against "his own people" (the Kurds of northern Iraq) and Iranian soldiers.

The Real Saddam: Sinister, Yes; Suicidal, No

The White House has been using a transparently manipulative and false historical argument whose primary purpose is to frighten the American people into war. A related goal is to divert the citizenry from the terrible shortcomings of domestic White House policies that exacerbate the growing social and economic insecurity of the population while distributing wealth and power upward.

The historical facts are clear.[15] When Saddam started a war with Iran in 1980, he did so because that nation faced a very real and serious threat from a zealous revolutionary nation (Iran) that was aggressively pursuing hegemony throughout the Middle East. He fought a strictly limited war seeking a large protective swath of expanded border territory. He never pursued the conquest of Iran or the overthrow of its revolutionary leader

Ayatolla Khomeini. His war was fought with the reasonable and realized expectation that other nations—including the United States, Saudi Arabia, Kuwait, and France—would offer considerable financial, diplomatic, and technical support to stem the spread of Iran's Islamic revolution.

When Saddam invaded Kuwait in the summer of 1990, his goals were far from reckless. He sought, after years of fruitless diplomacy, to punish Kuwait for its refusal to write off debts incurred in a war that arguably protected that nation's oil fields from Iranian conquest. He was also responding in arguably rational, Machiavellian ways to Kuwait's insistence on deflating world oil prices, which reduced Iraqi profits, by producing beyond OPEC quotas. When he invaded, he weighed his options carefully, concluding that he had definite reason to expect US approval, thanks to a now-famous communication from Bush I's ambassador to Iraq—April Glaspie. "We have no opinion on the Arab-Arab conflicts," Glaspie told Hussein, "like your border disagreement with Kuwait." Glaspie's State Department had earlier told Saddam that it had "no special defense or security commitments to Kuwait."[16]

Saddam proceeded, in short, on the assumption of a "green light" from Bush I. His invasion of Kuwait cannot reasonably be seen as proof of his nondeterrable nature since the US never attempted deterrence.

When the US responded with a devastating air campaign, Saddam communicated his willingness to retreat prior to the launching of a US ground war. But Bush I refused this option, unacceptably insisting that Saddam leave his military hardware behind in Kuwait. This impossible demand set the stage for an American massacre of Iraqi troops that is curiously deleted from the official record of "pathological" atrocities in the Middle East.

During the Persian Gulf "war," which Saddam curiously survived (contrary to White House doctrine on his "suicidal" nature), he never used chemical or biological weapons against Israel, Saudi Arabia, or the coalition forces that were pounding his military. He knew that using weapons of mass destruction would lead to his annihilation by the US. In addition, the mobilization of US troops deterred him from acting against the inspection regime in 1994.

What about Saddam's use of chemical weapons against "his own people" (if that's really what we want to call the minority Kurdish population he has long terrorized) and Iranian soldiers during the 1980s? Those actions certainly indicate Saddam's savagery, but they are not proof of his reckless and suicidal immunity to deterrence. There are two reasons for this conclusion. First, the people targeted were in no position to respond in kind. Second, Saddam gassed Kurds and Iranians with the support and assistance of the one country that happened and happens to possess the world's largest stockpile of deterrent weapons—chemical, nuclear, and biological. That would be the United States. During the 1980s, in fact, the US assisted Saddam's biological weapons program by providing him with American strains of anthrax, West Nile virus, and botulinal toxin.

WMD — America gave them to Saddam.

As for the nuclear threat allegedly posed by Saddam, there is no reason to think that he is willing to invite a devastating nuclear assault on Iraq and perhaps most significantly (for him) on himself—the certain result of starting a nuclear war in the region. Also preposterous is the notion that Saddam would "hand off" nuclear weapons to historical blood enemies in al Qaeda or other extremist Islamic terror networks. The Bush administration's abject failure to prove that Iraq is cooperating with al Qaeda is hardly surprising to any serious student of Middle Eastern politics.

The Homegrown Threat to Liberal Democracy

One does not have to be a radical critic of American imperialism to see through the transparent Orwellian absurdity of the White House's line about the Iraqi regime's nondeterrability. Even Thomas L. Friedman, foreign policy columnist of the *New York Times,* who is no friend to Arab causes, correctly notes that Saddam is "a twisted dictator who is deterrable through conventional means" and "loves life more than he hates us."[17] More substantively, the counterargument to Bush's claims of Saddam's reckless nondeterrability can be found in a recent article by two leading mainstream academics in the establishment journal *Foreign Policy* (John J. Mearsheimer and Stephen M. Walt, "An Unnecessary War," January–February 2003). It can also be found, in greater detail, in Carl Kaysen et al., *War with Iraq: Costs, Consequences and Alternatives* (December 2002), produced by no less of a "respectable" organization than the Committee on International Security Studies of the American Academy of Arts and Sciences.

What's missing in these very useful mainstream pieces is a broader framework in which to place and thereby understand the nature of the White House's deception. For that, we must consider the balance of global petro-capitalist relations that provide the basis for America's provocative presence in the Middle East in the first place. We should also consider the numerous domestic failures from which the White House wishes to divert popular attention in the industrial world's most unequal and incarceration-addicted nation—the "world's most prosperous state," where more than 45 million people lack basic health insurance.

Also recommended is an essay titled "The Orwell Diversion" (1986), written by the late Australian propaganda critic Alex Carey and included in his 1997 book *Taking the Risk Out of Democracy: Corporate Propaganda Versus Freedom and Liberty.* In that essay and elsewhere, Carey argues that the most relevant long-term threat to liberal democracy has never come from the state totalitarians of the Stalinist left or the fascist right. It comes instead from the homegrown, big business–connected "Respectable Right" that arose within the liberal-democratic societies of the West (chiefly the US) largely to protect concentrated corporate power against its natural homeland antagonist—the popular democratic tradition.[18]

More then fifteen years after the publication of Carey's essay, the Soviet Union has joined Nazi Germany in history's proverbial dustbin and the last classic *Nineteen Eighty-Four*–style regime (if such a thing has ever existed) bangs its little nuclear drum for global food assistance in North Korea. Meanwhile, a homegrown version of Big Brother stalks the corridors of domestic and imperial power in Washington, DC, wearing the uniform of the Respectable Right. He is deeply enabled by a corporate communications and entertainment empire that combines Huxley with Orwell to muddy the waters of popular perception in ways that the modern red- and brown-fascist state-totalitarians could only dream about. He is ineluctably, if perhaps unconsciously, drawn to the wisdom of Orwell's chilling axiom: "Who controls the past controls the future. Who controls the present controls the past."[19]

8
State of Deception: How Stupid Does the Bush Gang Think We Are?
January 28, 2003

New Uses for Duct Tape

What's the old saying—"A picture is worth a thousands words"? I've always been a little skeptical about that phrase, but it was borne out last Wednesday when George W. Bush's "Boxgate" incident hit the airwaves. There was Bush extolling "free trade" (corporate globalization) and his latest regressive tax cut in a St. Louis trucking company warehouse. He bragged about the superiority of the American System in front of "a printed canvas backdrop of faux cardboard boxes, which featured 'Made in America' in large black letters." The canvas read "STRENGTHENING THE AMERICAN ECONOMY." A handful of warehouse officials applauded in the background, framed by two American flags.[20]

The problem had to do with the only real warehouse boxes that White House "volunteers" could find to arrange in front of Bush. Each box had large pieces of dark-brown duct tape placed on their lower left corner. When reporters peeled the tape off, they found three magic words the White House wished to hide: "Made in China." It was difficult, the "volunteers" knew, to square such evidence (however anecdotal) of corporate America's reliance on cheap overseas labor with the pro-"globalization" and "Made in America" message intended by Bush's political mastermind Karl Rove. As a young man Rove, it is worth recalling, idolized Richard Nixon. He was reported by the *Washington Post* to have conducted training sessions for College Republicans in the art of Nixon-style dirty tricks.[21]

The corporate electro-"journalists" (CNN newscasters) who reported the version of the "Boxgate" story that I first encountered handled it in an interesting way—with a smile. They thought it was . . . *funny*. They read

73

the story, showed the clip, chuckled, and moved on to the next item. One suspects, however, that the bumbling little White House deception in St. Louis is no laughing matter to the millions of Americans who have lost manufacturing and other jobs to corporate globalization in recent decades. It is no laughing matter, either, to those concerned about the nation's costly trade and balance-of-payments deficit or "corporate America's" attraction to low-wage authoritarian states that deny elementary rights to their workers. It is no laughing matter to those who think that elected public officials in a "democracy" are supposed to speak honestly to the people rather than deceive them.

A Chronic "Disconnect Between Message and Reality"

"Boxgate" would perhaps be funny if it wasn't just a minor part of a much larger pattern of chronic disinformation and dishonesty in the Bush White House. Two years into the Bush-Rove presidency, the best question that a journalist could ask White House spokesman Ari Fleischer is something along these lines: "Mr. Fleischer, would you care to tell the American people just how stupid the White House takes them to be?" It's a question that won't be asked in quite those terms by the Washington press corps, which speaks in more polite terms, noting at its leftmost margins "the disconnect between [White House] message and reality."

By any reasonable standard, however, the scale of that "disconnect" under the current regime at 1600 Pennsylvania Avenue is exceptional. Let's examine just four examples.

Message: George W. Bush is a "populist" who sides with the "little guy" against Wall Street, is deeply concerned about the plight of the nation's poor, and seeks balanced economic growth that serves the entire US population.
Reality: Bush has consistently supported the interests of his class brethren in the corporate plutocracy. He has enacted and advocates further tax cuts that give the lion's share of benefits to the top 10 percent of "earners," do nothing to stimulate economic growth (as even conservative economists acknowledge), and undermine social programs needed by the nation's rising number of poor people.

Message: As "a uniter, not a divider," George W. Bush is strongly committed to racial justice in America and seeks to heal the racial rift in this nation. In line with Martin Luther King's belief in color-blind equality, he is opposed to the use of race for political purposes.
Reality: Bush appointed a Confederacy enthusiast as attorney general and refuses to apologize to African Americans for the crime and continuing legacy of slavery. He has needlessly antagonized African Americans by making racist federal judiciary nominations and filing a White House brief in the Supreme Court case against the University of Michigan's affirmative action program,

which he falsely accuses of mandating racial "quotas." His regressive domestic and imperial foreign policy agendas inflict disproportionate pain on African Americans and people of color at home and abroad. The White House routinely uses race for political purposes, spinning the presence of two African Americans in key foreign policy positions as proof of its racial sensitivity.

Message: The likely perpetrators of the September 2001 terror attacks (al Qaeda) attacked the World Trade Center and the Pentagon because they hate the "freedoms" enjoyed by people in American and Western "civilization."
Reality: The likely perpetrators are largely indifferent to domestic US society. Their real issues with America relate fundamentally to America's intrusive, imperial, and oil-driven foreign policy in the Middle East, which is why European nations (with the possible exception of American lapdog Britain) are much less likely to be targeted by terrorists. Their real goals are to spark jihad within the Middle East and to overthrow Arab regimes they see as insufficiently Muslim. Interestingly, the Bush administration has used 9/11 to roll back the very freedoms that it falsely accuses the terrorists of targeting.

Message: The Iraqi regime and its weapons of mass destruction (WMD) present a clear, present, and highly significant danger to the American people, making a new American "war" for regime change necessary in Iraq. Iraq is the single greatest threat to world peace and the American people by far.
Reality: The Iraqi regime is effectively disarmed and poses little if any threat to its own neighbors, much less to the US. Its "leader" Saddam is a vicious dictator, but there's nothing in his past record to indicate that he is suicidal, which he would have to be to use weapons of mass destruction against Americans or his neighbors. North Korea's declared intention to begin mass production of nuclear weapons is a much greater threat to world peace and American security. The single most important such threat at present is the bellicose imperial unilateralism of the world's leading manufacturer, possessor, and distributor of WMD—the United States, led by the arch-imperialist Bush gang.

The list of the Bush gang's deceptions, including the bizarre notion of the "Evil-Axis" and Rove's recent description of Bush as an "environmentalist," goes on and on. It should be fully compiled and juxtaposed against the Bush administration's forthcoming publication of Saddam's propaganda campaigns from 1990–2003. Surely the White House's effort to turn 9/11 and fear of al Qaeda into a rationale for war on Iraq and fear of Saddam should be counted as one of the most remarkable top-down propaganda operations in the modern record. In the meantime, we look forward to elaboration on the above and other forms of message-reality "disconnect" tonight, as George W. Orwell delivers what promises to be the most deceptive State of the Union address in memory.

Bush II likes to give his associates nicknames. Rove, for example, has received the clever moniker "Boy Genius." Here's one we ought to consider for our president: "Pinocchio," unless he actually believes the stuff his handlers have him saying to the people. In which case good old "Dubya" seems as appropriate as ever.

We Can See Through Your Lies

Fortunately, there is growing evidence that the American people are onto Bush's lies. A recent *Wall Street Journal*/NBC poll reports that a 49 percent plurality of Americans now disapprove of the way that Bush is "handling the economy." Fully 61 percent doubt that Bush's "economic stimulus package" will do much to stimulate economic growth. Bush's proposal to eliminate taxes on corporate dividends, the centerpiece of his package, is rated by poll respondents as the least productive among a set of potential actions the government might take to restore growth. By a 59 to 31 percent margin, respondents agree that the package would "benefit the most wealthy" rather than "all Americans equally"—a judgment that Bush has dismissed as "typical class warfare rhetoric."

Also interesting, the approval rating for Bush's handling of foreign policy has taken a considerable dive—from 75 to 52 percent—in the last three months, which cannot help but disturb White House strategists as the Bush administration enters its "endgame" in Iraq. *Washington Post* reporter Michael Dobbs notes that "*public opinion in the United States* and Europe is *closer to the French position*"—opposition to early military action on Iraq—"*than the U.S.* [well, White House] *position.*"[22] Not surprisingly, Bush's overall approval rating is falling. It currently rests at 54 percent, down from 82 percent one year ago and 62 percent one month ago. The proportion of Americans who express disapproval of Bush's job performance has risen to 40 percent.

"The Fetters Imposed on Liberty at Home. . . ."

The bad news is that these data probably speed up the war timetable in the Bush-Rove White House. The conventional political wisdom holds that the people will rally around the president once it becomes clear that "our boys" are entering combat. The Machiavellian counsel of Rove argues that saber-rattling against foreign Evil Others is a serviceable antidote to the domestic population's growing unrest over issues of socioeconomic homeland insecurity and related deep inequality. As James Madison once noted, "the fetters imposed on liberty at home have ever been forged out of the weapons provided for defense against real, pretended, or imaginary dangers from abroad."[23] Americans would do well to keep in mind this wise advice from the nation's revolutionary generation as they try to separate fact and reality from fiction and message in Mad King George's imperial State of Deception address.

9

Citizens or Spectators? Democracy Versus Empire on the Eve of "Inevitable War"
February 7, 2003

The White Man's Burden: "To Shock and Awe"

We are drifting quickly downstream toward a terrible historical waterfall. In "a matter of weeks, not months," America is *reported likely* to unleash world history's most lethal military machine on Iraq—a poor, battered, and effectively disarmed nation that poses minimal danger even to its own neighbors. Iraqi casualties in the event of this "war" could run well into the hundreds of thousands. One hesitates to estimate casualties if the killing machine's masters act on their threat to use nuclear weapons.

The US "Defense" Department plans to pulverize Iraq with *800 cruise missiles* in the space of *two days*. "There will not be a safe place in Baghdad," boasts a senior Pentagon official. The Pentagon is hoping for a "Hiroshima effect," leading Iraq to "quit, not fight."[24] It is forgotten or (more likely) never learned that Japan sought to surrender prior to the criminal Hiroshima and Nagasaki bombings, conducted to put the Soviets and other potential challengers in their proper postwar place.[25]

In a time when US policy planners feel free to speak in cavalier terms about reproducing a "Hiroshima effect," it is worth recalling the chilling reflections of the five-star US Admiral William D. Leahy, who headed the US Joint Chiefs of Staff and served as the chief of staff to the commander in chief of the Army and Navy from 1942 to 1949. "It is my opinion," Leahy wrote in 1950, "that the use of this barbarous weapon at Hiroshima and Nagasaki was of no material assistance in our war against Japan. The Japanese were already defeated and ready to surrender. . . . My own feeling," Leahy added, "was that in being the first to use it, we had adopted an ethical standard common to the barbarians of the Dark Ages. I was not taught to make war in this fashion, and wars cannot be won by destroying women and children."[26]

The openly expressed intent of the planned attack is to shatter Iraq "physically, emotionally and psychologically," consistent with American strategist Harlan Ullman's racist theory of "Shock and Awe."[27] By this theory, the non-Caucasian survivors of attack from the skies called upon by the Great White Masters of the World will climb out of their rubble to shake their heads in stunned admiration at the godlike capacities of the Great Men chosen to lead them into freedom. "Thank you," they will say, "for saving us by destroying our homes and communities, destroying our primary healthcare system, and denying clean water to our children."

Iraq's population, it should be recalled, is still reeling from an earlier American-led assault that laced parts of their country with cancer-causing Depleted Uranium and devastated basic civilian infrastructures, including water-treatment and electricity plants. The Iraqi people have also been living and dying for more than a decade under the American-led regime of economic sanctions—an officially unmentionable "weapon of mass destruction" (WMD) that particularly marks small children for passage to the hereafter.

Such is the White Man's Burden, shared by George W. Bush and his British "poodle" (a pit bull to weaker states) Tony Blair. They have the duty to inflict the necessary Judeo-Christian pain on unfortunate Arabs, tragically born into pre-"modern" lands that contain resources prized by "Western civilization." That "civilization" is led by the only nation to incinerate live human beings (non-Caucasians of course) with atomic ordnance, quite unnecessarily. It is useful, politically, that the burden can be carried with crucial assistance from two African American White House policymakers—affirmative action beneficiary/opponent Condoleezza Rice and "dove" Colin Powell, who recently shocked naive European leaders by joining the clamor for rapid "war" on Iraq.

As assistant operations officer of the US American Division in 1969, it is worth noting, Powell sought the good graces of the Great White Men by drafting the military's initial denial of the 1968 My Lai massacre, in which 400 Vietnamese civilians died at the hands of US soldiers.[28] In his overhyped United Nations speech this morning, Powell tried to further the prospect of new US-imposed atrocities, launched from a safer distance and sparing the executioners from having to see and smell the tragic consequences of their actions.

Demonstration Effect: "To Start the World Over"

The horrible possibilities for Iraqi civilians are of little concern to the White House. The Bush administration sees the forthcoming attack as essential to the attainment of three key objectives for which the supposed Iraqi threat is a useful pretext. It seeks, first, to divert the domestic population from its declining socioeconomic situation, worsened by regressive social policies imposed by the same gang running the nation's foreign policy. The second goal is to deepen US control over Middle Eastern oil resources, the world's greatest material prize in an age of global petrocapitalism. This aim burns with special intensity among the petroleum-soaked suits in the White House "oiligarchy."

The Bush administration's third aim is more grandiose. It is to seize on what it perceives as a historic opportunity granted by the collapse of Communism and the jetliner attacks of September 2001. The administration wants to make it clear to the *entire world* that there is, and can be for the foreseeable future, only one powerful state and that those who resist this reality can expect their lives to become hell. Iraq is "merely a convenient stage," notes John Pilger, for the demonstration of this lesson. As Pilger puts it, "the Bush cabal believe they are at a Hiroshima-like juncture in history—that they have at their disposal the means to start the world over in an apocalyptic spasm of swift and terrifying violence. The War Party believes itself to be embarked on an epochal, world-altering mission, and they are determined that this moment not be squandered." Iraqi oil, Pilger further notes, "is important," but the "real prize" is "nothing less than world domination: all the riches above and below the earth and seas." The main intent of the forthcoming war is "to break the will of the species."[29]

Irrelevant Complications: The Anglo-Saxons' "War Train Is Leaving the Station"

Recent reports suggest that the "Bush cabal" has already decided to seize the great historical moment. According to last Sunday's *New York Times,* discussion "in the corridors of the United Nations" has dropped the apparently obsolete question of whether or not Bush and Blair actually have a "war"-worthy case—fortunately, if true, for Powell, whose speech today made no such case. "The talk" now is only "about when the war [is] likely to start, and with whom [on board]. United Nations officials," the *Times* reported, "[are] *already looking past a war,* expecting a major role in helping refugees and rebuilding Iraq." The title of the article in which this observation appears is "All Aboard: America's War Train Is Leaving the Station."[30]

The fatalistic sentiment expressed in that title is validated by the comments of a senior French official who recently met with American officials, including Deputy Defense Secretary Paul Wolfowitz. "We got the impression," the French official told *Newsweek* (February 3, 2003), "that everything was already decided." In the minds of *les anglo-saxons,* as the French call the British and Americans, the "war" is "inevitable."[31]

Three days ago, in a column citing elite US scholarship that devastates the White House's strategic war argument, *Financial Times* columnist Martin Wolf concludes that "the war, it appears, is going to happen." He doubts that the "war" should be fought, but his only concern now is that Bush "be as committed to winning the peace as waging the war."[32]

For the Bush people, believing they are chosen by God and/or History to remake the world in the skies over Iraq, it is irrelevant, apparently, that

- no compelling evidence (despite Powell's unimpressive efforts today) supports their argument that Saddam poses a serious threat to the US or even the Middle East.
- Iraq is unlikely to use or hand off to terrorists (again, Powell aside) any of the WMD it may have, except as a desperate last response to US attack.
- containment has "worked" (from an amoral geopolitical perspective) regarding Iraq, and Saddam *can be deterred*. Saddam, as Wolf notes, is "brutal and rash" but "not mad. On the contrary, he is a calculator."[33]
- attacking Iraq will significantly increase the likelihood of new and terrible terror attacks and will spawn a new generation of Arab terrorists panting and planning for spectacular revenge.
- attacking Iraq may well destabilize the domestic and regional politics of the Middle East in ways that bode darkly for the effort to restrain terrorism.
- North Korea presents a much greater imminent threat to world peace than Iraq. So does nuclear-armed Pakistan, which could fall into extremist hands if the US attacks Iraq.
- attacking Iraq in the name of the doctrine of preemptive war will likely speed the global proliferation of WMD as the world's many potential US target states realize that possession of such weapons is the only effective deterrent to devastating US assault. This is a key lesson of the Bush administration's divergent responses to Iraq and North Korea.
- attacking and then (as Bush intends) occupying Iraq (for as long as ten years) will cost US taxpayers hundreds of billions of dollars they can ill afford as the Bush gang and its domestic allies deepen the skyrocketing federal deficit with plutocratic tax cuts falsely sold as "economic stimulus."
- the preponderant majority of Europeans are strongly opposed to Bush's plans. According to America-based *TimeEurope* magazine, four out of five Europeans now see the US as "the greatest threat to world peace,"[34] consistent with the British *Daily Mirror*'s proclamation last summer that "[t]he USA Is Now the World's Leading Rogue State."[35]
- *most Americans* disapprove of going to war alongside just one or two major allies and without UN approval. Two-thirds of Americans wish to "take more time" (*Newsweek*, February 3, 2003)—remarkable when we consider that, as Noam Chomsky notes, "the US is the only country outside Iraq where Saddam Hussein is not only reviled but also feared." Even Thomas Friedman, who supports the planned attack,

had to acknowledge today that "the base of [popular American] support" for what he call's Bush's "audacious project" is "incredibly narrow." Friedman's observation is worth quoting at greater length: "I've had a chance to travel all across the country since September and I can say without hesitation there is not a single audience I spoke to where I felt there was a majority in favor of war in Iraq. The dominant mood is: 'Mr. President, we don't want to be against you in a war on terrorism. But do we really have to do this? My 401 (k) is now a 201 (k) heading for a 101 (k). Osama bin Laden is still on the loose. The Europeans are uncovering new terrorist cells left and right. And I have walked through so many airport metal detectors in the last year that I now glow in the dark. I understand what the Afghan war was about and would have volunteered with a pitchfork—but I just don't get this war.'"[36]

- not surprisingly, a significant large-scale peace movement (opposing Bush's plans on moral as well as practical grounds) has already arisen in the West, including the US.
- Bush's war plans are opposed by many "elite" officials, intellectuals, and planners in the US as well as in Europe and around the world, making it easy for left critics to find "respectable" arguments against the "inevitable" assault. Bush's "war" plans and the doctrines guiding them came in for harsh criticism from various global elites gathered last week at the World Economic Forum in Davos, Switzerland. State Department Director of Policy Planning Richard Haass left Davos acknowledging that America "has yet to persuade the international community" that "war" is "necessary."

All of this appears to be irrelevant to the White House, except perhaps in *speeding the drive to "war."* In the view of American planners, it seems, these irritating little complications—including the opposition of most of the world's people, *even in the imperial state*—combine with seasonal weather patterns to put a premium on rapid deployment. As skepticism spreads, the political window on the Bush gang's perceived historic opportunity is seen by them as closing along with the meteorological one.

Cowboy Chutzpah: "Success Begets Success"

We should not, however, underestimate the White House's determination to move forward in the face of opposition at home and abroad. Beneath a populist veneer crafted by Republican political strategists, Bush and his "posse" (as he likes to call his White House team) are elitists who see themselves as born to rule. They imagine themselves beyond democratic constraint, like Wild West cowboys outside the reach of the law.

It is a sentiment borne out by the personally inept and broadly unpopular Bush's remarkable rise to power, consistently enabled by family riches, family name, and the special intervention of powerful allies in private (e.g., Enron) and public (e.g., the Governor's Office of Florida and the US Supreme Court) domains. And it doesn't help that Bush thinks of himself as the world's most powerful spokesperson for "Jesus Christ, the savior," whom he cited, during the Republican presidential debates in late 1999, as "the political philosopher or thinker" he most identified with.[37]

Whatever its members' feelings about God and Jesus, the Bush cabal has an abiding faith in the convenient capacity of saber-rattling and foreign policy crises, real or manufactured, to restart lagging approval numbers. It also believes in the providential power of such crises to divert the domestic population from nagging little problems like the disappearance of jobs, pensions, savings, and budget surplus. Such are the lessons of 9/11, which rehabilitated (or perhaps habilitated) a mediocre and illegitimate presidency, as well as the November 2002 midterm elections, when Bush's handlers kept media and electorate properly focused on Evil Others overseas.

Moreover, the Bush "posse" expects the "war" to be a quick and stunning victory that will erase significant opposition through sheer effectiveness. The predominantly Caucasian populace of the richest nations are included among the audience targeted by the White House for "Shock and Awe." Thus, for instance, Powell recently "stunned his fellow foreign ministers" at the UN "by comparing imminent war in Iraq to the US invasion of Panama in 1989." Powell, *Newsweek* reported, "dismissed French and German criticisms by saying that everyone complained, too, when Washington removed Noriega. But the outcome went well, as the country was returned, democratized, to its people." "Success begets success," Powell told the flabbergasted ministers, who should ask their aides to dig up some richer background material on the White House's "dove."[38]

Powell's Panama analogy is flawed in numerous ways, but it usefully reflects the dangerous, over-the-top arrogance of an administration that thinks its capacity for violence places it beyond meaningful popular and global restraint. Also likely entering the administration's calculations is its expectation that the official US "opposition" party (the Democrats) and America's "mainstream" corporate-state media (including one full-time "news" network [Fox] that openly pants for "war") will continue to enable the Bush war party. The "liberal" US media and Democrats do this by passing on the bizarre notion that Iraq somehow poses a serious and nondeterrable threat to the American people, significantly linked to 9/11's likely perpetrators and other nonstate terror networks.

Not in Democracy's Name: Citizens or Spectators?

The corporate-state media's antidemocratic role in the imperial "homeland" is multifaceted. It includes both the classic Orwellian task of misinformation and filtering and the more (Aldous) Huxley-esque role of diverting "the masses" through mind-numbing pseudo-entertainment and titillation. Especially noticeable in recent corporate-state coverage and commentary is the related tone of citizen irrelevance. Observing the "mainstream" media in America, we find it increasingly difficult not to cringe at the presentation of great events in a way that places history beyond the agency and input of the citizenry. Wars, tax cuts, welfare reductions, prison increases—as framed by dominant state-capitalist media, these and other developments are meant to be passively experienced by the populace, not to elicit citizen participation. There is suspense, perhaps, about certain outcomes, particularly those for which it is deemed necessary to rally mass consent (especially war). Still, the people in the audience (the citizenry) are not expected or supposed to significantly influence policy. The latter is left to the Great White Men who rule the world with occasional help from "experts" of color (e.g., Rice and Powell), in accordance with the mystical mandates of God and History.

The democratic tradition, in whose name America's policymakers speak, recoils in horror at this dark framing. History, this tradition teaches, is not ordained in advance and from above. Nothing in the realm of human affairs and public policy, it reminds us, is "inevitable." There is but one past, but the present and the future are indeterminate with real-life outcomes contingent upon numerous "factors," including the intelligence, consciousness, instincts, capacity, and will—the agency—of "we the people."

The point of democracy is not to plant citizens in front of an elite-programmed crystal ball, giving them instruction across the vast electronic coliseum on what is planned for their future so that they can properly and safely adjust. Rather, it is for them to be actively engaged, fully informed, and strongly empowered in shaping the future in accordance with their collective needs, aspirations, and capabilities.

We are not merely spectators; the democratic tradition beseeches us to remember the great events of our time. We are citizens, richly engaged, deeply implicated, and fundamentally accountable for the actions of our elected officials and other public servants. We are present at and involved in our own making and in the making of the world we share with others.

If ever there has ever been a time to revisit these democratic teachings, it is now, as the Bush cabal prepares to write its authoritarian notion of The Way Life Should Be into history, with horrible and unimaginable consequences for future generations.

10
It's the Empire, Stupid
February 13, 2003

It is hard not to notice the shift in emphasis of American left protest and activism since 9/11. The so-called new New Left is looking a bit more like the old New Left as "antiglobalization" Seattle Man makes way for or transforms into Anti-US War and Imperialism Woman. The leading targets of protest have changed from the World Trade Organization, the International Monetary Fund, and the World Bank to the White House and the Pentagon. The emphasis seems to have shifted from resisting transnational corporate and world financial domination of the planet to stopping a specifically American assault on one nation—Iraq. Important goals of the global justice movement—democracy, ecologically sustainable development, and the reduction of economic inequality within and between nations—seem to have been placed on the back burners. The leading pot on the front burner now is the urgent need to stop America's march to war. Also on the front at slightly lower heat is the related struggle against the homeland assault on people of color and economic disadvantage and on domestic civil liberties that accompanies the regressive, budget-busting "war on terrorism" like white on rice.

The antiwar movement, it seems fair to say, exhibits broader immediate appeal than the global justice movement. It is easier, after all, to talk about how the White House is preparing to quickly and directly kill and maim masses of innocent Iraqis than to explain how multinational corporations and global trade and financial institutions murder people and ecosystems a bit more slowly around the world. The peace movement presupposes much less knowledge about and explicit, conscious alienation from the "workings" of the dominant system of socioeconomic management (capitalism) than does the global justice movement. At the same time, the proposed forthcoming war's regressive domestic impact, diverting increasingly scarce (for social functions at least) public money from social to military expenditures, is more immediately and graphically evident than the undeniably negative domestic consequences of corporate globalization. And the drive for war is strongly linked to a specific illegitimate, widely unpopular (indeed unelected), offensively brazen, and shockingly corporate-plutocratic presidency in ways that redound to the benefit of the peace movement.

Is this seeming shift in focus a problem for the left? Has the left been set back, rolled back to the 1960s, so to speak? Has it been forced to step down from a promising movement for global democracy, equality, and environmental sustainability to mount a sadly elementary retro-struggle against one nation's imperialism and racism? Are we back to square one?

Not really. There are some reasons for concern along these lines, perhaps, but we should resist such pessimistic conclusions for at least six reasons. First, far from experiencing rollback, the current US peace movement is picking up where the movement against the Vietnam War left off. Even before the Bush attacks, hundreds of thousands marched in massive protests bigger than the largest anti–Vietnam War marches of the 1960s. And more than two-thirds of the American population oppose the White House's plans to unilaterally launch "war" on Iraq.

Second, given the greater transparency and simplicity of the antiwar cause, the peace movement provides an opportunity for global justice activists to make meaningful contact with progressively inclined people they would not otherwise meet.

Third, the Bush administration's push for war in the Middle East is significantly driven by modern capitalism's environmentally disastrous addiction to oil, gas, and the internal combustion engine. There is a significant progressive world-ecological dimension to the antiwar movement, which includes groups calling for the development of clean-energy alternatives.

Fourth, American global justice activists should welcome and learn from the peace movement's clearer connection to domestic poverty and race issues. Excessively white and middle-class, the global justice movement has failed to develop adequate linkages to the urban racial and social justice movements and to communities of poverty and color. Those communities experience more than their share of difficulties (racial profiling, crime, poverty, mass incarceration, gentrification, toxic waste sites, a shortage of affordable housing, etc.) right here at home, in the eye of the globalization hurricane.

Fifth, current US war plans are about *far more than Iraq*. Beyond Persian Gulf oil, the "real prize," as John Pilger was quoted as saying in chapter 9, is *"nothing less than world domination: all the riches above and below the earth and seas."*[39] Pilger's analysis might sound like an over-the-top left-dystopian fantasy, but it is based on a sober reading of US planners' documentary record. That record includes the White House's latest *National Security Strategy of the United States*, a pivotal September 2000 report issued by the Project for a New American Century, the United States Space Command's chilling *Vision for 2020* (advancing American global "Full Specter Dominance" in defense of transnational corporate interests), Paul Wolfowitz's 1992 Pentagon policy paper *Defense Planning Guidance*, and the book *Shock and Awe: Achieving Rapid Dominance*, penned by Harlan Ullman of the federally contracted "Defense Group, Inc.'s" Rapid Dominance Study Group and posted on the website of the US "Defense" Department's Command and Control Research Program.[40]

Sixth, the left's new confrontation with the tightening fist of specifically American state power is not really a diversion from the struggle against antidemocratic, regressive, and environmentally disastrous corporate globalization. According to many "antiglobalization" activists, modern transnational globalization has de-nationalized world power and stripped away the relevance of the nation state.

This judgment correctly observes that the architects of modern globalization seek to institutionalize and entrench the special rights and privileges of multinational corporations that owe allegiance to no single nation state. It rightly notes that globalization has reduced the policy leverage of national governments, even in the core (formerly called First World) states of the world capitalist system. It forgets, however, that globalization remains fundamentally imperial. Globalization continues to be all about enriching the First World relative to the peripheral and semiperipheral states. It is no accident that the dramatic expansion and acceleration of world economic activity during the last fifty years have been accompanied by a considerable widening of wealth disparities between the core and the periphery. Also more than coincidental to globalization are the emergence and expansion of giant First World and especially American corporations that dwarf corporations based outside the core.

No national business class has been more centrally involved in, and benefited more from, corporate globalization than that of the United States, which comprises 6 percent of the world's population but controls more than a third of the world's resources. This was acknowledged by foreign policy columnist Thomas Friedman in a *New York Times Sunday Magazine*[41] cover story published as the US prepared to bomb Serbia in the spring of 1999. Before the collapse of "communism," Friedman argued, the key justification for US globalism/imperialism was the protection of the world's "market democracies" through the "containment" of the expansionist Soviet Union. Today, however, Friedman continued, the justification proceeds from the United States' "over-arching interest" in guaranteeing the geopolitical stability necessary for "sustaining globalization." That "over-arching interest" consists of the fact that the "US wins" in a planet ruled by "free market" and "democratic" capitalism since it "had 200 years to invent, regenerate, and calibrate the checks and balances that keep markets free" and "has many of the most sought-after goods and services in the world market. . . . Globalization," Friedman cleverly concluded, "-is-US."

Friedman's analysis is flawed, reflecting its heavily ideological nature. The Soviets contained the Americans more than vice versa, and neither American nor global capitalism is "democratic" or based on "free markets." It's the leading sectors of the American business class that "win" most from globalization, not the falsely homogenized "US," which contains many workers who have been displaced and downsized by the workings of corporate globalization. Still, Friedman accurately senses the strong connection between that process and American power.

Global justice activists have also tended to downplay the significant extent to which modern capitalist globalization is shaped and underpinned by core and especially US state power and policy. The world's leading transnational corporations owe their very existence and much of their exalted market power to government charters and to numerous forms of core state protection (including, but hardly restricted to, tariffs and intellectual property rights) and subsidy (including the US "defense" budget).[42] At the same time, the great world financial institutions that do so much to impose the disastrous neo-liberal model on noncore states— kicking away the ladder of development by denying similar state protections, guidance, and subsidy to poorer nations—are the deliberate creations of the US government (specifically the US Treasury). It is with the blessing, directives, and funding of the US that the IMF and the World Bank impose the imperialist, First World–friendly "free trade, free investment" model of "investor rights globalization" on nations that need something very different—the very sort of protection against foreign economic penetration and domination that modern-day core states made sure to provide themselves in their time of economic modernization and industrialization—if they are ever going to join the club of wealthy nations.[43]

There is a strong military dimension to the predominantly American state power that "sustains globalization." Here again, Friedman is offensive but useful. "The hidden hand of the market," he wrote in the same piece cited above, "will never work without a hidden fist. McDonald's," he argued, "cannot flourish without McDonnell Douglas, the designer of the F-15. And the hidden fist that keeps the world safe for Silicon Valley technologies is called the US Army, Air Force, Navy and Marine Corps."[44] Friedman's imperialist candor resonates curiously with the following passage from the United States Space Command's recent Vision Statement for 2020, which dissents only from Friedman's notion that globalization provides great benefits for all world peoples and nations:

Historically, military forces have evolved to protect national interests and investments—both military and economic. During the rise of sea commerce, nations built navies to protect and enhance their commercial interests. During the westward expansion of the continental United States, military outposts and the cavalry emerged to protect our wagon trains, settlements, and railroads [and to kill the indigenous population that stood in the way of America's racist "Manifest Destiny," with its supposedly God and History–ordained right of conquest and appropriation, P.S.]. The emergence of space power follows both of these models. . . . [S]pace forces will emerge to protect military and commercial national interests and investment in the space medium due to their increasing importance. . . . Although unlikely to be challenged by a global peer competitor, the United States will continue to be challenged regionally. The globalization of the world economy will also continue, with a widening between "haves" and "have-nots."

Meanwhile, "the importance of space capabilities to military operations is being widely embraced by many nations" and weapons of mass destruction are undergoing "worldwide proliferation." In this context, the Space Command feels, it will be necessary for the United States to develop and maintain American "control of space," the capacity to undertake "global engagement of precision forces from, to, and through space," and the capacity for "the integration of space forces and space-derived information with land, sea, and air forces and their information."[45]

The terrible jetliner attacks of September 2001 have combined with the collapse of the Soviet deterrent more than a decade ago to provide the corporate-plutocratic arch-imperialists in the Bush administration an opportunity to brandish Friedman's "hidden hand" like no other time in recent memory. They are showing and flexing the iron fist of empire partly in defense, and partly in pursuit, of global economic interests. It is a mistake, however, to see the Bush group as little more than corporate lackeys who have surrendered state power to transnational energy, weapons, and financial corporations. They have attained significantly autonomous, unprecedented, and, for them, intoxicating military state power—far greater than anything they could ever expect to experience in the so-called private sector.

September 11th's imperial aftermath has reminded us that the state has yet to "wither away" and that capitalist economic globalization is still, as always, richly bound up with core-state militarism.

The nature of the complex relationship between that globalization project and the world state system will spark debate among left intellectuals for many more years. In the meantime, we would do well to appreciate the wisdom of a basic formulation from one such intellectual—veteran Egyptian Marxist Samir Amin. As Amin told fellow attendees at the World Social Forum in Porto Allegre, Brazil, "there is not on the one hand social and economic problems and on the other hand political and military problems. . . . One cannot defeat the IMF and other institutions that obey the United States without defeating the military strategy of the United States. As long as the aggressive, fascist strategy of the United States is not defeated, an alternative globalization will not be possible."[46]

11
Broadcast Priorities: Corporate Media Versus Democracy in the Streets
February 15, 2003

Strange Expectation

Let's start with four basic observations. First, by the widely accepted and often passionately embraced reckoning of its own citizens, media, and elected officials, the United States is a democracy. Second, a functioning democracy depends to no small extent on wide, intensive, and unbiased media coverage of important contemporary political developments at home and abroad. Third, few developments could be more worthy of such coverage than millions of Americans taking to the streets to resist their government's plans to attack a weak and impoverished nation in a "powder-keg" region full of terrible danger for Americans and others. The newsworthiness would only be enhanced if the largest protest were to occur in a city that had already experienced a horrible attack by terrorists from that region. Fourth, mass protest to prevent an action that will kill hundreds of thousands of people is at least as important as an accident that already occurred and cost seven lives.

Asleep at the Camera

On the basis of these observations, one might expect that Saturday's mass American protests against the Bush administration's planned attack on Iraq would receive in-depth, blow-by blow live coverage from the broadcast media. Many hundreds of thousands of Americans hit the pavement Saturday to protest the deadly, dangerous, and imperial plans of the White House—expected by the United Nations to kill as many as 500,000 Iraqis. Three hundred and seventy-five thousand braved freezing temperatures to protest in New York City, site of the terrible jetliner attacks on the World Trade Center. The numbers would have been considerably higher but for the efforts of city and local media authorities to repress attendance.

Well, the expectation of comprehensive media coverage would have gone unfulfilled. I was homebound yesterday but made use of my time by monitoring two different forms of media coverage. The first was Pacifica Radio through WBAI in New York City, available via the Internet. The second was my television. Thanks to a cable hookup that costs me $50 a month, I have access to fifty-seven stations. It's an exact numerical match to Bruce Springsteen's song about the nothingness of American television, titled "Fifty-Seven Channels/Nothing On."

The contrast was remarkable. Thanks to the comprehensive, in-depth "you are there" coverage provided by Pacifica/WBAI, it was clear that history was being made in New York City. The energy was unmistakable in the chants and cheers of the protestors, the passionate and articulate statements of the speakers, and the comments of demonstrators. Pacifica reporters' support for the protest was clear, but the events they related were so clearly momentous they would have struck even a reactionary listener as historically significant.

Things were different on the television. It would have been absurd, of course, to expect any kind of demonstration coverage on most of the stations. The preponderant majority of the broadcast spectrum is ceded to diverse demographic and cultural segments of the entertainment market.

But even on the seven or so stations where one might realistically expect ongoing live coverage of these momentous developments—the three major networks plus C-SPAN and the cable news channels—there was no such coverage. The protests were the number-one story, unavoidably, at CNN, which provided some remarkable protest footage from Europe and a poignant interview with a New York demonstrator who lost a relative in 9/11. And the story was covered somewhat grudgingly at the Fox News Channel, a veritable broadcast arm of the White House, along with reminders from former US military analysts and weapons inspectors–turned–Fox commentators that the White House "does not require consensus" to attack Iraq.

C-SPAN, the most progressive spot on the national broadcast spectrum, was asleep at the camera. As millions marched, it broadcast old tape from CIA Director George Tenet's recent Senate testimony on the supposed link between Saddam and al Qaeda.

Particularly at Fox News, the coverage downplayed America-specific dissent, giving considerably more attention to protests in Rome, Berlin, Paris, and London than to those occurring right in the imperial state's homeland. Fox made sure to tie it all to Saddam, linking American and European protests to suggestive clips of rifle-waving Iraqis carrying posters of their evil leader.

Mass Protest Versus the Exploding Space Shuttle and John John's Cessna

None of this is meant to discount the antiwar movement's success in making its story number one on the evening news and in the next day's newspapers. Still, it was hard not to notice the contrast between yesterday's noncoverage of live American protest and the corporate media's response to the space-shuttle tragedy just two Saturdays before. The latter was an essentially nationalist episode involving no real political controversy. It elicited an orgy of intensive "you are there" coverage, replete with exhausted anchors, a bevy of expert commentators, and details on all the latest developments. Film and photos of the disintegrating shuttle were played over and over. All the major networks and news cable stations stayed with the terrible story from morning until evening and well into the next day.

The contrast is reminiscent of the corporate media's response to the historic mass demonstration against corporate globalization that occurred in Seattle during November 1999. You could follow that remarkable development live on alternative Internet media. But when you searched your "fifty-seven channels" for live Seattle footage, you found anchormen still obsessed with John F. Kennedy Jr.'s demise. The nation's televisions had been "turned into fishbowls" (left media critic Robert McChesney quipped) as network cameras descended into the Atlantic for John John's sunken Cessna.

Down the Memory Hole in Just Twelve Hours

Further proof of the "mainstream" (corporate) media's reluctance to give Saturday's demonstrations their due came at 1:30 Sunday morning, when I resumed my position in front of the idiot box. A story on CNN informed late-night watchers that the basic factor determining the timing of an apparently inevitable US attack on Iraq is *climate*. We heard from "CNN Military Analyst" and "Brigadier General" David Grange, who reassured his audience that the "US military can attack in any weather." Still, he noted, US planners are concerned about the coming Iraqi heat, which will complicate the Army's "Mission Oriented Protective Posture" (military speak for special troop gear to guard against chemical and biological weapons). Another issue is sandstorms, which make it difficult "to engage targets with your optics"—tough, that is, to see the people you are trying to destroy.

I flipped to the Fox News Channel, where a panel of media experts was analyzing the media's "*Pre*-war Coverage." This segment was labeled "The Media Braces for War." Panel member and onetime Guggenheim fellow Neal Gabler argued that it would be a "tragedy" if the inevitable "war" becomes the "new reality tv." Gabler also worried about "a real possibility we won't get the whole [war] story" from "our media." Someone should look into that.

The panel's host suggested that the leading news channels, including Fox, will drop commercials during the war's initial days—a temporary cost that media corporations will gladly pay in pursuit of increased "market share."

Just half a day old, the historic mass demonstrations of 2/15/03 were already fading into history's ashcan, as far as CNN and Fox's experts were concerned. Perhaps Fox should run a segment labeled "The Media Help Generate 'War' [the graphic inequality of the supposed combatants requires quote marks] by Assuming That It Is Inevitable and Discounting the Massive Opposition of the Irrelevant People."

Things didn't get much better when I continued my deepening engagement with corporate television after some well-deserved sleep. On the fifteen minutes of NBC's *Meet the Press* I caught Sunday morning, yesterday's demonstrations had already been swept into the Orwellian memory hole. Tim Russert's discussions about the latest "war on terrorism" developments with National Security Adviser Condoleezza Rice and former US General Wesley Clark focused on strategic questions relating to Saddam's behavior, top European policymakers, the UN Security Council, and al Qaeda. Saturday's outpouring of citizen opposition to US plans at home and abroad was apparently irrelevant—a nonfactor in any serious discussion of current events.

It was the same everywhere I turned: Wolf Blitzer on CNN (interviewing Homeland Security chief Tom Ridge on the likelihood of domestic terror attacks), a PBS foreign policy expert panel, and an NBC media panel headed by Chris Matthews on NBC. None of the talking heads I encountered in my bleary-eyed television meanderings found the previous day's historic popular dissent worth mentioning as they discussed future US policy in the Middle East.

Perhaps I missed the standard obligatory comment on protest from Rice—the one where the White House notes how incredibly fortunate the American people are to possess the right of popular assembly. It's a favorite line from Rumsfeld and Rice, who seem to think Americans should be grateful that their masters permit them protest without the fear of being shot or thrown into concentration camps. Saddam, the Bush gang loves to remind us, permits no domestic opposition. The idiotic implication, never questioned by corporate media, is that Saddam is somehow at risk of bringing dictatorship to the United States along with his weapons of mass destruction.

Toward Media Reform

It has become common to note the growing disconnection between American public opinion and Bush domestic and foreign policy. Less commonly noted but equally relevant and also growing is the mismatch between that opinion and American corporate media. The second gap reflects the deep incorporation of America's "private" media oligarchy into an imperial state-capitalist project that seeks to advance a process of authoritarian corporate globalization richly favored by America's leading multinational media firms—giant publicly sponsored corporate hierarchies that fail to fulfill their duty to supply Americans with the information required for responsible democratic citizenship.

After we stop this horrible war, let's take up the cause of democratic media reform, helping thereby to prevent future imperialist campaigns.

12
"Ungrateful"? America, France, Hitler, and Debts of History
February 20, 2003

"We Saved Their Butts"

It is difficult to imagine the bitter irony with which many French people must be receiving the American charge of "ingratitude." For the last two weeks at least, leading members of the US Congress, editorialists, and others have been bashing the French for their supposed failure to support international "law and order" by joining America's reckless and dangerous campaign to needlessly massacre Iraqis. There is even talk of an American boycott of French goods. Much of the criticism has focused on the charge that France is "ungrateful" for America's heroic efforts to save them during the "Good War"—the great Allied struggle against German and Japanese fascism between 1941 and 1945.

Listen, for example, to Fred Barnes, executive director of the reactionary *Weekly Standard*. Last Thursday, he expressed his outrage that France would "actively try to undermine President Bush" on Iraq "after all we've done for them"—including "saving their butts" in World War II.

Behold the outraged former New York City Mayor Ed Koch. "I encourage everybody in America: do not go to France," Koch said last week. "These people were Nazi [collaborators] in large part. We saved them—and they turned on us." "Most of us," chimed in "war" enthusiast Rep. Gary Ackerman (D-Queens, New York), "believe [the French] would all be speaking German if it were not for US military intervention."

Nearly three weeks ago, US Senator John Kyl asserted that America "liberated" France from "Hitler's grip" in a statement denouncing "old Europe's" (France and Germany's) supposedly irrelevant opposition to American "war" (massacre) plans in the Middle East.

Deleting America's Fascist Accommodation and Emulation

History holds a less than exalted position in the nation that Michael Eric Dyson once aptly called "The United States of Amnesia." Still, it is interesting to note how consistently elite would-be architects of American opinion feel driven to construct fundamentally, albeit bad, *historical* arguments on behalf of their various projects at home and abroad.

A funny thing forgotten by practitioners of the new American sport of French-bashing is that US policymakers helped enable the rise of European fascism that culminated in Hitler's march of terror. As is apparent from the relevant historical literature, the US watched with approval as fascist darkness set over Europe during the interwar years. American policymakers saw Italian, Spanish, German, and other strains of the European fascist disease as a welcome counter to the Soviet threat—essentially the demonstration Russia made of the possibilities for modernization (industrialization, urbanization, and nation-building) outside the capitalist world system—and anticapitalist social democracy within Western European states.

In 1937, the US State Department's European Division argued that European fascism was compatible with America's economic interests. This key diplomatic agency reported that fascism's rise was a natural response of the "rich and middle classes" to the threat posed by "dissatisfied masses," who, with the "example of the Russian Revolution before them," might "swing to the left." Fascism, the State Department argued, "must succeed or the masses, this time reinforced by the disillusioned middle class, will again turn to the left." The French Popular Front government of the mid-1930s was an example of the popular left threat that made fascism acceptable to American officials before Hitler really launched *his* drive for a *New World Order.*

It is true that fascism became an avowed US enemy during WWII. This did not occur, however, until fascism, holding power in two leading imperialist states, directly attacked American interests. American policymakers intervened against fascism on the basis of perceived national self-interest, not out of any particular concern for the human rights of the French or, for that matter, the European Jews, or anyone else.

After the war, it is worth noting, America's accommodation of European and Asian fascism in the interwar period became the model for US Third World policy. In the name of resisting supposedly expansionist Soviet influence and anticapitalism, the US sponsored, funded, equipped, and provided political cover for numerous Third World fascist regimes. In doing so, it *protected and enlisted numerous Nazi War criminals* (e.g., Klaus Barbie) perceived to have special skills in antileftist counterinsurgency. And today, as it prepares a "preemptive" invasion of a weak state to advance an American-dominated New World Order, the US quite reasonably strikes many European and other world citizens as the closest thing in recent historical memory to Hitler's Third Reich.

Who Is Ungrateful?

The American right wants to view France's position on US Iraq policy as a French referendum on its historical debts to other nations. Fine—perhaps, then, we should see France's resistance to the Bush War Party as an expression of its deep gratitude to Russia, which opposes Bush's Iraq campaign and which lost *25 million lives* in the struggle against fascism-Nazism. No nation did more than Russia to stop the Nazis.

If their charges of French ingratitude are to be taken seriously, America's warmongers believe that a decent nation expresses proper gratefulness for a survival-enabling historical gift from another nation by embracing the savior nation's current policy agenda, whatever the widespread opposition of the saved state's population. By this standard, however, America ought to be *taking its policy cues from France*. After all, it is incontrovertible historical fact that French military assistance was crucial to America's victory in its War of Independence against the British Empire between 1776 and 1783. Perhaps the French should launch a public relations countercampaign, accusing American policymakers of being ungrateful for the heroic sacrifices made by France to enable *the very birth* of the United States.

The French do feel gratitude for the role Americans played in expelling the Nazis. When they see George W. Bush sneering from their television screens about the concocted threat posed by Iraq, however, they do not flash back to Franklin Delano Roosevelt and the heroic struggle against world fascism. They see a dangerous new potential world dictator, one who manufactures exaggerated foreign threats to justify a Nazi-like drive for unchallenged world power.

What is the moral calculus whereby one nation's historical debt to a stronger nation's past opposition to a shared monstrous enemy mandates the weaker state's supine subservience to the stronger state's current global agenda—even when that agenda puts the weaker state at significant risk?

Better Analogies

The charge of ingratitude was once leveled against America's Founding Fathers, in the aftermath of what American history texts call "The French-Indian War." The accusation came from King George's British Empire, aghast at the North American colonists' reluctance to pay the costs of supposed imperial protection. The ensuing struggle, sparked by British efforts to enforce proper imperial subordination, culminated in the American Revolution, successfully completed with crucial assistance from France—*something for which the American people should be eternally grateful.*

Here, perhaps, we find a somewhat more useful historical analogy than WWII to grasp "ungrateful" France's reluctance to jump on board the imperial campaign of history's new and more dangerous Mad King George.

Among the many reasons for people to know their history, few are as compelling as the power such knowledge gives them to critically scrutinize misleading historical statements made by policymakers to advance terrible agendas. The hysterical French-bashing historical propaganda recently spewed out by America's modern imperialists and their chauvinistic cheerleaders is an excellent example.

13
Moments of Truth, Masters of War
March 17, 2003

Across the nation, America's newspapers announce the same headline, handed, as is so often the case, to our media poodles by their masters in the White House: "Moment of Truth."

It *is* a moment of truth, a pivotal time, one of those fateful points where you have to decide—left or right, in or out, smile and play along or say "the hell with the Masters" and step down from your assigned spot on the killing line.

Bush and the other fundamentalist arch-imperialists and corporate-military plutocrats in the White House are prepared now to go beyond their bellicose Orwellian rhetoric. They are ready to enter the War Criminals' Hall of Fame by launching an unjust, illegal attack on a weak, impoverished, and effectively disarmed nation that poses no serious threat to the American people. They are prepared to initiate a truly terrible act of aggression, launching 800 cruise missiles into Baghdad in two days in a "Shock and Awe" campaign they openly compare to Hiroshima and Nagasaki.

Their Chicken Hawk hearts are quickening as they gear up to fight a "war" from behind their well-guarded desks, walls, and computer screens. To quote from Bob Dylan's "Masters of War," they've "fasten[ed] the triggers, for the others to fire." They will "sit back and watch while the death count gets higher."

Bush and Blair are prepared to destroy untold numbers of innocent Iraqi civilians—the United Nations estimates that 500,000 Iraqis are at risk—in the name of "democracy" and "freedom," code words for "empire" when uttered by American statesmen, as is well understood outside the United States. Bush and Blair see the civilians they are about to butcher in Iraq pretty much the same way al Qaeda saw the thousands of Americans it killed in September 2001—as expendable "offal" on the path to higher political and doctrinal objectives.

The Hiroshima and Nagasaki analogies are accurate, but not in the ways that the enforcers of the New World Order claim. Like those hideous 1945 atrocities, also falsely sold as necessary to "save lives," the forthcoming attack on Iraq is partly an experiment and partly a demonstration project to display current and future US power. As in 1991, cybernetic Masters of War, tucked behind computer screens, will test new weapons systems. They will try to make a chilling new statement to the entire world about America's superiority in the manufacture and deployment of the means of what they call "creative destruction."

It is a moment of truth for the world state system. Bush, Rumsfeld, and the rest are prepared to put the last nail in the coffin of a multilateral world order. At the moment that the first bombs land in Baghdad, "the United States, the most powerful nation in history, [will] no longer just be threatening to use its power internationally, with no nod to anyone else. It will be at the point of no return," writes *Chicago Tribune* correspondent R. C. Longworth, on the path to a unilateralist world order.[47]

The ultimate regime change the Bush cabal seeks is international. It wants to overthrow the last hints of serious global cooperation and undo international law. It seeks to enshrine America as the unchallenged hegemonic power, ruling alone, by sheer preponderance of military force.

It is a moment of truth for America's rising number of poor, stuck at the bottom of the industrialized world's most unequal and wealth-top-heavy nation—the leading prison state on the planet. The American rulers of the New World Order are happy to spend half a billion dollars a day on overseas conquest and empire even as the crises of their "homeland's" many impoverished communities grow deeper. The cries of those communities fail to elicit significant response beyond expensive mass surveillance, arrest, and incarceration from a supposedly "cash-strapped" public sector whose cup runs over when it comes to serving wealth and empire.

It is a moment of truth, a moment of terror, for the people of Iraq in ways too obvious to state and too painful to contemplate.

It is a moment of truth for America's corporate-state media, falsely labeled "mainstream." The owners and managers of the nation's "private" communications empire have emerged as full-fledged Masters of War with flying colors both print and electronic. They have enabled the imminent massive high-state crimes in numerous ways, conveying Bush's idiotic claims that Iraq threatens America and that Saddam was linked somehow to 9/11. They have worked to relegate the American citizenry to spectator status, treating fateful questions of state policy as if they are beyond the sphere of legitimate popular input and agency. They have treated the "war" (massacre) as "inevitable" even as millions march against it. They have failed to adequately register the protests and fears of the people in whose name they claim to speak. The blood of dead Iraqis is already showing on their hands.

Next to the White House and the Pentagon, I can think of no structures more deserving of massive citizen protest than America's great media corporations.

Now these great manufacturers of mass consent and diversion, these giant cultural charnel grounds, these massive, deadening structures of neo-Orwellian/Huxlean thought control, have another important task. They must work to provide ex post facto justification for the imminent war crimes by pretending to discover proof that Iraq really was a threat, that it really was connected to 9/11, that it really was building nuclear weapons, and so on. It is their job, as in 1991, to ignore and hide the mass civilian casualties, to relegate the crumpled bodies of Iraqi children, mothers, and grandfathers to history's dustbin while trumping the pyrotechnics above Baghdad as a glorious victory for human "civilization." It is their job, again, to drown the tears of Arab children and mothers in a sea of racist celebration and disproportionate concern for "our" troops.

Watch them as they work to manipulate mass opinion in defense of empire, slavish and supine before the awesome march of the Great White Men and the carefully chosen subordinates of color atop the world's leading rogue state. Behold the media Masters as they "lie and deceive" "like Judas of old" (Dylan, "Masters of War"). They manufacture images, transmit high-state falsehoods, and frame deceptions that promise to set the world on fire. Like the chiefs of Boeing, Lockheed Martin, and other "defense" contractors lining up to cash in on the New Imperial Century of Permanent War, the vampire corporate media executives will "hide in [their] mansion[s] while young people's blood flows out of their bodies and gets buried in the mud" (Dylan, "Masters of War").

It is a moment of truth for the citizens of the Western democracies. We are free to express our opposition to the plans of the warmongers without fear of being shot or incarcerated. But how shall we express our dissent in the wake of the decision for "war" (massacre)? Shall we remain content to write letters to our public officials? To write letters to the editor and to draft opinion-editorials for the newspapers? To write, perform, and applaud protest songs? To write articles in the alternative press and for antiwar websites and to speak at antiwar teach-ins and demonstrations? To hand out buttons, collect signatures, send out mailings, construct e-mail lists, and identify protest targets? To target prowar politicians for removal from office? To march and chant and hand out flyers in peaceful demonstrations?

We have done all of these things and much more, and we shall continue. Much has been accomplished and remains to be done through these timeworn means. But the Masters of War and Empire and Propaganda are undeterred by reasonable mass citizen action. Bush has dismissed responding to the many millions in the streets as "governing by focus groups."

The Masters are determined to carry out their hideous crimes in our name, regardless of what we say and feel. We have spoken truth to power, and power has refused to hear. We have said, "Please sir, listen" to the president, surrounded by his neo-fascist "posse," and he has responded with authoritarian disdain. The decision for "war" has been made, we are told, and now it is time for us to go home and line up obediently behind the bluebloods who alone are fit to make policy, grateful that we were benevolently granted the right to express our opinion. "Support our troops."

"The president, who's wanted war with Iraq all along," notes *New York Times* columnist Bob Herbert today, "has been unwilling to listen seriously to anyone with an opposing view." Further: "Mr. Bush has remained unmoved by the millions of protestors against the war who have demonstrated in the United States and around the world. If any one of these millions has had something worthwhile to say, the president hasn't acknowledged it. . . . The president's mind was made up long ago and all the chatter of pro and con was just so much smoke. Mr. Bush will have his war."[48]

It all brings supporters of peace and justice to a very different moment of truth than the sort contemplated by Bush. It brings us to the point where we are compelled to embrace extralegal direct action and open civil unrest to undo the new slaughterhouse of Empire.

14
Resist Despair
March 25, 2003

Our Streets, Their Telescreens

For two straight nights, we filled the streets of downtown Chicago, tens of thousands for peace, justice, and democracy—for life. "What do we want? *Peace!* When do want it? *Now!*" "*Tell* me what democracy looks like. *This* is what democracy looks like." "One, two, three, four, we don't want this racist war." "*Whose* streets? *Our* streets!"

We marched and chanted, drums beating and whistles blowing, angry but determined and completely nonviolent. The second night we were closely monitored every step of the way by a giant sullen army of jackbooted gendarmes, metropolitan soldiers in the proposed new century of Permanent Imperial War. Behind and above, office workers peered out of their corporate skyscrapers, curious about this outbreak of passionate mass dissatisfaction in the streets of a leading world city. "Look, that one there, five floors up in the fifth column, she just gave us the peace sign."

We passed on numerous occasions Friday night beneath the "L," the city's famous Elevated Train system. More than once the conductor of a moving train stuck his or her hand out of the window, flashing two fingers in the air. We had seen the same symbol of solidarity from bus drivers marooned the night before by marchers on the city's Lake Shore Drive.

Writing four days later, I still feel the waves, the rhythm, and the roar of the crowd, which included people from every racial, ethnic, religious, and age group in Chicago—far more than the usual white college-educated suspects.

It was a good decision to turn off my computer, leave my office, and attend those marches. I made a critical mistake, however, on Friday night.

I turned on my television to watch the local ten o'clock news. I wanted to see what kind of impact we had made according to the holy, all-knowing corporate-state media that so powerfully shapes the hearts and minds of my fellow citizens/spectators.

The beginning of the newscast was dedicated to the shocking and appalling pyrotechnics above Baghdad, focusing discussion on the official state targets and deleting the likely consequences for civilians below. We learned that President Bush's approval ratings were rising in response to the beginning of the barbarism.

The Chicago march was covered ten or so minutes into the broadcast by a smiling anchorwoman whose opening line was "What a difference a day makes!" The hook of her story was the supposed contrast between a terrible Thursday, when 20,000 protestors overwhelmed overmatched police, and a thankfully tamer Friday, when the cops came out in full riot gear to protect the city—from itself. Order restored.

I flipped to the non-news programming that runs on most of my fifty-seven stations. How many people, I wondered, are enjoying basketball, sitcoms, and fitness infomercials as their tax dollars and soldiers are being used to enshrine the imperial rule of sheer force and to crumble the governing edifices of a sovereign nation in the cradle of ancient civilization?

Do Mourn, Do Organize

My mind flashed to the woman in an elevator I rode on Thursday. "We lost," she told me, showing me her "No War" button on the lapel of her coat. Her companion grimaced and stared at the floor. "Time to go home and lick our wounds," he weakly joked.

I felt their despair. I breathed it in and then . . . it was gone. We must mourn the lives that have been lost and the many more that will disappear because we have been unable to stop the invasion of Iraq. The grief demands to be felt; otherwise it will fester beneath our rugged public exteriors, poisoning our activism in ways that can only serve the Masters of War.

The old Industrial Workers of the World slogan—"Don't Mourn, Organize"—is more than just half-wrong. You don't have to choose. And you'll organize more effectively if you acknowledge and process the reality of the defeats that you and others have suffered.

Reasons to Resist Despair and Keep Fighting

At the same time, there are a number of sound empirical reasons to think that antiwar activists have already won significant victories and can expect more triumphs—just as there are other reasons to keep resisting that have nothing to do with past victories or the objective balance of forces. In what follows, I give arguments for Americans who hate the war to resist defeatism and stay energized against Bush foreign policy and for the causes of peace, justice, and democracy at home and abroad.

1. *Unprecedented Early Resistance.* The depth, breadth, and scale of the domestic, overseas, and popular resistance to Bush's war are remarkable—unprecedented at this stage of an American military campaign. The numbers of antiwar activists in the streets *even before the conflict formally opened* were phenomenal. Despite the best jingoistic efforts of the White House and corporate-state media, popular antiwar activism is already at a level that peace organizers were unable to attain until many years into the Vietnam War.

2. *Lives Saved.* Peace demonstrators at home and around the world have already saved Iraqi lives by contributing significantly to the creation of a political climate in which "mass civilian casualties" are feared as "a public relations disaster for Washington" (Reuters).

3. *No Quick and Easy Victory.* A key part of the sales job for this war has been the promise of rapid, total victory. Bush never leveled with the American people regarding projected deaths of Iraq civilians or US soldiers and the length and danger of the war and the occupation. So where are all the grateful, welcoming, self-consciously "liberated" Iraqi civilians predicted by the Bush administration? This Sunday's CNN coverage acknowledged "unexpectedly strong resistance" from Iraqi forces. Invading Iraq to install a new regime without any real support from other Arab states and other leading world nations may prove to be a long and bloody struggle. The fierce determination of Iraqi leaders is combining with resurgent Iraqi nationalism and Kurdish distrust of US intentions to prevent easy and rapid imperial triumph. This works against the quick disappearance of the peace movement on the model of 1991, when Daddy Bush achieved the basic objective (Iraq out of Kuwait) in short order with a "Nintendo War" and when there was no question of a long and difficult occupation following "regime change."

4. *Where Are All Those Terrible Weapons of Mass Destruction (WMD)?* Another key part of the White House's sales job is the notion that Saddam possesses huge and threatening stockpiles of major, state-of-the-art chemical and biological weapons and the potential to develop nuclear weapons. The Pentagon will pressure the media to play along with the doctrinal requirement that Saddam be shown to have possessed truly fearsome caches of WMD. There is potential for welcome White House embarrassment here, thanks to the monumental deception involved in the claim, well understood by serious investigators.

5. *Soft, Passive, and Qualified Support for Bush's Unnecessary War.* Many Americans express outward support for the president because they think they should "support our troops" in a moment of crisis and have been led

to believe that the war will be quickly won and concluded. Privately, however, many Bush supporters don't get the president's obsession with Saddam Hussein and his determination to put our soldiers in harm's way for incredibly murky reasons. Their assent is full of misgivings, reflecting a sneaking and accurate suspicion that they have been fed bad information to convince them that Saddam represents a serious threat to people outside Iraq.

As the struggle extends and costs more American as well as Iraqi lives, with the justifications unclear and questionable, some of this outward support will erode. It won't help the White House that America's incredibly unequal political economy continues to wallow in pseudo-recovery, its top-wealth-heavy torpor furthered by the regressive domestic policies Bush hopes to advance with his imperial agenda.

It is an indication of the soft and passive nature of the president's support that prowar rallies put merely hundreds into public squares while antiwar activists marshal tens and even hundreds of thousands of passionate marchers.

6. *The "Vietnam Syndrome" Is Not Dead.* Bush's father spoke too soon when he claimed that the Persian Gulf War (during which the US and its allies dropped 84,200 tons of munitions on Iraq and Kuwait) put the "Vietnam syndrome" to rest. The "Vietnam syndrome" refers to the American population's reluctance to sustain mass American casualties in overseas conflicts of dubious defensive necessity. The high-altitude bombing of Iraq and the horrific slaughter of Saddam's defeated troops in 1991 hardly qualified as a serious test of the "syndrome's" strength.

The father of one of the first US soldiers killed in "Operation Liberate Iraq" accused the president of essentially taking his son's life for no good reason. This mourning father is rightly unconvinced that Saddam Hussein represents the sort of danger that might justify such a sacrifice. The Bush administration will elicit more such bitterness among grieving families and communities as it continues to wage its unnecessary imperial war of occupation on sullen, unwelcoming, and heavily armed Iraqis.

7. *Domestic Failures and a Peace Movement That Is Making the Connections.* Today the White House went to Congress requesting and certain to quickly receive a "supplemental" (on top of a $360 billion "defense" budget) appropriation of $74 billion to pay for the Iraqi war and homeland security.[49] Sixty-three billion will go to the Pentagon and $8 billion to "coalition partners," leaving just $4 billion for protecting the domestic population from terrorist attack. The extravagantly expensive war of occupation is making the radically regressive essence of the Bush regime more evident than ever. How can the American government afford to spend hundreds of billions of dollars on empire while slashing taxes for the super-rich and deepening the crisis of America's growing number of poor at home? It lacks the money to adequately fund education for all of the country's

children or for universal health coverage, but it can spend more on the military than do all possible US enemy states combined many times over. It can spend hundreds of billions on the occupation of a distant nation that poses minimal risk to the US.

This is an opportune moment to criticize and connect two great paralyzing myths foisted on the American public by "conservative" ideologues, neo-liberal policymakers, the corporate-state media, and even some segments of the left. The first myth claims that the essential political choices we face are between the supposedly liberating, democratic, and "free" market and the supposed dead hand of an inherently authoritarian and hyperbureaucratic public sector. The second myth claims that the state is too weak and cash-strapped to carry out relevant functions in support of the common good: adequate school funding, drug treatment, national health insurance, and much more.

In reality, the really relevant choices are between regressive, authoritarian public policies that serve heavily concentrated and highly bureaucratic corporate power and social-democratic policies that serve the common good, reduce disparity, and advance democracy. In really existing American society, moreover, the public sector is weak and cash-strapped only when it comes to social democracy for the people. Its cup runs over in powerful ways when it comes to serving wealth, empire, and racial disparity at home and abroad.

This great double standard is becoming increasingly evident to the American peace and justice movement. Relating Bush's dangerous overseas agenda to the White House's class war against America's poor and working people ("the War at Home," as it was called in a recent massive Chicago demonstration), this movement is making the connections between empire abroad and repression (including racially disparate mass incarceration) and inequality at home.

It is worth recalling that Daddy Bush's high wartime (Desert Storm) approval ratings fell quickly because of his failure to address deepening domestic economic insecurity. Also meriting remembrance is the fact that American policymakers were forced to scale back and ultimately call off their military crucifixion of Southeast Asia by their realization that the War on Vietnam was significantly feeding a homeland rebellion against hierarchy and injustice *at home.*

8. *Ruling-Class Fractures.* A significant portion of the US business, intellectual, and political establishment does not support Bush's foreign policy. This opposition is based less on morality than on practical and conservative calculations. For some parts of the ruling class, including possibly Bush I, Bush II and his neo-fascist "posse"—this, as noted, is what the Fundamentalist Cowboy from Crawford likes to call his White House team— are following a reckless and radical course which threatens to destabilize a system that was serving the privileged quite well. This can only be positive

for peace and justice activists. Such activists have always exploited divisions among the Masters to win important victories like the legalization of labor unions, the creation and expansion of public family cash assistance, the passage of Civil Rights legislation, and the end of the Vietnam War.

9. *The Growing Revolt Against Corporate-State Media.* Posters denouncing the warmongering role and related concentrated nature of the corporate-state media are widely visible at recent peace demonstrations. With good reason: Bush would not have been able to whip up enough public American support to go over the head of global allies and a significant component of his own nation's establishment in attacking Iraq without the complicity of the corporate-state media. Permitting the White House to disseminate frankly preposterous lies about the dangers posed by Iraq and the real nature of US objectives abroad, the owners and managers of those media have emerged as full-fledged Masters of War in the post–September 11 era. The jingoistic performance of the Corporate-State Communications and Information Empire during Operation Dominate Iraq/Global Regime Change should put to rest once and for all the idiotic right-wing myth of the "liberal" and even "left" media. This can only encourage peace and justice activists' growing propensity to identify and challenge America's vast corporate-media manufactories of mass consent, diversion, and desensitization.

10. *Post-Invasion Concerns.* Antiwar activists were naturally insulted by the disturbing propensity of government officials and the media to discuss the invasion of Iraq as a *fait accompli* before it happened. Now that the invasion is under way, we need to mourn our defeat and realize that the nature of occupied Iraq is *also contested terrain.* We should demand a decent flow of humanitarian aid for Iraqis; adequate care for the victims; Iraqi oil wealth for Iraqis; elimination of the genocidal US-imposed economic sanctions that have killed more than a half-million Iraqi children; self-determination and basic human rights and dignity, including a decent welfare state and reconstruction of civilian infrastructure for the Iraqi people; and much more.

11. *Beyond Iraq: Against War on the World.* Iraq is the first target for a proposed new global campaign of empire. The Bush administration's ultimate aim is more grandiose than diverting the America population from domestic inequities or deepening US control over strategic Middle Eastern oil resources. As John Pilger noted weeks before the invasion, Iraqi oil is important, but the overall objective is "world domination."[50] If all "goes well" in Iraq, the Bush team and successor imperial regimes will most certainly be targeting other states for "preventive war"—that is, unwarranted imperial invasion.

12. *World Opinion on Our Side.* If "my fellow Americans" is your only reference group, things can get rather depressing in the United States. Switch or broaden your reference group to *the human race* and you will

find some inspiration. The White House's claim to be backed by a "broad" overseas "coalition" is transparently false. Its leading global partner is the disappointing Tony Blair, whose early enlistment in the war on Iraq is opposed by the preponderant majority of England's citizens. Blair has been compelled to justify his position with the insistence that he would move Bush toward moderation and multilateralism—a claim that Washington has undermined with impunity. Beyond Blair, Bush's international support is unenthusiastic and obviously purchased with US taxpayers' hard-earned dollars. The great majority of the world's people, including those in "coalition" states, oppose Bush's war. That opposition is hardly irrelevant.

13. *Beyond the Crystal Ball.* The most compelling case for staying positively energized and organized against the Bush White House does not rest on our sense of the alignment of forces and chances for success. It does not rest on speculation—on what the crystal ball predicts for our causes. It is a matter of moral commitment and faith-based determination rather than objective assessment and practical calculation. It rests on the heartfelt knowledge that the Bush administration and its allies and enablers are doing something terribly, tragically wrong and dangerous to humanity. It is based on concerns that should remain intact even if 95 percent of the US population were solidly behind the self-infatuated Masters of War.

The Larger War

Those Masters and their subordinates worship the ancient authoritarian doctrine that political power grows out of the barrel of a gun. They see the people of the Middle East as irritating subhuman sideshows on the petroleum-soaked road to a doctrinally mandated New World Order of permanent unilateral US military supremacy. At home, their perverse moral calculus elevates bombs above books and makes them more willing to cut taxes for the unimaginably rich than to provide basic social protections for millions of very disproportionately nonwhite poor and working-class children. There is more than a tinge of fascism in the currently reigning Masters' way of looking at themselves, their own society, and indeed the world.

We can be certain, however, that many more innocent people would have been slaughtered by the policies of Bush, Rumsfeld, Rice, Cheney, Wolfowitz, Perle, and their followers were it not for the activism of people turning out en masse even here in the eye of the imperial hurricane. We American resisters of empire owe it to the people of the world and to ourselves not to back down, tragically despondent because the bullies in the White House have won an early battle in their projected endless war on the world. As Bush is telling us just today, the war is only beginning. It will not be fought in our name.

15
Bad War: Read "All About It" in the Establishment Press
March 30, 2003

More than some left commentators may like to acknowledge, the claims of the Bush War Party and its warmongering friends at the Fox News Network regarding "Operation Iraqi Freedom" are significantly contradicted by findings and commentary in the establishment print media. American antiwar activists and citizens must by all means press the corporate-state press to tell the whole truth and draw the responsible conclusions about the horrible injustices and tragedies that are being exacerbated and inflicted in our name. At the same time, we can usefully mine a considerable amount of rich and useful information from the mainstream press, reflecting various conflicts and requirements of class, faction, and thought control.

Acknowledging Iraqi Nationalism

Didn't buy the war masters' knee-jerk identification of Iraqi resistance to the American invaders with loyalty to and/or fear of Saddam? Your suspicions were supported by a number of establishment press reports acknowledging that many Iraqis fighting back are responding to an outraged sense of national pride, not to the allure or threats of Saddam's regime. A front-page story noting that "the Iraqis appear more committed to the fight than the Pentagon strategists expected" in last Friday's *Wall Street Journal (WSJ)* quoted a former leading US military strategist to interesting effect. "It's turned out," the strategist observed, "that the Iraqis are going to fight for the motherland."[51]

"A Wider Principle"

Didn't accept the masters' claim that the rest of the Arab world would be grateful that America has taken it upon its (supposedly benevolent) self to remove a threatening tyrant? Your suspicions were borne out by last Wednesday's *WSJ*, which included a front-page article titled "On Arab Street, Iraqi Resistance Strikes a Chord." The "sometimes lethal resistance U.S. troops have encountered in places such as the port of Umn Qasr and the southern Iraq city of Nasiriyah," the paper reported, has "fueled nationalistic pride and popular anger" among "Arab populations." It has also "pierced a post–Cold War myth of American invincibility, already dented by the Sept. 11 attacks." Among the expressions of this officially unexpected Arab response, the article continued, are an official Arab League statement condemning US aggression and a growing movement of Arabs volunteering for service against America's King George.

The *WSJ* provided an especially instructive quote from a Palestinian shopkeeper named Ehap al Ali, who says he "would go fight with the Iraqis" if he could. "Saddam isn't as bad as the Americans say he is," Ali told the *WSJ*, "and he isn't as good as the Iraqi government says he is. But that's not the point. There is a wider principle—we have an obligation to fight against foreigners who invade Arab lands." Such sentiment is increasingly widespread around the Middle East.[52]

Politically Skewed War Games

Skeptical about the Bush administration's claim that victory over Iraq would be quick, easy, and glorious—an awesome exercise in the display of overwhelming US power? The establishment press has no choice, of course, but to report that this has not occurred. Still, some of the mainstream coverage and commentary have shown welcome candor on the degree to which the US disappointment reflects poor planning and the extent of the difficulties facing US troops. Last Friday's *New York Times* gave page-one coverage to the forthright comments of Lt. Gen. William Wallace, commander of Army forces in the Persian Gulf. Wallace acknowledged that "the enemy we're fighting against is a bit different than the one we war-gamed against."

Citing Wallace and other Army sources, the *Times* went on to note numerous serious problems beyond the unexpected heroic resistance of Iraqis—travel delays, fierce weather, overextended supply lines, communications breakdowns, and insufficient food supplies for troops. "No matter how politically appealing a quick, decisive victory would be, the simple physics of the battlefield are making that less likely," the *Times* concluded.

An opinion-editorial that appeared the next day in the *Times* even raised the specter of Mogadishu. "No matter what kind of power can be rolled into Baghdad," Mark Bowden wrote, "if it faces a hostile population . . . the scene could turn into a nightmare. Soldiers would be moving in a 360-degree battlefield with obstructed sight lines and impaired radio communications, trying to pick out targets from civilian populations determined to hide, supply and shield the enemy, unable to attack Iraqi firing positions without killing civilians."[53]

In this as in numerous other mainstream reports and commentaries, Dick Cheney and Richard Perle are revealed in horrible, narcissistic, blood-soaked splendor. In making their case for the current butchery in Iraq, these and other leading proponents of the New World Order promised jubilant, welcoming masses and rapid, total victory over territory, hearts, and minds.

According to a front-page story in yesterday's *Chicago Tribune*, America's armed forces weren't even allowed to "war-game" against the real "enemy." This interesting article reports that Paul Van Riper, "a Pentagon consultant considered a top strategist in asymmetric warfare," quit mock prewar battles because Pentagon planners dismissed the threats he posed in his assigned role as a "rogue Persian Gulf dictator." The planners refused to acknowledge the hits he scored by using tactics like suicide bombers and guerilla harassment of US supply convoys.[54]

WMD Still AWOL

Questioning the pivotal war-justificatory notion that Saddam possesses huge and threatening stockpiles of major, state-of-the-art chemical and biological weapons of mass destruction and the potential to develop nuclear weapons? A story titled "Troops Haven't Found Chemical Arms" in last Thursday's *WSJ* offered some reasons for healthy skepticism. It quoted retired Army colonel David Franz, who said that he was "not counting on" the US military's ability to uncover biological agents being used or developed by Iraq's regime. The paper also noted that US soldiers recently "found nothing suspicious" in a chemical plant outside Najaf "that US intelligence agencies had thought for years was manufacturing chemical weapons." The nuclear question doesn't even merit coverage.[55]

"Sorry, but the Chick Was in the Way"

Worried about the ethical blank check given to US military forces by blindly approving "support our troops" (at all costs) sentiment? Concerned that supporting soldiers to carry out orders to slaughter might not be the best way to foster basic mental health among military personnel who will become returning veterans in our midst? Your concerns are borne out by two front-page articles that appeared in last Saturday's *New York Times*. The first article is titled "Either Take a Shot or Take a Chance." It quotes Marine "sharpshooter" Eric Schrumpf to chilling effect. "We had a great day," Schrumpf told *Times* reporter Dexter Filkins. "We killed a lot of people." According to Filkins, Schrumpf "recalled one such incident, in which he and other men in his unit opened fire. He recalled watching one of the women standing near the Iraqi soldier go down. 'I'm sorry,' [Schrumpf] said. 'But the chick was in the way.'"

The second article is titled "Haunting Thoughts After a Fierce Battle." It relates the moral crisis Sgt. Mark N. Redmond faced after killing untold numbers of Iraqi fighters heroically resisting the invasion of their home-land by superior American forces. "I mean, I have my wife and kids to go back home to," Redmond told *Times* reporter Steven Lee Myers. "I don't want them to think I'm a killer." Redmond "did not," Myers noted, "want to dwell on the details of the deaths his weapons caused."

The article concludes with the comments of Army chaplain Mark B. Nordstrom, who happens to belong to a branch of the Mennonites with a pacifist theology. Noting that American troops had "killed thousands" in the "last few days," this "pacifist" comforter of troops charged with murder observes that "nothing prepares you to kill another human being. Noth-ing prepares you to use a machine to cut someone in two." (Well, we can think of a few "things" that do, including the US Army and Marines. . . .) "It bothers" US soldiers, Nordstrom told Myers, "to take life, especially that close." It is apparently easier on the soul to kill from 30,000 feet or from a distant air-conditioned missile targeting office. "They want to talk to me so that they know that I know they are not awful human beings."[56]

Social service agencies and law enforcement back home, get ready. And remember, America: your president, as reported in the mainstream press, is proposing to significantly cut veterans' benefits.

"You Realize It Was Real"

Concerned about the moral implications of modern satellite-guided "war," where masses are dispatched to the grisly hereafter at the tap of a comput-er key by indifferent technical personnel in distant antiseptic command centers? Your anxiety finds justification in a front-page *WSJ* story that appeared last Thursday. It related the comments of an officer in a Hawaii-based US Navy Strike Center, where "planners stare at screens, outwardly oblivious to the havoc they were wreaking far away." "It was surreal," the officer told *WSJ* reporter David S. Cloud, speaking of his experience dur-ing the initial cruise missile strike on March 21. "It was no different than exercises we've practiced again and again. . . . Hours later you take a step back and see the video and see the hits coming in Baghdad and you realize it was real."[57] Take note, American mental health practitioners.

No Vile Self Interest?

Skeptical of official White House claims that Operation Dominate Iraq is unrelated to something as petty as economic self-interest on the part of key US policymakers and the massive corporations they represent? Your suspicion that some of the warlords might be acting on what Adam Smith called "the vile maxim of the masters"—everything for me and nothing for anyone else—will find reinforcement in the March 24th issue of the *New Yorker.* Writer Seymour Hersch, no radical, detailed Perle's vested interest in the terrorism that can be expected in the wake of current US assaults on the Arab world, very much in line with the hopes of Osama bin-Laden. Perle, it turns out, is a managing partner in Trireme Enterprises, a venture-capital company that invests in technology, goods, and services of value to "homeland security and defense" around the world. Its projected clients include Saudi Arabia, a leading bin-Laden target.[58]

A story that appeared in last Thursday's *WSJ* under the title "Perle's Conflict Issue Is Shared by Other Defense Panel Members" will further reinforce your suspicions. It shows that numerous members of the Defense Policy Board, a key Pentagon advisory body that has argued effectively for war on Iraq, work for corporations poised to make considerable sums in the areas of homeland security and "national defense." Well before the beginning of the war, moreover, the *WSJ* reported that a small number of politically connected American firms (including Cheney's own Halliburton) were situated to make hundreds of billions off the task of rebuilding the very Iraqi infrastructure the White House and Pentagon were planning to bomb.[59] A rather instrumentalist new wrinkle on the economic theory of "creative destruction."

Wondering if the world's millions of antiwar protestors might be on to something more than a just a catchy phrase when they chant "No Blood for Oil"? Evidence that they are was presented last fall by reporters for the online version of MSNBC News. In an article titled "Iraqi Oil, American Bonanza," MSNBC quoted industry analysts who "say that it's unlikely that American firms will be left empty-handed if the U.S. follows through on military action."[60] There is not room here to recount the large number of mainstream stories that have detailed the considerable and diverse ways that American oil and other corporations can expect to benefit from the projection of US power in the Middle East.

Military Globalism Versus Recovery in an Age of Economic Multilateralism

Don't buy the administration's rosy forecasts of a strong recovery once the war is (not so quickly) concluded? Your skepticism is supported by an opinion-editorial in last Monday's *New York Times* written by James Grant, editor of the respectable *Grant's Interest Rate Observer.* According to Grant, no radical, "the war didn't cause America's financial and economic problems. But it's not so far-fetched to assume it may soon worsen them." Grant's pessimism rests on the simple observation that the costs of the war are going to be met by the printing of more dollars, leading to inflation and the cheapening of American currency. That cheapening is going to reduce America's ability to finance its massive foreign current account deficit (the US imported $500 billion more than it exported in 2002) with dollars. "Up until now," he notes, "the rest of the world—America's creditors—was more than happy to exchange its merchandise for our currency, a currency they have coveted both as a medium of exchange and a store of value." This will change with the officially mandated superabundance of dollars required to pay for this and "future . . . wars, pacifications and occupations" (Grant), something that will deepen related underlying US economic problems of excess capacity and stagnant stock shares.

An interesting line appears in Grant's sixteenth paragraph, where he argues that "unilateralism in military affairs may be necessary and expedient. But the relationship of a debtor nation to its creditors is necessarily multilateral. This is especially true in the case of a debtor nation that prints the money with which to service its debts."[61] Hmm . . . maybe the Europeans aren't as irrelevant as Bush and Rumsfeld want us to believe. One can find numerous similar negative economic judgments in the mainstream press (especially the *Financial Times*), suggesting a conflict between the global militarism of the White House and the "rational" economic globalism of cooler-headed American and world-systemic corporate minds.

"Budgetary Shock and Awe"

Wondering about the domestic social-democratic opportunity costs of the extravagantly expensive war of occupation the Bushies are determined to pursue as countless American communities slip further into poverty and isolation? Wondering about the true "patriotic" priorities of a government that spends hundreds of billions of dollars on foreign conquest while slashing taxes for the super-rich and claiming to lack the money to adequately fund education, provide universal health coverage, and adequately match unemployment benefits to the numbers out of work? Questioning the sincerity of the White House officials and congressional allies who pontificate on behalf of "shared wartime sacrifice" by all Americans?

Your concerns were seconded by a strident, outraged *New York Times* editorial that appeared last Tuesday under the title "Budgetary Shock and Awe." "The country," noted the *Times'* editors, "is facing plenty of financial problems: the economy, the cost of the war on terrorism and the war in Iraq. Stunningly, Congress is prepared to make things worse, far worse, with more than $500 billion in tax cuts for the upper 1 percent of taxpayers. To finance these spoils for the wealthiest Americans, House leaders ... plan deep cuts of $475 billion in vital programs for the bottom 99 percent. These direct hits will range from Medicaid to child care, education to food stamps, environmental protection to emergency doles for the poor."[62]

No, It's Not a Left Press

What's going on here? Are the American print media acting in accordance with a liberal and even "left" bias, as posited by "media critics" working for various assorted radical-right groups like the Heritage Foundation and the American Enterprise Institute? Hardly: the majority of opinion-editorials in the mainstream press was prowar in the months leading up to the unjust and unnecessary invasion of Iraq. It remains taboo in that press to honestly acknowledge the underlying crypto-fascist immorality and, indeed, insanity of the war and the doctrines that inform US policy. Strong moral criticism of domestic policy is permissible, but such criticism of related, deadly foreign policies is not. The criticism of war conduct remains essentially practical, not moral in nature: it's about whether and how the military campaign is "working" and not about whether it's right or wrong. It is unthinkable, of course, for a mainstream reporter to acknowledge the heroic nature of the resistance being carried out by many Iraqi fighters.

The few horrific actions of US forces that are acknowledged appear as tragic, inevitable anomalies, inherent in the fateful logic of war, where losses are to be expected and "The Wheel in the Sky Keeps on Turning." As presented, they appear largely devoid of connection to any living human agents that might be traced to the White House, where top officials have emerged as certifiable war criminals by any reasonable world standard. Stories that might seem to question the administration and Pentagon often seem lost in a bigger sea of war stories that do no such thing. The massive coverage (it practically takes hours to wade through it all now) is loaded with respectfully treated rationalizations and disinformation from the dominant ideological authorities.

It is left to the reader to discern the broader moral implications of unpleasant items like the story of the sniper who shrugged off his murder of an Iraqi "chick." A morally responsible journal might have titled that story "Mennonite-"Pacifist" Army Chaplain Helps Soldiers Feel Better About Murders They Are Ordered to Commit by George W. Bush."

There's a general tone of denial in the establishment US press about the incredible fact of what we are in fact witnessing—imperialist gangsters gone wild. Their global wilding is being aided and abetted by a morally spineless press. You will find no reasonable recommendations in the mainstream press for the obvious citizen response to the immoral madness of their current US government: mass action to disrupt "business as usual."

Interesting, in that regard, to read a recent *New York Times* article praising the antiwar movement for toning down its supposedly original "wild-eyed" response to Bush's war to embrace more orderly and respectful patterns of resistance.[63] The same issue of the *Times* in which this condescending article appears gave indications that US military planners were responding to the unexpected Iraqi resistance by upping their already-considerable level of thoroughly illegal barbarism, in accordance with commanders' insistence that the "rules of engagement" be loosened to permit more civilian casualties.

A Useful Dichotomy: Grassroots and Treetops Audiences

To understand the significant extent to which peace and justice activists can nonetheless find useful information in the establishment American press, it is important to realize that the American mainstream media craft two different versions of US policy for two different audiences. The first audience, call it the "grassroots" (following the work of the late Australian propaganda critic Alex Carey), comprises the general mass of citizens whose essential role in society is to keep quiet, work hard, be entertained, and do what they're told. In rare moments when media managers feel the need to do more than just divert this sorry human "rabble" (to use Noam Chomsky's term characterizing the masters' view of most of the populace) from thinking about policy at all, as during times of US-led war, they feed it nonsense about America's supposed global humanitarianism, supposed freedom, and supposed great threats from overseas. The "Wizards of [corporate] Media Oz" did precisely that during Operation Desert Storm and they are doing it today. The leading tools of ideological population control for this audience include major spectator sports, sit-coms, reality TV shows, and the FOX News Network.

The second target group comprises the relevant political class of Americans from at most the upper fifth of society. Call this audience (again, following Carey) the "treetops"—the people who matter and who deserve and can be trusted with something approximating the real story because their minds have been properly disciplined and flattered by the processes of higher education and professional certification. This segment includes such privileged and heavily indoctrinated persons as corporate managers, lawyers, public administrators, and (most) university professors. Since these people carry out key societal tasks of supervision, discipline, training, and indoctrination, they cannot be too thoroughly misled about current events and policy without deleterious consequences to the smooth functioning of the dominant social and political order. At the same time, information and commentary for the political class sometimes reflect a degree of reasoned debate among its members about how best to manage the world in its interests.[64]

More than many in the activist left may know, there is considerable such debate at present. A portion of the US business, intellectual, and political establishment does not support Bush's foreign policy. Its opposition is based less on morality than on practical and conservative calculations. As noted in chapter 14, for some parts of the ruling class Bush and his "posse" are following a reckless and radical course which threatens to destabilize a system that was serving the privileged quite well. There is an interesting tension, as William Greider notes (and probably overstates) in a recent issue of the left-liberal *The Nation,* between the "free-market corporate globalization" embraced by key segments of the ruling class and the over-the-top military globalism on which Bush has audaciously bet his political future and historical legacy.[65]

The Grant editorial quoted above is an example of this tension. Another example is found in the March 17th issue of the establishment magazine *Business Week,* where Jeffrey E. Garten, dean of no less a respectable establishment institution than the Yale School of Management, criticized the current "disconnect between national security strategy and economic policy." According to Garten, "a foreign policy that involves continual military interventions abroad while securing the U.S. itself is bound to erode economic vitality," reflecting a new chapter in historian Paul Kennedy's "imperial overstretch" hypothesis.[66]

For these and other reasons, we should survey the mainstream press carefully, always reading between the lines to extract the kernels of politically useful information. It is often helpful, of course, to be able to cite the establishment press in making the cause for radical-democratic criticisms of US policy: "don't take it from me—you can look it up in the *Wall Street Journal.*" It is ultimately left to activists (whose willingness to question received wisdom does not stop at the door of risk to their careers and savings accounts) to provide the necessary overall moral and political context and to draw the obvious conclusions for responsible citizen action.

16
"Down the Memory Hole" with Weapons of Mass Destruction
April 11, 2003

"Who Controls the Past . . ."

In *Nineteen Eighty-Four,* George Orwell's haunting dystopian novel set in a totalitarian state called Oceania, the government and its informational apparatus have a chilling knack for instantaneous historical revision. Whenever Big Brother, the all-powerful outer face of the ruling circles of the Inner Party, changes the official government line on some area of foreign or domestic policy, closely monitored functionaries in the Ministry of Truth are put to work transforming the official record of the past. Historical facts that seem to contradict or otherwise challenge the new turn(s) are thrown "down the memory hole." New facts are invented to create the illusion of flat continuity between past, present, and future, consistent with a key party slogan: "Who controls the past controls the future. Who controls the present controls the past."

For most of his adult life, chief *Nineteen Eighty-Four* protagonist Winston Smith knows, Oceania had been at war with rival totalitarian state Eastasia and allied with a third similar nightmarish formation called Eurasia. In 1984 ("if it was 1984"), however, Oceania was now officially at war with Eurasia and allied to Eastasia. Winston and other ideological functionaries work to annihilate all record and consciousness, including their own, of the earlier alignment, now embarrassing to the Party, official "guardian of democracy" and practitioner of "Permanent War."

Most of *Nineteen Eighty-Four's* many readers in the Western, liberal-capitalist world shuddered at the horror depicted by Orwell. We were certain, however, that the threat Orwell described found its only relevant real-life representation or potential in the pseudo-socialist Soviet empire that provided the main living model for *Nineteen Eighty-Four.* Orwell's novel fears externally—the totalitarian threat was "over there." Surely, we liked to think, the threats he pointed out collapsed with Stalinism.

We might want to rethink that. Consider, for example, the impressive rapidity of the recent shift in Big Brother Bush's party line on why the current Oceanic "coalition" (America, England, and a ragtag scrum of the "bullied and bribed") illegally invaded and overthrew the government of a formerly sovereign nation in a tinderbox region of the world. The essence of the shift is suggested in the recent comments of official Chicago Police Department (CPD) spokesperson Pat Camden, explaining why the CPD arrested hundreds of protestors the day after the bombing of Baghdad commenced. According to Camden, who apparently enjoys a long leash from city police superintendent Terry Hilliard, "You have to ask yourself, what's the cost of liberty? What's the cost of protest? We're sending people to Iraq to put their lives on the line so that the people of Iraq can exercise liberties," says Camden,[67] brushing aside the opinion of most of the politically conscious human race, who think the White House is driven by less elevated objectives related to the projection of American power.

There's a lot to question in Camden's remarks, including the appropriateness of local law enforcement editorializing on the purposes of US foreign policy. The most remarkable thing about Camden's statement, however, is the expeditious ease with which it pours that policy out from the new mould manufactured by the White House and its corporate-state media in the postinvasion era. Wasn't this hopelessly one-sided "war" on Iraq sold to the American people first and foremost as self-protection against a "reckless" regime that intended to attack us with an awesome stockpile of deadly chemical, biological, and (someday soon) nuclear weapons and its supposed alliance with al Qaeda and other terrorists?

Yes, and it remains entirely possible that the US and its compliant media will find or claim to find some significant stock of WMD, but that's all pretty much over for now, for reasons that are easy to guess. These include the simple absence of serious evidence of WMD (hardly surprising to those who read between the lines of US propaganda during the already apparently ancient pre-invasion era that ended nearly three weeks ago) so far. Also relevant is the need to construct new justifications for a transparently illegal and monumentally expensive occupation. The White House hopes, further, to set up new invasions of countries not so strongly linked in the admittedly ever-changing public mind to WMD. It is relevant, finally, that recent polling data is giving the Bushies a green light to downplay WMD. As noted in chapter 6, a recent *Newsweek* survey found that *83 percent* of American "war" supporters will continue to support the military action "even if the [US and UK] forces don't find weapons of mass destruction."[68]

So here's an interesting research project for all your junior-high social studies students. Go to the website of the United States White House (www.whitehouse.gov), click on the president's radio addresses over the last six months (upper-left section of the website), and print each one that relates in any way to Iraq. Read all of the addresses (they usually run less than a page) with two magic markers on your desk—one yellow and one blue.

Mark with yellow every time you see the president mention Saddam's "weapons of mass destruction," Saddam's link to al Qaeda or other terrorists, Saddam's "threat" to Americans and/or the world, or the goal of "disarming" Saddam. Mark with blue every time you see the president speak about the struggles or difficulties of the Iraqi people, the domestic oppression practiced by Saddam, or the goal of freeing or liberating those people. The mostly yellow-marked printouts are basically about protecting ourselves from the ruler of Iraq. The mostly blue-marked ones are about freeing the Iraqi people. I could be wrong, but I'm pretty sure your students will be marking their printouts up with a lot more yellow than blue until maybe just the last two radio addresses.

On the Saturday prior to the commencement of American bombing, the presidential radio address Camden might have heard mentioned Saddam's "terrible" "weapons of mass destruction" at least five times and claimed that Saddam "sponsors terror." Bush specified "mustard agent, botulinal toxin and sarin, capable of killing millions," though the previously standard nuclear threat was absent. He spoke of Saddam only as a threat to Americans and others outside Iraq.

As portrayed in Bush's address, the goal of the then still impending "war" was thoroughly defensive: it was to "protect ourselves" from a reckless maniac determined to attack us and destroy "the peace of the world." Neither the situation of the Iraq people nor the goal of liberating them was mentioned even once, unless we want to count Bush's credible claim that Iraq was using innocent people as human shields.[69]

In his last radio address (April 5), Bush used the phrase "weapons of mass destruction" exactly once, and only once did he suggest a link between Saddam and global terrorism. The "Iraqi people," by contrast, were mentioned seven times, and words relating to the "freedom" or "liberation" of Iraqis occurred five times. The no longer imminent "war" is now being sold as a practically selfless campaign on behalf of what Bush rightly calls "the long-suffering people of Iraq," victims of what Bush rightly terms "one of the cruelest regimes on earth." Bush naturally deletes the powerful role that American policy has played in entrenching that very regime not only before but also after its invasion of Kuwait.[70]

Back in the already officially ancient Pre-Invasion Era (a bit more recent than the Age of Mesopotamia), when America was content to merely contain Saddam, other Orwellian deletions were required in relation to Iraq by the White House and agreed to by the US media. The leading erasure concerned America's critical support of Saddam and his various weapons programs prior to the Iraqi invasion of Kuwait, which was carried out with a green light from the US State Department. The support included the US-approved export of deadly biological agents and the personal hand of Donald Rumsfeld.

Then as now, honest discussion of that history was forbidden not simply because it contradicted America's false and narcissistic image of itself as the benevolent historical homeland and exporter of democratic civilization. Equally if not more significant, that history contradicted the official line that Saddam was a "reckless," practically suicidal fanatic determined to risk his life and regime to strike his hated American enemy. It may be disgusting but it isn't suicidal or reckless to use chemical weapons against defenseless Kurds or Iraqis when you do so with the approval and support of the most powerful nation on earth.[71]

For these and other reasons, Reagan, Bush 41, and "Rummy's" little affair with Saddam is a little bit like Oceania's previous alliance with Eurasia—best swept into history's ashcan in light of current events.

Of course, Camden doesn't need instruction from the White House to spout the new official justification for an illegal war on Iraq and mass political arrests on American streets. He only needs to watch CNN (the supposed "fair" alternative to the openly crypto-fascist Fox News), observing its anchors and carefully selected commentators jump to the snap of their masters' doctrinal whip like the finely trained neo-Orwellians they've allowed themselves to become. They zeroed in on the oversold drama of Saddam's falling statue (near a hotel where Western reporters had just been slaughtered by "errant" US artillery) as American personnel scoured the grounds of ancient Mesopotamia for evidence of the practically forgotten weapons that supposedly necessitated the "war" in the first place. They and other parts of the Corporate Communications Empire make up the new millennium's de facto Ministry of Truth. Their owners and managers have moved decisively into the vanguard of the Permanent Warrior class.

17
Rachel Corrie, Jessica Lynch, and the Unequal Worthiness of Victims
May 12, 2003

You can learn much about the toxic and authoritarian role of the American "mainstream" (corporate-state) media by asking a representative sample of Americans to identify and tell you what they know and think about two young women recently in the news—Rachel Corrie and Jessica Lynch. Your respondents will certainly know and care a great deal more about Jessica than Rachel, for reasons that bode poorly for the state of American civilization and hence the fate of the world.

"I Wonder About These Children"

Rachel Corrie died at the age of 23 on March 16th in Rafah, a Palestinian city on the southern tip of Gaza. A senior at Evergreen State College in the state of Washington, Rachel lost her life trying to stop the demolition of a Palestinian home, murdered by an Israeli bulldozer driver. The driver rode his machine *twice* over her clearly visible body. Rachel became one of many killed in Gaza and the West Bank, victims of a racist occupation that provides the single greatest source of Arab bitterness in the tinderbox that is the Middle East. Hers was the first death of a foreigner in Palestine to protest Israeli actions.

Rachel Corrie was a "shining star, a wonderful student, a brave person of deep convictions," according to Evergreen, which bucks the conservative trend of American higher education by nurturing concern for oppressed people at home and abroad.[72] The excellent quality of the thought that informed her schoolwork is displayed in an e-mail message sent out five weeks before her death. In one section of this message, Rachel reflected on the difference between Americans' life situations and that of

Palestinians, children especially, living under the iron heel of a leading terrorist US client state:[73]

> No amount of reading, attendance at conferences, documentary viewing and word of mouth could have prepared me for the reality of the situation here. You just can't imagine it unless you see it, and even then you are always well aware that your experience is not at all the reality: what with the difficulties the Israeli Army would face if they shot an unarmed US citizen, and with the fact that I have money to buy water when the army destroys wells, and, of course, that I have the option of leaving. Nobody in my family has been shot, driving in their car, by a rocket launcher from a tower at the end of a major street in my downtown. I have a home. I am allowed to go see the ocean. Ostensibly it is still quite difficult for me to be held for months or years on end without a trial (this because I am a white US citizen). When I leave for school or work I can be relatively certain that there will not be a heavily armed solider waiting halfway between Mud Bay and downtown Olympia at a checkpoint—a soldier with the power to decide whether I can go about my business, and whether I can get home again when I'm done. So, if I feel outrage at arriving and entering briefly and incompletely into the world in which these children exist, I wonder conversely about how it would be for them to arrive in my world.
>
> They know that children in the United States don't usually have their parents shot and they know they sometimes get to see the ocean. But once you have seen the ocean and lived in a silent place, where water is taken for granted and not stolen in the night by bulldozers, and once you have spent an evening when you haven't wondered if the walls of your home might suddenly fall inward waking you from your sleep, and once you've met people who never lost anyone—once you have experienced the reality of a world that isn't surrounded by murderous towers, tanks, armed "settlements" and now a giant metal wall, I wonder if you can forgive the world for all the years of your childhood spent existing—just existing—in its attempt to erase you from your home. That is something I wonder about these children. I wonder what would happen if they really knew.

These and other parts of her message put celebrated imperialist authors like Robert Kagan to shame. Still short of her bachelor's degree, Rachel left Kagan and other academically certified apologists, planners, and propagandists of racist "war" and empire in the moral-intellectual dust.

Her courageous capacity for critical thinking and morally engaged activism reflected her family's values as well as her undergraduate experience at Evergreen. "We've tried to bring up our children to have a sense of community that everybody in the world belonged to," said Rachel's father, an insurance actuary—an atypical occupation, perhaps, among the middle-class liberal and left "war" opponents that American rightists blast as overprivileged "un-Americans."[74]

Rachel's murder received brief attention in the "mainstream" American media. Her story was rapidly eclipsed, however, by the "war" on Iraq, which Rachel naturally opposed.

"Saving Private Lynch": Celebrating an Expendable American

Things are very different with the media's treatment of the rescued POW Pfc. Jessica Lynch. Like Rachel, Jessica before the "war" was young, pretty, blond, interested in seeing the world, concerned for children (before joining the Army she was planning to teach kindergarten), and admired for her determination. After those similarities, however, key differences emerge.

Jessica is only 19, too young to be a college senior. She comes from a blue-collar family (her father is a self-employed truck driver) in a tiny West Virginia town named—hauntingly enough—Palestine. Palestine is located in Wirt County, where the poverty rate was 20 percent (26 percent for children) and median household income was below $31,000 at the end of the twentieth century.[75] Unlike Rachel, Jessica lacked both middle-class pathways to American career success and access to the world of critical reflection and inquiry that reveals the full story of US foreign policy. She is one of the Americans whom George W. Bush, Donald Rumsfeld, and other members of the American super-rich see as expendable in their rush to imperial expansion. Like numerous other young Americans from her socioeconomic cohort, Jessica joined the predominantly working-class ranks of the armed forces looking for more than immediate employment. She was also pursuing college tuition assistance to attain the educational certification so essential to making a decent living in the United States, the most unequal nation in the industrialized world. Military service is the price she and many other Americans pay for being born into the lower ranks of the American hierarchy.[76] As one iconoclastic West Virginian puts it, "here in West Virginia, we have the highest enlistment per capita of any state. I suppose that speaks volumes about the opportunities this economy offers the young in these parts. Jobs in the coalmines aren't even very plentiful anymore. Jessica was one of the hopeful, looking for a way to get the skills and education she needed and eventually to return to her beloved mountain home. She sure got more than she bargained for in more ways than one."[77]

In paying that price, Jessica and her comrades in the US Army 507th Maintenance Company found themselves caught behind "enemy" lines in Iraq on March 23rd, one week after Rachel's murder. As a result of the battle that ensued, Jessica is recovering from multiple injuries, including a head wound, a spinal injury, and fractures to her right arm, both legs, and her right foot and ankle. She has already been through multiple surgeries.

From the moment of her rescue, Jessica has been hailed as a true American heroine. She has been offered college scholarships and honored for emptying her weapons into Iraqi capturers. Already, she has been the subject of a *People* magazine cover story and a recent "A&E" television special titled "Saving Private Lynch." There will be books and movies, with corporate moguls offering lucrative contracts for the story of her life and ordeal (mega-publisher HarperCollins has already announced a book contract for the Iraqi lawyer who is credited with helping rescue Lynch).[78] Still, no financial compensation can overcome the damage she experienced in service to the imperial dreams of Bush, Rumsfeld, and other "Chicken Hawk Masters of War," who "hide in [their] mansion[s]," as Bob Dylan ("Masters of War") put it forty years ago, "while young people's blood flows out of their bodies and gets buried in the mud."

Look for the masters in the White House to richly mine Jessica's story for domestic political advantage. The corporate-plutocratic Bush administration is perversely drawn to Jessica's working-class origins, which fit nicely with its disingenuous effort to sell Dubya's regressive domestic policies—tax cuts for the super-rich and social service cuts for the poor and the rest of us—as an expression of populist concern for the Little Guy.

Worthy and Unworthy Victims

Those who honestly scrutinize the Orwellian machinations of the White House, the Pentagon, and America's corporate-state media will hardly be surprised to see Rachel's tragic story slip further into the corporate-crafted "popular culture's" historical dustbin while Jessica's harrowing tale is highlighted for months to come. The relevant text here is the second chapter, titled "Worthy and Unworthy Victims," of Noam Chomsky and Ed Herman's path-breaking *Manufacturing Consent: The Political Economy of the Mass Media,* published as the Cold War was nearing its partial conclusion with the collapse of the Soviet deterrent to American global ambitions. "A propaganda system," the authors noted, "will consistently portray people abused in enemy states as worthy victims, whereas those treated with equal or greater severity by its own government or clients will be unworthy."[79]

As the different media treatments accorded to Rachel and Jessica suggest, this analysis continues to hold relevance in the "post–Cold War era" and applies to American as well as overseas victims.

The Rachel-Jessica dichotomy is hardly the only example of the living propagandistic distinction made between "worthy" and "unworthy" victims by recent US media. As American bombs rained upon innocent Afghans during the initial campaigns of George W. Bush's post–September 11 "war on terrorism," the *New York Times* and other newspapers provided detailed and highly personalized obituaries of individuals killed in the 9/11 attacks—the ultimate officially worthy victims in American history (millions of African American slaves and obliterated Native Americans would certainly be just as deserving in an honest and nonracist record). These write-ups were sensitive, compelling, and appropriate; but no major American media outlet saw fit to provide comparable, individualized treatment for the thousands of Afghan civilians who lost their lives as "collateral damage" in America's war on the Taliban and al Qaeda.

In the current "war," Americans have learned a great deal from "their" media about the Kurdish and Iranian victims of Saddam's past and *US-approved* gassings. They learn next to nothing, however, about Israel's many past and contemporary Palestinian victims, including *2,000 people killed just since 9/11*. The Palestinians' situation remains hopelessly mysterious and devoid of meaningful context for Americans, thanks to biased US coverage and commentary. Americans have seen what ought to be heartwrenching images of killed and injured Iraqi civilians. But the most terrible images are filtered out for fear of their potential effect on world and US opinion, and Americans never hear or read the compelling life stories of innocent Iraqi victims of the American invasion. Things are different for US casualties and POWs, featured and honored in national and local media, which dutifully played along with the Big Bush Lie that put Jessica and other expendable Americans in harm's way in Iraq in the first place— the preposterous idea (taken seriously nowhere outside the US) that Saddam represented some kind of serious threat to Americans and the world.

This is hardly surprising. To this day, the US populace is being trained by the American corporate communications and entertainment empire to think of the Vietnam War in terms of the pain it inflicted on American psyches and not in terms of what it did to the Vietnamese, *millions* of whom died as the price for daring to resist invasion by the most powerful nation on earth. American losses in Vietnam—including 58,000 dead— were considerable and disproportionately concentrated among the poor and working classes, but they paled by comparison to those experienced by the people of Vietnam.

18
It Hurts to Kill: "Like I Just Did What the Lord Says Not to Do"
May 12, 2003

"A Picture in My Head I Will Never Be Able to Get Rid Of"

Consistent with this perversely narcissistic American "Vietnam syndrome" [discussed in chapter 17], reporters covering "Operation Iraqi Freedom" have generated sensitive reports on the difficulties faced by US soldiers handling the emotional trauma that results from killing Iraqis. Two such reports, summarized in a *New York Times* article titled "Haunting Thoughts After a Fierce Battle," are discussed in chapter 15.[80] And even more chilling is an April 11th *Wall Street Journal* story by war correspondent Michael M. Phillips. Phillips told the story of a group of Marines sharing experiences and reflections sitting in a circle in the ruins of the Iraqi Oil Ministry's employee cafeteria. He related the anxieties of Marine Cpl. James List, 21, who was "worried that for the rest of his life he'll be haunted by the image: a clean-shaven, twenty-something Iraqi in a white shirt, lying wounded in an alleyway and reaching for his rifle—just as Cpl. List pumped two shots into his head. 'Every time I close my eyes I see that guy's brains pop out of that guy's head. . . . That's a picture in my head that I will never be able to get rid of.'"

Another Marine interviewed by Phillips reported "an eerie feeling" after shooting a wounded Iraqi in the back of the head. It was "like," Sergeant Pierre reflected, "I just did what the Lord in the Bible says not to do." Pierre carried out the traditional "eye-thump" procedure whereby US troops make sure that freshly killed enemy soldiers are "really dead" by poking them in the eye with a rifle muzzle.

Cpl. Anthony Antista initially celebrated after he shot dead two Iraqi soldiers, "but the exhilaration quickly gave way to guilt." His comrades misunderstood him when he repeatedly told them, "Hey, I shot two people." Fellow soldiers thought he was "bragging," but "what he was really doing," notes Phillips, "was trying to find someone who might understand how bad he felt."[81]

Dying Arabs as Twitching Game Animals: "It Went Away and I Shot the Guy Some More"

According to Phillips, the members of Bush's invasion force were "only beginning to deal with the psychological pain" resulting from "having inflicted [mass] death" on civilians and soldiers in a poor and practically defenseless land. But some of the cafeteria circle's participants seemed, well, okay with the experience. The low point of Phillips's article is provided by a Lt. Moore, 26, who "tried to comfort his troops by relating his own experience as a hunter, growing up in Wasila, Alaska." According to Phillips, in a passage worth quoting at some length, Moore

> shot his first caribou at the age of seven or eight, he told them. It was thrilling to see the animal fall. When he got closer, however, he saw the caribou was still alive, still convulsing in pain. The boy was unsure whether he was supposed to feel good or bad. Over years of hunting caribou, bear, and other animals, he grew accustomed to eye thumping and death. So when Lt. Moore looked down from a staircase in the building in Baghdad and saw three Iraqis below, he didn't hesitate. The men had been wounded by a burst of machine gun fire, but they were still moving [twitching perhaps like freshly shot Alaskan game]. The lieutenant shot one man point-blank and then watched the results; the next man was twitching and got the same treatment. "It's gross, but here's the thing," the lieutenant told his Marines. "That queasy feeling—I don't get that at all."

By Phillips's coolly crafted account, Moore's cold-blooded sentiments were shared by Marine Sergeant Timothy Wolkow, 26, who reported an initially "queasy feeling" after the first time he shot an Iraqi. "It went away," Wolkow related, "and I shot the guy some more."[82]

One wonders—did the Israeli bulldozer driver feel at all "queasy" when he first drove over Rachel Corrie? If so, the feeling must have passed because he quickly put his machine in reverse to crush her "some more." Perhaps the Pentagon should reach out to Israel, offering some of its pastoral services and encounter-group techniques to this undoubtedly troubled victim of the homicide he carried out against an unworthy victim resisting racist aggression in the Middle East.

A Modest Proposal

God knows we should provide therapy for veterans returning from Iraq—especially the Moores and Wolkows among them: it's the soldiers who *aren't* haunted by their assignment in Iraq we ought to be most worried about. Returning veterans could also use a scholarship to Evergreen State College or some other academic institution where they might receive an honest education in the real purposes and antidemocratic makings of US foreign policy (all too rare in American "higher education"). Such an investment would help them develop Rachel's capacity to exchange herself for official, state-designated enemies and to resist George W. Bush's determination to wage permanent war on the Arab world and other future unworthy victims of American empire. Perhaps no group needs such an education more urgently than the owners, managers, and other key staff members of the American corporate-state media, which deserve special credit for enabling and indeed driving the horrifying new wave of US imperialism.

19
Systematic Distortion: Nonrandom Material Falsification and the White House Agenda
August 27, 2003

As George W. Bush sets new campaign fundraising records, reflecting dedicated service to the wealthy few, the threat of being removed from office ought to be the least of his worries. Title 18, part 1, chapter 47, section 1001 of the United States federal statutory code mandates fines and imprisonment up to five years for a federal office-holder who "knowingly and willfully falsifies, conceals, or covers up by any trick, scheme, or device a material fact; makes any materially false, fictitious, or fraudulent statement or representation; or makes or uses any false writing or document knowing the same to contain any materially false, fictitious, or fraudulent statement or entry."[83]

Practicing damage control in the wake of the dominant media's curiously belated and partial recognition that Operation Iraqi Freedom was based on spectacular high-state dishonesty, the Bush War Party rushed to limit the public dissection of its shamelessly mendacious war propaganda to its claim that Iraq had tried to purchase uranium for a nuclear bomb from Africa. But this hopelessly discredited allegation was just one of many "materially false, fictitious, or fraudulent statements and representations" made by Bush and his "posse" to sell their falsely labeled "preemptive" attack on Iraq as the only to way to ensure that "the people of the United States and our friends and allies will not live at the mercy of an outlaw regime that threatens the peace with weapons of mass murder."[84]

Among the other unproven and discredited allegations related to the fictitiously labeled "Operation Iraqi Freedom":

- Iraq possessed 30,000 liters of anthrax and other lethal biological agents.

- Iraq attempted to buy aluminum tubes to be used to construct nuclear weapons.
- Iraq had "in fact reconstituted nuclear weapons" (Cheney).
- Iraq possessed a "growing fleet of manned and unmanned aerial vehicles" that could be used to dispense chemical weapons against US targets within and beyond US soil.
- Saddam possessed 30,000 munitions capable of delivering chemical agents and inspectors had recently turned up 16 of them (Powell, to United Nations).
- Saddam was building ballistic missiles that could fly 620 miles, nearly seven times the range permitted by the United Nations (Powell).
- Saddam's regime possessed several mobile biological weapons labs.
- Saddam removed United Nations weapons inspectors from Iraq during the late 1990s without any provocation, seeking to hide a resurgent program of weapons of mass destruction (WMD) reconstruction.
- During the recent crisis leading to US invasion, "we gave [Saddam] a chance to allow the inspectors in, and he wouldn't let them in . . . so we decided to remove him from power."
- Iraq had strong and long-standing ties to al Qaeda and was linked to 9/11 and a serious threat to hand off WMD to Islamic militant terrorists like bin-Laden.
- Saddam's past horrific (and US-funded and -approved) use of chemical weapons against Iraqi Kurds and Iranian soldiers and his invasion of Kuwait (with perceived US approval) proved his reckless (even suicidal) willingness to use WMDs against the US and/or other states.
- The Bush administration wished to avoid military action against Iraq, seeing the use of military force against that nation as "a last resort" and only "reluctantly" engaging in war.
- The US invaded Iraq out of respect for international law, the United Nations, and international democracy and in opposition to the use of violence in international affairs.
- Invading US troops would certainly be welcomed by grateful, joyous Iraqi masses, celebrating the freedom granted them by George W. Bush and his "liberating" armies.

Even as he and his subordinates made such strikingly misleading claims in preparing and conducting an illegal invasion of a sovereign state—an action opposed by the preponderant majority of the human species, which sees the US as the leading threat to world peace—Bush had the audacity to include the following quotation from John F. Kennedy in the text of a pivotal war speech given in October 2002: "Neither the United States of America nor the world community of nations can tolerate deliberate deception and offensive threats on the part of any nation, large or small."

The above deceptions are a small fraction of the total number of materially false, fictitious, and fraudulent statements made by Bush and his administration. A recent example from a list that is frankly exhausting to track (monitoring current White House misinformation is a full-time job) is Bush's claim that the US government "has a deficit because we have been through a war." As the Congressional Budget Office has shown, Bush's harshly regressive tax cuts for the affluent have "cost," writes *Newsweek* columnist Jonathan Alter, "the [United States] Treasury nearly three times as much as the wars in Afghanistan and Iraq, reconstruction after 9/11, and homeland security measures combined."[85]

Also literally false was Bush's claim in January 2003 that his latest tax cut would provide "tax relief for everyone who pays federal taxes." The Tax Policy Center, a sophisticated research arm of the Brookings Institution and the Urban Institute, quickly discovered that 8.1 million federal taxpayers, predominantly low-income, received no such relief from the proposal.

The deeper deception, however, lay in Bush's repeated insistence that his plan was designed to help ordinary, hard-working Americans with modest incomes—a claim buttressed by his technically accurate assertion that the federal tax bill of an average American family would fall by $1,600. In a report that has gone curiously unchallenged, Citizens for Tax Justice found that half of all taxpayers would receive less than $100 of relief this year. It also learned that two-thirds of the federal tax savings go to the wealthiest 10 percent of taxpayers and that the richest 1 percent receive an average cut of nearly $100,000 a year under Bush's plan. Also missing from Bush's statements: the cost of increased local and state taxes, levied to make up for federal dollars squandered by Bush's determination to reward his well-heeled comrades in the unmentionable domestic class war—the top-down version.

As for concealment of key material facts, we have—again, among many examples—the White House's literally sickening decision to strike out important sections on the possible human effects of global warming from a major report issued by the Environmental Protection Agency last June. The White House also deleted reference to a study demonstrating dramatic increases in world temperatures over the last ten years. It added a reference to a study questioning those findings by the corporate-funded American Petroleum Institute.[86]

Bush's defenders will argue that the president's false statements are not technically illegal because he did not "knowingly and willfully" make false claims. The president of the United States, we are informed by the White House, cannot be expected to be a "fact-checker." He relies on the information his "experts" dig up, and some of these data are inevitably and unfortunately bad. At the same time, some of his supporters admit, the president himself is, well, not the sharpest person to ever hold the nation's highest office. He is especially prone to "regular guy" confusion when it comes to handling the countless facts that cross his desk. This is part of his appeal and popularity.

But do we really want a man of such apparent limitations at the head of the most powerful assemblage of military force in history? And why, moreover, do the president's supposed "mistakes," "exaggerations," and "overstatements" always serve empire abroad and inequality at home? And how bad is the intelligence these days? Why, for example, did the White House never seem to "err" in the direction of the considerable number of respectable intelligence experts who—taking seriously their professional responsibility to discover and report on what's actually going on in the world, without primary consideration to political concerns—questioned the claims made by war hawks like Rumsfeld, Perle, and Wolfowitz, for whom facts are little more than Orwellian playthings?

As Noam Chomsky noted more than thirty years ago in a book that dissected the delusional mindset of the people who brought us the Vietnam War, "mere ignorance or foolishness" on the part of US policymakers "would lead to random error, not to a regular and systematic distortion" that always favors military action. Now, as during the Vietnam era, reports illustrating the truth beneath official deceptions go essentially unchallenged by the White House because the government "does not really hope to convince anyone by its arguments, but only to sow confusion, relying on the natural tendency to trust authority and avoid complicated and disturbing issues. The confused citizen turns to other pursuits, and gradually, as government lies are reiterated day after day, year after year, falsehood becomes truth." The citizen is "whipped into line by fear that we will be overwhelmed by an external enemy if we let down our guard."[87]

That analysis from the Cold War period provides a pretty good description of the Bush administration's political hopes and strategies for 2004 and beyond. Those hopes are framed by an Orwellian mindset that merges darkly with a number of toxic homeland tendencies—for example, corporate/big-money domination of the candidate-selection and policy-formation processes, the corporate stranglehold on dominant media, and the chronic overwork of the US population, to mention just a few—to raise disturbing questions about the degree to which democracy survives within the world's most powerful and dangerous state.

Notes for Part II

1. Bob Dylan, "Masters of War" (1963), lyrics available at http://www.bobdylan.com/songs/masters.html.

2. Rumsfeld and Powell are paraphrased in Bob Woodward, *Bush at War* (New York: Simon and Schuster, 2003), p. 49.

3. Scowcroft is quoted (from an op-ed he published in the *Wall Street Journal* in August 2002) in The World Policy Institute, *Arms Trade Resource Center,* "Current Updates," available online at www.worldpolicy.org/projects/arms/updates/08002html#1, and in John Derbyshire, "Management or Confrontation?" *National Review Online* (August 20, 2002), available online at http://online.com/webjournalism/Texts/commentary/scowcroft.htm.

4. CBS News, "Plans for Iraq Attack Began on 9/11" (September 4, 2002), available online at www.cbsnews.com/stories/2002/09/04/september11/main520830.shtml.

5. Bob Woodward, *Bush at War* (New York: Simon and Schuster, 2003), p. 49; emphasis added.

6. John Pilger, "The New Pearl Harbor," *New Statesman* (December 16, 2002), available online at http://pilger.carlton.com/articles/124759.

7. Glen Kessler, "U.S. Decision on Iraq Has Puzzling Past," *Washington Post* (January 12, 2003), p. A1; Anthony Lewis, "On the West Wing," *New York Review of Books* (February 13, 2003), p. 4.

8. Quoted in Kessler, "U.S. Decision on Iraq."

9. Project for a New American Century, *Rebuilding America's Defenses: Strategy, Forces, and Resources for a New Century* (Washington, DC: PNAC, September 2000), available online at www.newamericancentury.org/RebuildingAmericasDefenses.pdf; Pilger, "The New Pearl Harbor"; Research Unit for Political Economy, "Real Reasons for the US Invasion: The Current Strategic Agenda of the United States," *Aspects of India's Economy,* Nos. 33 and 34—Special Issue on the US-Iraq War (December 2002), available online at www.rupe-india.org/34/agenda.html.

10. Henry Giroux and Susan Searls Giroux, "Cultural Studies and Critical Pedagogy in the Academy"(July 8, 2003), in the author's possession.

11. Norman Solomon, "U.S. Media Are Too Soft on the White House," *Newsday* (August 1, 2003).

12. For some early discussion, see Paul Loeb, "Hope Out of Quagmire" (July 30, 2003), available online at http://www.soulofacitizen.org/Iraq.htm; Bob Kemper, "Chapter 3 of Term Is a Cliffhanger," and William Neikirk, "Big Shoes to Fill and Not His Father's," both in *Chicago Tribune* (August 19, 2003), sec. 2, p. 1; and John Nichols, "The Heat Is On: As Questions Grow, So Does Bush's Vulnerability," *The Nation* (August 18/25, 2003), pp. 13–15.

13. Richard Bernstein, "Foreign Views of the U.S. Darken Since September 11," *New York Times* (September 11, 2003), p. A1.

14. Patrick E. Tyler, "A New Power in the Streets," *New York Times* (February 17, 2003), p. A1.

15. This chapter relies heavily on John J. Mearsheimer and Stephen M. Walt, "An Unnecessary War," *Foreign Policy* (January–February 2003); and Carl Kaysen et al., *War with Iraq: Costs, Consequences and Alternatives* (Cambridge, MA: The Committee on International Security Studies of the American Academy of Arts and Sciences, December 2002), available online at www.amacad.org/publications/mono graphs/War_with_Iraq.pdf. Thanks to Noam Chomsky for referring me to the Kaysen et al. piece.

16. "Excerpts from Iraqi Document on Meeting with U.S. Envoy: Special to the *New York Times*," *New York Times* (September 23, 1990), reproduced online at http://www.chss.montclair.edu/english/furr/glaspie.html.

17. Thomas L. Friedman, "Thinking About Iraq (I)," *New York Times* (January 22, 2003), p. A21.

18. Alex Carey, *Taking the Risk Out of Democracy: Corporate Propaganda Versus Freedom and Liberty* (Urbana and Chicago: University of Illinois, 1997), pp. 11–17, 109–139.

19. George Orwell, *Nineteen Eighty-Four: A Novel* (London: Secker and Warburg, 1949), p. 32.

20. Photograph with subtitle "Tale of the Tape," *New York Times* (January 23, 2003), p. A1.

21. Lou Dubose, Jan Reid, and Carl Cannon, *Boy Genius: Karl Rove, the Brains Behind the Remarkable Political Triumph of George W. Bush* (New York: Public Affairs, 2003).

22. Michael Dobbs, "Willing to Go to War With or Without the UN," *Washington Post* (January 28, 2003); emphasis added.

23. James Madison, "Political Reflections," February 23, 1799, quoted in John Samples, "James Madison's Vision of Liberty," *CATO Policy Report* (March/April 2001), p. 12, available online at www.cato.org/pubs/policy_report/v23n.2/madison.pdf.

24. Andrew West, "800 Missiles to Hit Iraq for 48 Hours," *Sydney Morning-Herald* (January 26, 2003), available online at http://www.smh.com.au/articles/2003/01/25/1042911596206.html; CBS Evening News, "Iraq Faces Massive US Missile Barrage" (January 24, 2003), available online at http://www.cbsnews.com/stories/2003/01/24/eveningnews/main537928.shtml. See also Paul Richter, "US Weighs Tactical Nuclear Strike on Iraq," *Los Angeles Times* (January 26, 2003).

25. Gar Alperovitz, *The Decision to Use the Atomic Bomb* (New York: Vintage, 1996).

26. William D. Leahy, *I Was There: The Personal Story of the Chief of Staff to Presidents Roosevelt and Truman, Based on His Notes and Diaries Made at the Time* (New York, 1950), quoted in Alperovitz, *The Decision to Use the Atomic Bomb,* p. 3.

27. Harlan Ullman et al., *Shock and Awe: Achieving Rapid Dominance* (Washington, DC: Center for Advanced Concepts and Technology, 1996); CBS Evening News, "Iraq Faces Massive US Missile Barrage."

28. Elaine Brown, *The Condemnation of Little B* (Boston: Beacon Press, 2002), p. 227.

29. John Pilger, "The Mother of All War Shows," *The Black Commentator,* Issue 27 (January 30, 2003).

30. Serge Schmemann, "All Aboard: America's War Train Is Leaving the Station," *New York Times* (February 2, 2003); emphasis added.

31. Richard Wolffe et al., "War and Consequences," *Newsweek* (February 3, 2003).

32. Martin Wolf, "US Must Commit to Winning the Peace," *Financial Times* (February 4, 2003).

33. Ibid.

34. *TimeEurope,* "Poll: The Biggest Threat to World Peace" (January 2003), available online at http://www.time.com/time/europe/gdml/peace2003.html.

35. *Daily Mirror* (July 4, 2002), p. 1. According to John Pilger, "The front page of the *Daily Mirror* was as powerful as any I have known, a tabloid at its best. George W Bush was flanked by a row of Stars and Stripes, chin up, eyes misted. 'Mourn on the Fourth of July,' said the banner headline. Above him were the words: 'George W Bush's policy of bomb first and find out later has killed double the number of civilians who died on 11 September. The USA is now the world's leading rogue state.'" Pilger, "Freedom of the Press," *SOAS Stop the War* (July 10, 2002), available online at http://www.soasstopwar.org/pilger1.htm.

36. Thomas Friedman, "Little Domestic Support for Iraq Action," *Salt Lake Tribune* (February 9, 2003), available online at http://www.sltrib.com/2003/Feb/02092003/commenta/27529.asp.

37. Lucas Morel, "Faith and Philosophy Take Center Stage in Iowa," The Ashbrook Center for Public Affairs (December 1999), available online at http://www.ashbrook.org/publicat/oped/morel/99/iowa.html.

38. Wolffe et al., "War and Consequences."

39. Pilger, "The Mother of All War Shows."

40. The President of the United States, *The National Security Strategy of the United States* (2002); Ullman, *Shock and Awe;* Project for a New American Century, *Rebuilding America's Defenses;* Armstrong, "Dick Cheney's Song of America"; United States Space Command, *Vision for 2020,* available online at http://www.fas.org/spp/military/docops/usspac/visbook.pdf.

41. Thomas Friedman, "A Manifesto for the Fast World," *New York Times Sunday Magazine* (March 28, 1999).

42. Noam Chomsky, *Profits Over People: Neoliberalism and Global Order* (New York: Seven Stories Press, 1999), pp. 28–40.

43. Among many possible cites see Ha-Joon Chang, *Kicking Away the Ladder: Development Strategy in Historical Perspective* (London: Anthem Press, 2002). Chang is a member of the faculty of Economics and Politics at the University of Cambridge. See also Chomsky, *Profits Over People,* pp. 65–118; Paul Street, "'People Profit from Trade,'" posted March 9, 2003 at http://www.zmag.org/content/showarticle.cfm?SectionID=13&ItemID=3210.

44. Friedman, "A Manifesto for the Fast World."

45. United States Space Command, *Vision for 2020.*

46. Quoted in Mark Rupert, "The Global Justice Movement in a Neo-Imperial Moment," available online at http://www.maxwell.syr.edu/maxpages/faculty/merupert/Neoimperial%20Moment.htm.

47. Quoted in Jim Lobe, "Costs of War Far Outweigh Benefits," *Asia Times* (March 21, 2003), available online at http://www.atimes.com/atimes/Middle_East/EC21Ak06.html.

48. Bob Herbert, "With Eyes and Ears Closed," *New York Times* (March 17, 2003), p. A23.

49. Lawrence McQuillan, "Bush Seeks $ Billions for War's Opening Stages," *USA Today* (March 24, 2003), available online at http://www.usatoday.com/news/world/iraq/2003-03-24-bush-cost-war_x.htm.

50. Pilger, "Mother of All War Shows."

51. *Wall Street Journal* (March 28, 2003).

52. Quoted in Yarislov Tromifov, "On Arab Street, Iraqi Resistance Strikes a Chord," *Wall Street Journal* (March 26, 2003), p. A1.

53. Mark Bowden, "Will Baghdad Fight to the End?" *New York Times* (March 27, 2003), p. A23.

54. Douglass Holt and Cass Simpson, "Critic: US Took Guerillas Lightly," *Chicago Tribune* (March 30, 2003), sec. 1, p. 1.

55. Christopher Cooper, "Troops Haven't Found Chemical Arms," *Wall Street Journal* (March 28, 2003), p. A8.

56. Dexter Filkins, "Either Take a Shot or Take a Chance," and Steven Lee Meyers, "Haunting Thoughts After a Fierce Battle," both in *New York Times* (March 29, 2003), p. A1.

57. David S. Cloud, "Before Missiles Fly, Global Network Gleans the Data," *Wall Street Journal* (March 27, 2003), p. A1.

58. Seymour Hersh, "Lunch with the Chairman," *New Yorker* (March 17, 2003), pp. 76–78.

59. Tom Hamburger and Dennis K. Berman, "Perle's Conflict Issue Is Shared by Other Defense Panel Members," *Wall Street Journal* (March 27, 2003), p. A4.

60. Michael Moran and Alex Johnson, "Oil After Saddam: A Great but Quiet Rush Is On for Stake in Iraq's Huge Oil Reserves," MSNBC News (November 7, 2002), available online at http://www.msnbc.com/news/823985.asp?0cb=-115114700; John W. Schoen, "Iraqi Oil, American Bonanza? In the Postwar Iraq, US Companies Could Be Major Players," *MSNBC News* (November 11, 2002), available online at http://www.msnbc.com/news/824407.asp.

61. James Grant, "Battling the Fog of Finance," *New York Times* (March 24, 2003), p. A15.

62. "Budgetary Shock and Awe," *New York Times* (March 25, 2003), p. A16.

63. Kate Zernick and Dean E. Murphy, "Antiwar Movement Morphs from Wild-Eyed to Civil," *New York Times* (March 29, 2003), p. B1.

64. Carey, *Taking the Risk Out of Democracy*, pp. 87–108; Chomsky, *What Uncle Sam Really Wants* (Berkeley, CA: Odonian, 1993), pp. 94–95.

65. William Greider, "Military Globalism," *The Nation* (March 31, 2003).

66. Jeffrey E. Garten, "Bush's Guns-and-Butter Dilemma," *Business Week* (March 17, 2003), p. 76.

67. Quoted in Ben Joravsky, "Taken by Surprise," *The Reader* (Chicago, April 4, 2003).

68. Elaine Povich, "Support Grows for Bush, War," *Newsweek* (April 6, 2003).

69. George W. Bush, Presidential Radio Address (March 15, 2003), available online at http://www.whitehouse.gov/news/releases/2003/03/print/20030315.html.

70. George W. Bush, Presidential Radio Address (April 5, 2003), available online at http://www.whitehouse.gov/news/releases/2003/04/20030405.html.

71. See Mearsheimer and Walt, "An Unnecessary War"; and Steven Miller, "Gambling on War: Force, Order, and the Implications of Attacking Iraq," chapter 2 in Carl Kaysen et al., *War with Iraq: Costs, Consequences and Alternatives* (Cambridge, MA: Committee on International Security Studies of the American Academy of Arts and Sciences, December 2002), available online at www.amacad.org/publications/occasional.htm.

72. Evergreen State College, "Rachel Corrie, 1979–2003," at http://www.evergreen.edu/news/mar03/rachelcorrie.htm.

73. "Rachel Corrie in Her Own Words," at http://italy.indymedia.org/news/2003/03/209033.php.

74. Nicole Brodeur, "In Death a Martyr Is Born," *Seattle Times* (March 18, 2003), available online at http://seattletimes.nwsource.com/html/nicolebrodeur/134655424_brodeur18m.html.

75. United States Census, *Census 2000 Summary File 3—Wirt Country, West Virginia,* available online at http://factfinder.census.gov/bf/_lang=en_vt_0name=DEC_2000_SF3_U_DP3_geo_id=05000US54105.html.

76. David M. Halbfinger and Steven A. Holmes, "Military Mirrors Working-Class America," *New York Times* (March 30, 2003).

77. Anne Tatelin, "The Gospel According to Jessica Lynch," available online at http://wheresmypants.net/jessica.htm.

78. See http://abclocal.go.com/wpri/news/5903-iraqlynch.html.

79. Noam Chomsky and Ed Herman, *Manufacturing Consent: The Political Economy of the Mass Media* (New York: Pantheon, 1988), p. 37.

80. Stephen Lee Myers, "Haunting Thoughts After a Fierce Battle," *New York Times* (March 29, 2003), p. 1.

81. Michael M. Phillips, "Hoping to Fend Off Traumas, Marines Share Horror Stories," *Wall Street Journal* (April 11, 2003).

82. Ibid.

83. *US Code Collection,* available online at http://www4.law.cornell.edu/uscode/18/1001.html.

84. George W. Bush, Presidential Radio Address (March 22, 2003), available online at http://whitehouse.gov/news/releases/2003/03/print/20030322/html.

85. Jonathan Alter, "Let Them Eat Cake Economics," *Newsweek* (June 28, 2003).

86. Dante Chinni, "Bush Credibility Gap—a Slow, Quiet Rumble," *Christian Science Monitor* (June 24, 2003).

87. Noam Chomsky, *For Reasons of State* (New York, NY: Pantheon, 2002 [originally published in 1971]), p. 53.

PART III
"The Beacon to the World of the Way Life Should Be"

The level of culture that can be achieved in the United States is a life-and-death matter for large masses of suffering humanity.

—Noam Chomsky, 1966[1]

Mr. President, we are going to meet this test of our generation. We are going to protect the freedom and the way of life that the beacon to the world of the way life should be. We can do no less.

—US Senator Kay Bailey Hutchison (R-Texas), 2002

How you gonna export something you ain't even got at home?

—Tony, doorman in Chicago, 2003

Introduction to Part III

Among the many disturbing characteristics of American imperialism is the way it at once reflects and reinforces powerful Americans' dangerous indifference, ignorance, and/or denial as to the nature of their own society. An excellent example is provided by a commentary that appeared in June 2003 in the *Sunday New York Times'* "Week in Review" section. This thought-piece, by *Times* writer David Rhode, bore the interesting title "Managing Freedom in Iraq—America Brings Democracy: Censor Now, Vote Later." In what amounted to an apologia for George W. Bush, Rhode held that American officials' decision to cancel key elections in Iraq was essentially "the right thing" to do, since "the contestants" in the fledgling Iraqi "democracy" weren't "standing on a level playing field and many of them don't even know the rules." Rhode then amplified his basic premise: "Some argue that holding a vote now would favor a handful of groups in Iraq—well-organized religious fundamentalists, politically sophisticated exile groups and anyone with cash to burn. The voice of the average Iraqi would be lost." To further support his argument that American officials are "right" to suspend "Iraqi freedom," Rhode noted examples of "recent post-conflict elections gone wrong," particularly citing the Bosnian elections that "returned nationalists to office instead of the moderates favored by American officials."[2]

By Rhode's democratic criteria—a "level playing field," with an equal chance for all "ordinary citizens" and no disproportionate influence for those with "cash to burn"—elections should be suspended in the United States, where the top 1 percent of the population owns more than 40 percent of the nation's wealth and possesses vastly greater capacity to fund campaigns, elect appropriate candidates, and contour policies to their own interests rather than to those of the nonaffluent majority. In fact, the top 1 percent—the truly super-rich—makes more than 80 percent of campaign contributions above $200 in the US, helping contribute to America's reputation as the "best democracy that money can buy." The disproportionate power these people are able to wield plays no small role in generating remarkable levels of voter disengagement and political apathy among the vast majority of the American electorate—those without similar clout. Thanks in part to the massive media-driven costs of American campaigns, the candidates who win the race for private dollars tend to win elections in the great preponderance of cases. It almost goes without saying that candidates serious about winning are beholden to wealthy corporate donors, who possess colossal stashes of political cash that they use as investments in the policy process. Thanks to this and a host of other factors—campaign finance is only one of many ways in which concentrated wealth dominates American politics and policy—it is absurdly difficult for people who challenge this money-driven structure (and its social and policy consequences) to seriously contest for elected office and policy "say" (influence). The democratic ideal is widely understood by Americans to have been negated by the harsh plutocratic realities of "dollar democracy" and the "golden rule" ("those who have the gold, rule"). And, of course, the US can boast of its own recent example of a horribly corrupt "election [presidential, no less] gone wrong" that brought "dangerous nationalists to office, instead of moderates"—with terrible consequences that extend far beyond the immediate issues related to Iraq, thanks to America's global power. It almost seems like overkill to add that George W. Bush owes part of his de facto presidency to the disproportionate political influence of "well-organized religious fundamentalists" (the Christian right) and even some "politically sophisticated exile groups" (Castro-haters in Florida).

Should American reformers appeal to the international community for a liberating military intervention and occupation of their damaged homeland? The occupation forces could remain until social, economic, and related communications/media-ownership conditions have been established to level the political playing field and establish an adequate voice for ordinary Americans.

I can think of no better example of imperial blindness to homeland reality, however, than the speech delivered on the US Senate floor by Senator Kay Bailey Hutchison (R-Texas) in support of the fall 2002 congressional resolution that gave George W. Bush unlimited authorization to attack Iraq. After reciting numerous White House deceptions relating to alleged threats posed by Saddam to America and the world in general, Hutchison came to a stirring rhetorical climax. "Mr. President," she announced, "we are going to meet this test of our generation. We are going to protect the freedom and the way of life that the beacon to the world of the way life should be. We can do no less."[3]

This mangled formulation epitomized the oratorical statecraft of Texas, perfected by that legendary serial killer of spoken English, George Junior.[4] Syntax aside, however, the deeper horror in Hutchison's speech was its shameless embrace of the narcissistic belief, shared by her president and most of her congressional colleagues, that America is the embodiment of human existence at its best. Her statement expressed a venerable American faith (predating literal nationhood) that our country is a God-and/or History-ordained City on a Hill, one that "stands taller and sees farther" than the rest of the world, as Madeleine Albright put it years ago.[5]

Given America's genuinely exceptional capacity to shape the future, a product of its extraordinary global power, this faith needs to be scrutinized with deadly seriousness. It needs to be scrutinized with particular attention to social, economic, cultural, and political conditions on the home soil of the world's supposed beacon of civilization. The chapters in part III confront American narcissism with reflections and statistics illustrating domestic nightmares that live on in the shadows of the American Dream—rich continuities of homeland misery that have deepened beneath the widely advertised notion that "everything changed" on 9/11.

These examples throw, I think, interesting light on a statement made by James F. Dobbins, director of the Rand Corporation's Center for International Security and Defense Policy and a former special White House envoy during US interventions in Somalia, Haiti, Bosnia, Kosovo, and Afghanistan. "The partisan debate" within the US "is over," Dobbins proclaimed just before the US invaded Iraq. "Administrations of both parties are clearly prepared," he continued, "to use American military forces to *reform rogue states and repair broken societies.*"[6]

In ironic contrast to Dobbins's facile assertions concerning US policy toward "rogue states," the majority of the world's politically conscious people view the United States as the world's chief rogue state, and with good reason. The US, moreover, owes Iraq['s] "broken society" not so much a policy based on "repair" as reparation—for the million-plus Iraqis who have died because of American policies (including our murderous encouragement of Iraq's war with Iran in the 1980s, Desert Storm, Desert Fox, and the deadly and socioeconomically crippling sanctions imposed from 1991 to 2003). At the same time, the United States is itself a "broken society," one torn by savage inequalities of class, race, and ethnicity, to mention only the most obvious fault lines of fractured human misery in the "homeland" of "freedom." Thinking especially of the racial fissure (a daily professional preoccupation of mine), I can only wonder, following Dobbins, when US military forces will be deployed on the streets of America, implementing the sort of deep social repair and reconstruction unsuccessfully advocated by black ex-slaves and their allies during and after the Civil War.[7]

Alas, the only domestic deployments of American gendarmes I was able to write about in the post–September 11 era (the repression of civil disturbances in the black ghettoes of Cincinnati and Benton Harbor, Michigan) were ordered to enforce obedience to the dominant system of institutions and doctrine, a system of hierarchy that has imposed suffering on countless citizens (of the US and beyond) and destroyed communities across the globe, from the ghettoes of Chicago, Harlem, and Watts to the bombed-out neighborhoods of Baghdad. This is the same system that the White House's 2002 *National Security Strategy* calls the "single, sustainable model of development" for the human race.

* * *

The point of the chapters in this part of the book is not simply to discredit imperial pretensions with uncomfortable homeland facts. Empire abroad and inequality (and repression) at home are inseparably linked and mutually reinforcing at various levels, including the political calculations currently being made by the war party in power. That party includes its chief domestic political adviser (Karl Rove) in foreign policy deliberations and sees the portrayal of imperialist success abroad as vital to the success of its authoritarian and regressive agenda at home.

Domestic inequality, plutocracy, repression, racism, and violence provide the homeland origins, the native taproots, of empire. At the same time, empire in all its permutations feeds back on domestic desolation and social hierarchy in numerous ways—profoundly encouraging, and providing cover for, the regressive, reactionary, racist, and repressive policies directed at the homeland population. Empire abroad and inequality/repression at home are caught up in a dialectical death grip that is having disastrous consequences for human civilization, both at the margins and in the hegemonic eye of the world-systemic hurricane. Empires, which often break the societies of subject states (India in the eighteenth and nineteenth centuries and Iraq in the 1990s, for example), are the product of broken policies grown and nurtured in domestic soil. The center and the "periphery" cannot be separated—they are components in a singular process. To be real and lasting, repair and reparations abroad must be combined with reparations and repair at home.

20
The Readily Available Reality of American Policy in an Age of Empire and Inequality
January 9, 2003

Empire Abroad, Inequality at Home

The harsh realities of American life and policy don't appear much more clearly in the nation's mainstream (corporate) media than they have during the last few days. We can look, for example at the January 6th *New York Times*. In the top left-hand column of page A1 of the nation's "paper of record" that day, we learned that the Bush White House is "assembling plans" for an eighteen-month occupation that will "promote a democratic Iraq." White House officials are researching, the *Times* reported, "the legal basis for taking control of the country." Plans are fluid and contingent upon numerous factors, the *Times* continued, but under all scenarios imagined by White House planners, "the American military would remain the central player in running the country for some time." There will also be a "quick takeover of the country's oil fields to pay for the [democratic] reconstruction of Iraq."[8]

We can then turn to a story in the upper right-hand column of the same day's *Times* to learn about Bush's proposal to eliminate taxes on corporate dividends paid to America's corporate shareholders. The proposed measure "could cost the government $300 billion over 10 years" and will "create much bigger budget deficits for the future," reported the *Times*. "Analysts," the *Times* elaborated, "have estimated that more than half the tax benefit of eliminating dividend taxes would flow to the wealthiest 5 percent of taxpayers."[9]

Another story on page A15 of the same paper on the same day provided some context for the Bush proposal, whose regressive radicalism surprised some of his advisers. It noted that America's corporations are "switching from defense to offense" in pursuing their policy agenda in a Republican Congress. "Counting on receptive ears in the new Congress," the *Times* reported, the business class sees the current alignment in Washington as its "chance to be heard." It is therefore moving forward aggressively in pursuit of business- and privilege-friendly "tax-cuts, deregulation, changes in tort law and *new profit opportunities from the war on terrorism.*"[10]

Key Deletions

To be sure, there were a few key things missing from the *Times*'s coverage of these stories that day. Regarding the occupation plans, there was no honest discussion of what the Bushies mean by "democracy." Noam Chomsky makes a useful distinction between the "dictionary" meaning of "democracy" and the operative "doctrinal" meaning used by the architects of American policy and opinion. The former involves "one-person, one vote," de-concentrated power and equal policymaking influence for all, regardless of wealth and other distinctions. The latter meaning "refers," in Chomsky's words, "to a system in which decisions are made by sectors of the business community and related elites" and in which "the public are to be only 'spectators of action,' not 'participants.' They are permitted to ratify the decisions of their betters and to lend their support to one or another of them, but not to interfere with matters—like public policy—that are none of their business."[11]

Leaving aside the absurdity of the idea that one nation can militarily impose democracy on another nation, we can be sure that the "democracy" promoted by the Pentagon will be restricted to the second definition, with crucial ethnic and imperial qualifications. American occupation authorities would have no interest in empowering Iraq's Shiite and ethnic Kurdish populations, and they would certainly subordinate Iraqi business interests to those of American and international corporations.

Of course, the *Times* could not note the underlying absurdity of a nominally bipartisan corporate plutocracy like the US claiming the right to export "democracy" to anyone. The first place to install democracy would be at home in a nation where 1 percent of the population owns roughly 40 percent of the nation's wealth and probably even a larger share of its policymakers. Big business's voice is always the loudest one in Washington's corridors of policy power, no matter which wing of the US Chamber of Commerce Party happens to hold sway in Congress.

And does anyone seriously believe that the White House wants to take over Iraq's rich oil fields only to "pay for reconstruction" and, in the *Times*'s words, "to protect [the oil] for the Iraqis?" Curiously absent here was any reference to the considerable French and Russian investment in Iraqi oil, something that bothers the petroleum-soaked suits in the White House. It is probably unrealistic to expect the establishment media to discuss these issues in honest, meaningful, and comprehensive ways.

Available Truths

A second thing missing from the January 6th *Times* was any sense of what the occupation of Iraq will cost American taxpayers. This, however, can be found in the establishment press. A recent analysis in the *New York Review of Books* by William D. Nordhaus, Sterling Professor of Economics at Yale, estimates that over the next decade a US occupation of Iraq would cost no less than $120 billion and could cost *as much as $1.6 trillion*. Nordhaus thinks that the Bush administration's "obsession" with Iraq carries an unjustifiable price tag in a time of "slow growth, fiscal deficits, a crisis of corporate governance and growing health care problems" in the American "homeland."[12]

A third omission concerns the unnecessary nature of the war being planned by the White House—the madness of King George's insistence that Saddam Hussein represents a serious threat to Americans or even his own neighbors in the Middle East. Again, however, that is an open topic for honest mainstream commentary for those who are willing to look. See, for example, the recent essay by distinguished University of Chicago political scientist John J. Mearsheimer and his Harvard colleague Stephen M. Walt in the most recent issue of the establishment journal *Foreign Policy*. Titled "An Unnecessary War," this excellent if rather narrow article skewers the transparently manipulative Bush line on Saddam as an inveterate, irrational, and even suicidal aggressor who is oddly hell-bent on exploding weapons of mass destruction. It reviews the historical record to show that the Iraqi regime is entirely deterrable and extremely unlikely to use chemical, biological, or nuclear weapons or to hand off such weapons to Saddam's historical blood enemies in al Qaeda or other terrorist groups.[13]

A fourth item missing from the January 6th *Times* was any discussion of the absurd notion that Bush's proposed giveaway to the rich will stimulate the nation's economy. This, however, is quite readily acknowledged in mainstream media in general, including the *Times* itself later in the week. Among the Bush plan's problems that were easy to learn about without reaching for the radical press, none is more glaring than its failure to put significant money in the hands of those most likely to spend it—the majority of lower- and middle-income Americans. The morally and fiscally irresponsible Bush package will only exacerbate the economy's basic underlying problem of excess capacity—too much capital relative to real purchasing power. Coupled with massive "defense" expenditures, it deepens the federal government's ever-growing deficit, pushing the bills for today's spending on the shoulders of subsequent generations.

Columnist Paul Krugman provided useful context for understanding this non-stimulus plan in the January 7th *Times*. White House officials, Krugman noted, are "betting that the economy will recover on its own" and "intend to use the pretense of stimulus mainly as an opportunity to get more tax cuts for the rich." Krugman rightly wondered if those officials "will ever decide that their job includes solving problems, not just using them" and chided reporters for being too frightened of the charge of "liberal media bias" to tell the full story on the plan.[14]

Chicago Tribune analyst R. C. Longworth, too, put Bush's plan in useful perspective yesterday (January 8, 2003) in a front-page report on Bush's recent visit to Chicago. "In his speech Tuesday at the Economic Club of Chicago," Longworth wrote, "Bush called his proposal a 'jobs and growth plan' and said it would stimulate a sluggish economy with tax-cuts aimed mostly at 'middle-income Americans.' But most economists said the cuts actually would largely benefit the super-rich. Even conservatives doubted the cuts would offer much stimulus. But this misses the point, the economists said. The real story, they insisted, is the guiding philosophy behind the cuts, which is a shift in the American tax burden from earnings by business and investors, toward taxes on income and consumption."[15]

An unusually sophisticated journalist who writes to the left of his paper's reactionary editorial board, Longworth understands quite well Bush's dark agenda: using the people's difficulties to distribute wealth yet further upward in the industrialized world's most unequal nation.

It's all very consistent with the underlying motif of American policy in the post–September 11 world. The jetliner attacks of 9/11 and the fear and insecurity they deepened have been a windfall for an administration whose essential mission has always been to deepen the concentration of wealth and power and to marginalize dissent at home and abroad. This is the unmentionable truth behind Bush's words uttered just three days after the tragic events: "through the tears," Bush told the American people, he saw "*an opportunity.*"

The Myth of the Powerless and Cash-Strapped State

With all the relevant qualifications and limits, a dark and significant story about American society and policy is largely there for the taking *by those with the time and energy* (key qualifications on which the ruling class counts heavily) to dig around a little in the establishment informational outlets.

In the wealthiest but most unequal and fiscally regressive nation in the industrialized world (the US), this story runs, the public sector lacks the money to properly fund education for all of the country's children. It lacks the resources to provide universal health coverage, leaving 42 million American without basic medical insurance. It cannot properly match unemployment benefits to the numbers out of work.

It lacks the funds to provide affordable childcare, housing, and prescription drugs for those on the bottom of its steep socioeconomic hierarchies. It lacks the money to provide meaningful rehabilitation and reentry services for its many millions of very disproportionately black prisoners and ex-prisoners, marked for life with a criminal record. It lacks the money to provide adequate job-training benefits and family cash assistance grants for the inner-city and rural poor, to protect consumers and the environment, and to shield minorities from discrimination in crucial labor and real estate markets. It lacks the money for publicly financed elections and free television time for candidates, both necessary to counter the corrosive impact of private wealth invested in our "dollar democracy"—the "best that money can buy." The list of basic social, economic, and civic needs that the American government cannot meet goes on and on.

There is much, however, that policymakers seem to think that American government *can* and *should* pay for. It *can* somehow afford to spend trillions on Fat Cat Tax Cuts that reward those who are least in need. It *can* spend more on the military than do all of its possible enemy ("evildoer") states combined many times over, providing massive subsidies to the high-tech corporate sector, including billions on weapons and "defense" systems that bear no meaningful relation to any real threat faced by the American people. It *can* afford to incarcerate a greater share of its population than any other nation in history and to spend hundreds of millions each year on various forms of corporate welfare and routine public subsidies to not-so-"private" industry.

American government *can* somehow afford hundreds of billions and perhaps more than a trillion dollars for an openly imperialist invasion and occupation of a devastated nation that poses minimal risk to the US and its own neighbors.

The American public sector is weak and cash-strapped when it comes to social democracy for the people, but its cup runs over when it comes to meeting the needs of wealth and empire.

Contrary to one type of analysis on the left, the state is not powerless in the face of the market. It is actually quite powerful, but its capability is exercised in authoritarian and regressive rather than democratic and egalitarian ways. It is highly effective in state-capitalist service to hierarchies of private power sustained by the interplay of private and public privilege in an age of empire and inequality. Such is the harsh truth of American policy, readily available to those with the time, energy, and desire to look, in these dark times.

21
Just Don't Call It "Class Warfare": Invisible Neighborhoods, Irrelevant People from Chicago to Baghdad
January 16, 2003

A Selective Audience

According to the White House, George W. Bush flew to Chicago last week to sell an "economic stimulus plan" to the people of the "American heartland." As always with the current administration, the reality is rather different. Truth is, Bush flew over most of Chicago to the ritzy Sheraton Chicago Hotel & Towers in the city's affluent North Loop to sell a tax cut for the wealthy to rich people in the Economic Club of Chicago. His speech was received by what the *Chicago Sun Times* called "a crowd of cheering businessmen."[16]

The Economic Club, whose terse website (http://www.econclubchi.org) pronounces "MEMBERS ONLY," is "not," that site's content providers explain, "a club of, or for, economists or economics majors." It is, rather, "about leadership . . . the 'Who's Who and Who's to Be' of Chicago's business and professional life." It has worked "for over 70 years" to "foster the development of civic-minded executives who embrace their broader role in helping build a better, more productive society." Members "must be sponsored and approved by a committee of their peers."

Translation: The Economic Club of Chicago is a metropolitan civic agency of, for, and by the corporate-connected super-rich and selected public, civic, and professional servants loyal to the corporate plutocracy that owns America's "democracy." It works for social and policy developments that preserve and expand the special wealth and privilege of leading segments of the business class.

"We're All in This Together" and "I Don't Think It Was Rich versus Poor"

Insisting that "we're all in this together" (United We Stand), Bush accused those who claim his plan is overly friendly to the rich of engaging in "class warfare." He received support in this regard from Chicago Mayor and Economic Club member Richard M. Daley. According to Daley, who rode with Bush in the presidential helicopter from O'Hare to the Loop, Dubya's speech was a winner. "I believe he hit a home run," the mayor told reporters, "in that he talked to Middle America. It don't think it was good versus evil, 'rich versus poor.'"[17]

But of course, "class warfare"—of the unmentionable top-down variety—is exactly what "it" is and always has been about with Bush. Bush's plan contains some proportionately small measures for poor and ordinary working people. It increases the child-tax credit, provides some small assistance to the states, and creates small unemployment accounts to help jobless workers whose unemployment benefits have run out.

Still, consistent with his hosts' "members only" mission, the cornerstone of Bush's package is the elimination of taxes on American corporate dividends—a measure that "could cost the government $300 billion over 10 years" and will "create much bigger budget deficits for the future," according to the *New York Times*. "More than half the benefit of eliminating dividend taxes," the *Times* reported, "would flow to the wealthiest 5 percent of taxpayers."[18] That may understate the proposal's regressive impact, since just 1 percent of investors receives more than 40 percent of stock-market income and the top 10 percent receives nearly 90 percent.

According to the Urban-Brookings Tax Center, thankfully created "to clarify and analyze the nation's tax policy choices" (http://www.taxpolicycenter.org), the liquidation of dividend taxes translates into an extra $45,000 for people making more than $1 million and $6 for people earning less than $10,000.

Bush also called for the acceleration of preexisting income tax cuts and the repeal of the estate tax, which affects only a tiny and superprivileged segment of the population. According to Citizens for Tax Justice, in a sophisticated analysis that has gone unchallenged, roughly half of the overall benefits of Bush's "bold plan" would go the wealthiest 10 percent of taxpayers. The wealthiest 1 percent of taxpayers, who "earn" $1 million annually, would save $32,000 a year, compared to a savings of $400 for a single parent with one child making $40,000 a year.[19]

Just don't call it "class warfare" or "rich versus poor."

Inverted Gramscianism

Chicago Tribune reporter Bob Kemper, no Marxist class warrior, provided a serviceable framework for understanding the real purpose and nature of

Bush's visit to Chicago. He noted that the Economic Club gave Bush a "high-profile and sympathetic forum" to "*symbolically wrap* a controversial plan that directs most of its money to the wealthy in the conservative, common-sense values of the American heartland."[20] This analysis reminded me of twentieth-century Italian Marxist Antonio Gramsci's notion of ruling-class cultural "hegemony" as the incorporation of social and political arrangements serving the interests of the privileged few into the "common-sense" worldview of ordinary folk.

Consistent with its inverted Gramscian project, the White House has been framing its proposed dividend tax cut as directly beneficial to the broad stock-owning middle-class. This spin deletes the fact that a small percentage of the population still owns most of the nation's corporate stock, however commonplace it has become for Americans to own some stock. It also merits mention that ordinary middle-class 401(K) accounts are already tax-sheltered until their owners withdraw their money, which then gets taxed as regular income.

Stimulus as Pretense for Regressive Tax Policy

New York Times columnist Paul Krugman also put the plan in useful context. The president, he argued, was trying to "use the pretense of stimulus mainly as an opportunity to get more tax cuts for the rich"[21]—an evaluation shared by "most economists" according to the *Tribune.* Even economic "conservatives" (translation: those who support the *radical* upward distribution of wealth and power) doubt the plan will offer any real systemic stimulus anytime soon. The *Tribune* quoted economist Kevin Hassett, of the "conservative" American Enterprise Institute, who acknowledged that "it's a tax reform [one that Hassett supports], rather than an economic stimulus. . . . That's how to think about it."[22]

A tax reform for the super-rich, it is worth noting, on top of a previous massive Bush tax reform for the super-rich. Just two years ago Bush asked for and received from Congress a mammoth ongoing income tax cut that directed 70 percent of its benefits to the top 5 percent of taxpayers in what was already by far the industrialized world's most wealth-top-heavy nation. This gift to the privileged few, too, was sold as essential for economic growth and jobs, but the results so far have been less than encouraging—2 million more jobless Americans and 4 million more without health insurance.

It's a tax reform for the rich, also worth noting, in a time of massively escalating imperial ("defense") expenditures. The price tag for the White House's obsessive, unnecessary Iraq campaign, which includes a possible eighteen-month occupation to install "democracy" (or whatever), runs well into the hundreds of billions.

Right out of the Reagan playbook, it's a deliberate combination—regressive tax cuts and massive Pentagon extravagance—guaranteed to further eviscerate the federal budget surplus Bush inherited, undercutting social programs and leaving an intolerable debt for generations to come.

Sheer Class (and Race and Gender) Venom

Adding insult to injury, Bush yesterday urged the Congress to tighten the nation's "welfare-to-work" requirements. Recycling old Reagan-Clinton rhetoric about "getting [poor] people to work" (*for someone else* at low wages and without union protection, healthcare, and other benefits) and making them "less dependent on government" (the wealthy are exempted from that stricture), Bush wants to increase the (paid) work requirements for the single-mother heads of highly disadvantaged public cash assistance households from thirty to forty hours a week. Current law under the harsh Clinton-Gingrich welfare bill of 1996, passed in the middle of a booming economy, is already the toughest in the industrial world. Meanwhile, the unemployment rate (considerably lower than real unemployment) has risen from less than 4 to more than 6 percent during the last two years. That rate is much higher in the unskilled labor market inhabited by most welfare recipients and is higher still in the neighborhoods housing the highest concentrations of the remaining public assistance caseload.

It takes no small measure of sheer top-down class (and related race and gender) antipathy to call for a tightening of the "work" requirements on welfare mothers in a time of rising joblessness. To do this while pushing massive tax cuts that will slash funds for childcare, job training, and other services needed to move from welfare to "work" requires a transparent class arrogance that is beginning to seep through the protective corporate media filters, as with the more obviously aristocratic Bush I.[23]

City of Neighborhoods

Chicago's boosters speak of it as "a city of neighborhoods." In a spirit of democracy befitting a "benevolent" empire preparing to export freedom and liberty to the Arab world, then, the president and the mayor might have made a neighborhood detour on their way to the Economic Club. They could have visited forgotten neighborhoods like North Lawndale, Garfield Park, Englewood, Oakland, and Grand Boulevard to view some of the "collateral damage" produced by an elite class and a related race war that has been waged with little publicity for the last three decades.

In Chicago's ten poorest neighborhoods, all located on the predominantly black South and West Sides and collectively containing 212,000 people, there was a distinct shortage of social and economic Homeland Security well before 9/11. Forty-five percent of those people lived in poverty at the time of the 2000 census. Median income was $17,320 and the youth mortality rate was 76 per 100,000.

Moreover, in the city's ten poorest zip codes in 2000, also all on the South and West Sides, more than a fifth of the civilian workforce was unemployed (not counting the large number of incarcerated persons) and the child poverty rate was *47 percent.*

These numbers come from the peak of the Clinton economic boom; things are worse in these communities now, thanks to the recent acceleration of paid work's long and ongoing flight disappearance from the inner city.

Life was very different at millennium's turn in the ten most affluent Chicago neighborhoods, disproportionately located on the more Caucasian North Side. In those select communities, just 4.6 of the people lived in poverty, median income was $60,187, and youth mortality was 1 per 100,000.[24]

But, of course, many Economic Club members probably do not reside in Chicago at all. They likely inhabit super-affluent Chicago suburbs like Lake Forest (with a median household income of $136,462), Winnetka ($167,458), and Kenilworth (*more than $200,000*), where well-kept avenues are dotted with palatial mansions, stock equity flows freely, and marvelously entitled children attend the state's finest and most well-funded schools.

Since they generally own no stock, the people in Chicago's bottom-end neighborhoods do not lose much sleep over the "double taxation" of corporate dividends denounced in outraged terms by the Bushies, forgetting that wages are levied at least twice by government in the form of payroll and sales taxes. Many in the city's poorest communities have never been employed long enough to receive unemployment and thus to become eligible for Bush's proposed small ($3,000) "jobless accounts." Many would be happy if they could just get felony drug convictions expunged from their records, like the president is said to have done, so they could be in the running to get a job to lose.

Priorities and Response

What do the Bush administration's actions, very different from its language of "togetherness," say to the residents of the nation's poor communities? Essentially, that

- they simply don't work hard enough and their needs do not (cash) register when compared to those of strategically placed businessmen who know how to put inherited fortunes and other people's money and labor to work for them—and whose "success" the government must "reward" (and create) with wealth-fare.
- solving their problems is not a public priority relative to fantastically expensive overseas projects to serve wealth and better supervise a

global system that drains the lifeblood out of their communities. World history's wealthiest nation *can't* afford to provide them with adequate job training, childcare, healthcare, environmental protection, drug treatment, and recreation but *can* afford $200 billion or more for attacking and then "reconstructing" (or whatever) Iraq. Taxpayer money that might be spent to educate their children, keeping them perhaps out of the nation's burgeoning and expensive hyper-incarceration system, is earmarked for darker global purposes.

- they are, in short, barely more visible than the people of Iraq and the neighborhoods of Baghdad, whose real situation and likely wartime fate are banned by Bush doctrine from the bizarrely obsessive White House campaign against Saddam—as if world history's most powerful military machine could launch a massive assault on just one man.[25]
- to identify and denounce these and other stunning American disparities is to prove yet further one's undeserving nature, marking one as an unpatriotic proponent of class warfare.

Criticisms of Bush policy at home and abroad are useful only in the context of resistance and the development of meaningful alternatives. Without the latter, criticism tends to reinforce the widespread fatalism, apathy, despair, and exhaustion (widespread in a nation with the industrialized world's longest working hours) upon which the ruling class relies heavily. A more fully responsible and appropriate response goes from understanding to changing the dark historical moment. Bush and his horrid collection of corporate-plutocratic and arch-imperialist fundamentalists must be compelled to stand down from their excessive, inseparably linked pursuits of empire abroad and inequality at home.

Major demonstrations against the currently planned war on Iraq and the related domestic assault are being held in the nation's capital and at other sites throughout the US this Saturday. Let the battle begin, and remember—if it feels like class warfare and if it talks and walks like class warfare, well, then, maybe that's just exactly what it is.

22
Mirror, Mirror on the Wall . . .
March 8, 2003

"People Are Going to Die"

So that's it then. George W. Bush can put his hand on his Holy Bible and repeat as often as he likes that "war" is his "last option" in his obsession with "disarming Saddam."[26] Truth is, the people who matter most in the most powerful military state in history are determined to launch a massive and devastating assault on a weak and impoverished nation that poses minimal risk to its own neighbors, much less the American people. Even in the antiwar movement, many of us candidly can't see how Mad King George W. Bush can back down now from his imminent "war," really a massacre under any likely scenario. He has painted himself into a very ugly corner, making the successful slaughter of Iraqis a requirement for American imperial "credibility" and the success of his regressive domestic agenda.

As Air Force General Richard Myers, chairman of the Joint Chiefs of Staff, put it Tuesday, "people are going to die." By "people," Myers means droves of innocent Iraqi civilians, slated for elimination in what he calls a "shock and awe" campaign to quickly overwhelm Iraqi opposition. The guiding idea, taken from military strategist Harlan Ullman, is to "unleash 3,000 precision-guided bombs and missiles in the first 48 hours of the campaign." "It's not going to be like 1991," Myers told reporters Tuesday, warning them to "be very, very careful about how you do your business" in Iraq.[27]

The "campaign" is modeled on the atomic terror attacks in Hiroshima and Nagasaki, both of which were supposedly launched in order to "save lives" by speeding Japanese surrender at the end of World War II. The plan is to jolt the Iraqi leadership into rapid submission, thereby reducing damages to people, buildings, and infrastructure—an expression of loving kindness from an administration whose leader claims to pray for the children of Baghdad. We can start dusting off a special new spot for George W. Bush in the War Criminals' Hall of Fame, right next to Daddy 41.

A New Low

Last night, in a painfully dull-witted prime-time press conference—a miserable new low in the public presentation of the American presidency—Bush trotted out the standard justifications. We heard that the White House wants to protect Americans and the civilized world from the threat of terrorism, to rid the Middle East of a terrible tyrant, to free the Iraqi people, and to stop the proliferation of weapons of mass destruction. Again and again, *as if he were trying to convince himself,* the president strained to make the great, false Orwellian link—the one that draws a firm line between Saddam, September 11th, weapons of mass destruction, al Qaeda, and international terrorism. Again and again, as if he had a hard time believing it, Bush repeated his faith-based belief that Saddam is a serious threat to "the American people."

He refused to directly answer reporters' questions about the reasons for mass opposition to his Iraq policy at home and abroad. Following standard White House doctrine, he told us how lucky we are to possess the right to protest, as if this were granted to us by benevolent masters and not a freedom to be asserted as our birthright. And as if it was seriously endangered by Saddam Hussein instead of by the Fundamentalist Confederacy enthusiast John Ashcroft and other sponsors of the Patriot Acts I and II and Total Information Awareness.

We heard that Bush sleeps well at night, soothed by his daily dialogue with a "comforting" God. Apparently, he is unconcerned about the mangled bodies of Arab children.[28]

"The Single Sustainable Model" of Proper National Development

Throughout the whole crisis, we have been lectured over and over about the greatness and benevolence of the United States. We are instructed that America seeks to export the beautiful, inseparably linked benefits of democracy, free markets, and freedom—great virtues that find their homeland and guardian in the United States of America. Last night, Bush repeated a favorite Orwellian White House line, claiming that those virtues were the terrorists' real targets on September 11, 2001. The jetliner attacks, he wants us to believe, had nothing to do with US empire in the Middle East.

Bush did not make any reference last night to his administration's declared belief, expressed in its recently released *National Security Strategy of the United States,* that the United States represents and epitomizes the "single sustainable model" of social and political development.[29] That idea, however, lurked behind his comments. Bush has received a heavy dose of the American power elite's narcissistic belief that their nation is the embodiment of social and human existence at its very best. His faith in the US as the "single sustainable model" of social development reflects a deeply rooted American faith that America is a God-ordained City on a Hill, one that "stands taller and sees farther" (as Madeleine Albright put it years ago) than the rest of the world. It is a belief shared by past American rulers of considerably greater intellectual capacity, including John F. Kennedy and Bill Clinton.

In trying to forge a coherent basis for lasting and powerful opposition to all of this, we should remember that domestic ("homeland" in current parlance) inequality/repression is the "*taproot*" (in J. A. Hobson's excellent word choice) of imperialism.[30]

Forget for a moment, if you can, that Japan was already defeated and seeking surrender before the A-bombs fell; that Saddam poses no serious threat to the United States or anyone else beyond his own subject population; that US troops are being needlessly placed in harm's way. Forget, briefly, if you can, that the United States itself is the greatest source of the world's weapons, including the mass destruction variety; that America is the main state responsible for initiating and sustaining the cancer of proliferation; that the "democracy" the Bush gang seeks to impose on Iraq and the rest of the planet is the sort that deepens inequality of wealth and power within and between nations, pushing the nonwealthy majority to the margins and handing the world's resources over to American and other Western investors. Forget for a minute the large number of terrorists (for instance John Negroponte, of Central American shame) the Bush administration employs, the numerous war criminals the US harbors, and the terrorist regimes (Colombia, Turkey, Israel, Saudi Arabia, and Indonesia for starters) that are sponsored and protected by the US. Forget for a second that North Korea poses a monumentally greater threat to world security. And forget, if you can, the farcical nature of the notion that one nation could impose "democracy" on another through savage bombardment, invasion, and occupation.

A Look in the Mirror: "The Way Life Should Be"

Put all these and other foreign policy absurdities aside, just for a moment, to scrutinize the idea that the internal American society represents democracy, freedom, and sustainable, happiness-generating social and political development. Reverse the evasive, permanent frontier-seeking flight mechanism at the heart of the imperial impulse[31] and hold America up in front of the mirror. It is a moment, one would hope, for something that

Bush claims to abhor: "introspection." (On this point, see *USA TODAY*'s obsequious interview with Bush in the February 28th edition of "The National Newspaper.")[32] As Bush prepares to shed Iraqi blood and further destabilize an already dangerous world in the declared name of American "democracy" and "freedom," Americans would do well to consider some unflattering facts of life in the nation that claims to show the world "the way," as Senator Kay Bailey Hutchison put it last summer, "life should be." Consider:[33]

- Even prior to the passage of George W. Bush's regressive 2001 tax cut, which gives the top 1 percent of taxpayers a nearly 40 percent tax reduction that will cost the US Treasury at least $1.8 trillion, the US was the most unequal of all industrialized societies. The richest 10 percent of the population owns more than 70 percent of the nation's wealth and the richest 5 percent of families receives as much income as the bottom 50 percent.
- In 2000, at the peak of the heralded Clinton economic "boom," 11 million households (10.5 percent of all US households) were food insecure; black and Hispanic households had hunger and food insecurity rates three times greater than those of whites. Things have worsened considerably since the onset of the Bush administration.
- More than 12 million (17 percent of) US children live in poverty, including more than 4 million under the age of 6, and the US child poverty rate is substantially higher than that of other industrialized nations.
- More than one in three US children live in or near poverty, and more than 8 million people, including 3 million children, live in homes that frequently skip meals or eat too little.
- America's Second Harvest, the nation's leading network of food banks, reports that more than 23 million Americans rely on their agencies; 40 percent of those come from working families.
- One in eight US households have reduced the quality of their diet to utilize financial resources in other essential areas (rent, day care, clothing, medical care, transportation, and utilities).
- As much as 20 percent of America's food goes to waste annually, with an estimated value of $31 million in lost food being thrown out.
- Forty-two million Americans (more than 16 percent of the population), including more than 8 million children, lack health insurance.
- Nearly eight out of every ten US adults (79 percent) think that their healthcare system requires either fundamental reform (51 percent) or complete rebuilding (28 percent).
- Under the rules of the plutocratic American mode of politics, the leading predictors of election success are (1) total campaign spending and (2) being an incumbent. As it happens, incumbents out-raise challengers

by more than 4 to 1 in the House of Representatives and more than 5 to 1 in the Senate, reflecting the greater ability of current office-holders to raise funds from corporations and people seeking to shape policy.

- The winners of the political finance race (the "wealth primary," in the words of American campaign finance reformers) win 92 percent of the races for the US House of Representatives and 88 percent of the races for the US Senate.
- The average amount spent by the winners in the US Senate races of 2000 was $7.2 million; the average spent by losers was $3.8 million.
- George W. Bush raised more than $191 million, compared to the just over $133 million raised by Gore.
- Less than 1 percent of the US population contributes more than 80 percent of all money in federal elections in amounts of $200 or more. The vast majority of such wealthy contributors are wealthy white men with annual family incomes higher than $100,000.
- Americans have the longest working hours and commuting times in the industrial world, further degrading capacities for civic engagement that are already gravely challenged by corporate media and the wildly disproportionate political and ideological influence exercised by the wealthy owners and managers of giant corporations. Long working hours also exacerbate widespread job dissatisfaction among the US population.
- Nine corporations own more than 50 percent of all American media (including both print and electronic), exercising a degree of concentrated private influence over public information, imagery, and consciousness that is without historical precedent.
- Reflecting mass disillusionment with big-money and media-dominated politics, American citizens boycott the ballot box in huge numbers, exhibiting the lowest voter turnout in the "democratic" world. By the 1990s, US turnout even in presidential elections had fallen to less than half of the adult population.
- While white men make up 43 percent of the Fortune 2000 workforce, they hold 95 percent of the Fortune 2000 senior management jobs.
- American schools and communities are so racially segregated that the average American black child's school is 57 percent black even though blacks make up only 12 percent of the nation's population.
- A typical black individual lives in a neighborhood that is only 33 percent white and more than 50 percent black.
- African Americans are twice as likely to be unemployed as whites. To attain equal employment in the US between blacks and whites, 700,000 more African Americans would have to be moved out of unemployment and nearly 2 million African Americans would have to be promoted into higher-paying positions.

- The poverty rate for blacks in the US is more than twice the poverty rate for whites.
- Black families' median household net worth is *less than 10 percent* that of whites. The average white household has a net worth of $84,000 whereas the average black household has a net worth of only $7,500.
- Nearly three-fourths of white families but less than half of black families own their homes.
- In 1999, there were 28,784 gun-related deaths in the US—over 80 such fatalities each day. Fifty-eight percent of these deaths were suicides and 38 percent were homicides.
- Firearms killed 3,365 children and teens aged 19 and under in 1999. Of these, 1,990 were murdered, 1,078 committed suicide, and 214 were victims of accidental shootings. (Details are not available for the balance of 83 fatalities.) Every day in the US, 9 children are killed by gun violence.
- In 1997, 6,416 young people 15 to 24 years old were murdered, and 6 percent of students reported carrying a firearm at least once in the previous thirty days.
- Almost two-thirds of children 7 to 10 years old in the US fear that they might die young.
- Domestic violence is the single greatest cause of injury to women in the US; four American women are murdered by a relative or a partner each day.
- More than 40 percent of US rivers, lakes, and estuaries are too polluted for safe fishing or swimming, and industry was allowed to legally dump more than 260 million tons of toxic chemicals directly into American waters in 2000.
- Each year, an estimated 18 million Americans suffer from depression and more than half of these people have major or clinical depression. Depression costs US business an estimated $70 billion in medical expenditures, lost productivity, and other expenses.
- Suicide took the lives of 29,350 Americans in 2000. It was the eleventh highest cause of death for all Americans but the third highest cause for 10– to 14–year-olds, 15– to 19–year-olds, and 20– to 24–year-olds.
- Sixty percent of marriages in the US end in divorce.
- Every year, 40,000 Americans, including 7,000 teenagers, die in automobile accidents.
- Only China, Saudi Arabia, and Iran execute more prisoners than the US.
- The US has the highest known death-row population in the world: thousands await execution.
- The nation that proclaims itself the homeland and headquarters of world freedom comprises 5 percent of the world's population but houses more than 25 percent of the world's prisoners.

- The rate of incarceration in the US is 699 per 100,000, up from roughly 100 per 100,000 in 1970. The next highest rate in the world is Russia at 644, and the American rate is six times higher than that of Britain, Canada, or France. "No other Western democratic country has ever imprisoned this proportion of its population," says Norval Morris, a professor emeritus at the University of Chicago Law School. He considers the high number of people held behind bars in the United States to be "appalling."
- Blacks are 12.3 percent of the US population, but they comprise roughly half of the approximately 2 million Americans currently behind bars.
- On any given day, 30 percent of African American males aged 20 to 29 are "under correctional supervision"—either in jail or prison or on probation or parole.
- In particular, huge numbers of Americans today are locked up for drug offenses and other transgressions that would not have met with the same punishment twenty years ago.
- Nearly one in five black men has a prison record, *an "astounding" one in three black men* now possesses a felony record, and one in four black adult males is an ex-felon, no longer serving time in prison or jail or on probation or parole.
- Blacks use roughly 15 percent of the illegal narcotics in the US but make up 60 percent of the nation's drug prisoners.
- George W. Bush owes his presence in the White House to the illegal removal of thousands of black ex-felons from voter rolls in Florida, a state run by his brother Jeb Bush. This pivotal purge, curiously downplayed by liberals who can't stop blaming Ralph Nader for the outcome of the 2000 elections, is recounted in sickening detail in the first chapter of Greg Palast's astonishingly good book *The Best Democracy That Money Can Buy*.[34]

"How You Gonna Export Something You Ain't Even Got at Home?"

The lists of social, economic, political, psychological, and ecological failures and of unmet civic and social needs in the US go on and on. These are enough, however, to suggest that America's power elite is in no legitimate position to make decisions of life, death, and sociopolitical development for the masses of the Middle East or anywhere else. What, after all, does it say about their plans for Iraqis and other world citizens when the Bush administration views a society with such grave internal problems (its own) as the "single sustainable model" of human and social development—the "beacon to the world," in Hutchison's words, "of the way life should be"?

On page 6 of Wednesday's *Chicago Sun Times,* I learned that "U.S. Will 'Shock and Awe' Iraq: General Says Civilians Almost Certain to Die." Further down, on page 22, I learned that "Chicago Will Choke." The story on that page reported that the disappearance of open space, the decrease in public transit use, and the addition of 1 millions cars will push the Chicago metropolitan area over the brink of ecological livability by 2030.

The United States, it seems to me, has got a few things to take care of at home before it has anything to tell others about how to pursue life, liberty, and happiness. As a doorman named Tony said to me the other day in a brief conversation about Bush's declared desire to bring democracy and freedom to the Iraqi people: "How you gonna export something you ain't even got at home?" Tony lives in a 95 percent African American neighborhood on Chicago's West Side, home to massive poverty, endemic violence, and five of the ten city zip codes that together receive nearly a fourth of Illinois' 20,000 released prisoners each year.[35]

As detailed in chapter 21, President Bush flew over the West Side last January on his way to a lakeshore meeting of the "Members Only" Chicago Economic Club. There he unveiled his plans to slash corporate and other taxes on the super-rich, throwing the country further into deficit even as he escalated the expensive, taxpayer-financed investment expected to bear fruit upon its initial return in the form of untold numbers of Iraqi corpses. Tony is from one of America's many invisible neighborhoods, bereft of campaign-finance clout, lacking lobbyists' pull. Like the invisible masses of Iraq, his community is not taken seriously by the regime that rules his "homeland." His community, too, is ready to have its already-considerable difficulties exacerbated by the plutocrats in the White House—the Great White Men who, with their assistants of color, scorn the habit of introspection. These power members of the "elite" see no use for the mirror other than to deflect light from the terrible truths of our time.

"How you gonna export something you ain't even got at home?" It's a damn good question, far better than anything I hear from people with advanced and professional degrees, crippled by the ideological discipline inculcated in those trusted with hierarchy's "creative" tasks of supervision, indoctrination, and strategic planning.

As we do our best to stop and, failing that, scale-back Mad King George's murderous attack on Iraq, we must also work to prevent future imperial projects by building a real and lasting democracy at home. For the good of the world at home and abroad, we Americans need to rip Hobson's taproot out of the ground. We need to create a genuinely democratic and sustainable model for all, starting with ourselves.

23
Deep Poverty, Deep Deception: Facts That Matter Beneath the Imperial Helicopters (Comments to the Illinois Welfare Reform Symposium)
June 17, 2003

I want to open with five quotations, all from Texas Republicans, three from the president of the United States, that speak to the dark and dubious times in which we live. The first, which we've seen before in this book, is from US Senator Kay Bailey Hutchison, making her case for authorizing George W. Bush to attack Iraq last fall. At the end of a five-minute oration that repeated many of the standard false reasons for assaulting that impoverished and defenseless nation, Hutchison came to an interesting and grammatically challenged conclusion. "Mr. President," she said, "we are going to meet this test of our generation. We are going to protect the freedom and the way of life that the beacon to the world of the way life should be. We can do no less."[36]

The second quote belongs to George W. Bush and was made six days ago at the Chicago Hilton, where the president promoted changes in Medicare to move more seniors into the private, for-profit health insurance system. Making reference to his last visit to Chicago, when he came here to sell his latest regressive tax cut, Bush claimed that "since I was here, thanks to the bravery of our military, the regime of Saddam Hussein is no more," and "the world is peaceful and free." "There are still terrorist networks which hate America," Bush claimed, "because of what we love. They hate us because we love our freedoms."[37]

The third quote also comes from Bush Junior and was made during his previous Chicago visit in January. Thanks to the efforts of its "business leaders and entrepreneurs," Bush told his audience then, "Chicago" is "a prosperous and energetic city." "We cannot be satisfied," he added, "until every part of our economy is healthy and vigorous."[38]

The fourth quote likewise comes from the lips of Bush the Lesser. It was uttered on the occasion of the national holiday honoring Martin Luther King, Jr., one week after Bush made public his decision to intervene against affirmative action for African Americans at the University of Michigan. "Even though progress has been made," Bush told a black church in Landover, Maryland, "there's more to do. There are still people in our society who hurt. There's still prejudice holding people back. . . . There's still a need for us to hear the words of Martin Luther King to make sure the hope of America extends its reach into every neighborhood across this land."[39]

The ff... recently been usefully rescued from the dustbin of novelist and activist Arundhati Roy. It comes from es parental context for the sharp disconnects be- and some of the facts I am about to present. The sh the First was campaigning for the presidency nent on the notorious Persian Gulf incident in r accidentally murdered 290 civil passengers on 't care what the facts are," the older Bush said; "I r the United States."[40]

to debate foreign policy or the reasons that for lo not hate us, but I do want to raise some qu ...ent to which America is a "beacon to the world" of the way life should be." I want to present some facts from Chicago that suggest both the limits of Chicago's "prosperity" and the considerable extent to which American freedom is translating into the "liberty" to be desperately poor for a considerably and very disproportionately black share of our city's children. And I'd like to say an unpleasant thing or two about the extent to which the Bush administration is concerned with helping the "people in our society who hurt" or with bringing health, vigor, and hope to "every neighborhood across this land."

The United States, the nation that shows the rest of the planet "the way life should be," is the industrialized world's most unequal state by far. The richest 10 percent of the population owns more than 70 percent of the nation's wealth, and the richest 5 percent of families receives as much income as the bottom 50 percent.

It would be one thing if this gross inequality were not accompanied by massive and increasing poverty at the bottom of the pyramid. But serious poverty is deeply, widely, and increasingly evident across the United States. Last year, as Hutchison called us the world's role model, America's Second Harvest, the nation's leading food-bank network, reported that 23 million Americans relied on its agencies in 2001. The year before that, the US Department of Agriculture reported that the number of Americans who were food insecure or hungry or at the risk of hunger was 34 million. And a couple of weeks before Hutchison's speech, the US Census Bureau reported that the proportion of Americans living in poverty had risen during the previous year to 33 million and from 11.3 to 11.7 percent of the population.[41]

There are two basic problems with using the poverty level to measure how badly poor people are faring in Bush's America. The first is that it is widely recognized to be an outdated and inappropriate measure of true hardship. Without getting into the methodological details, let me simply tell you that the official poverty threshold for a family consisting of one mother and two children in the United States is only *$14,494.* I defy anyone here to try to live decently at that level in Chicago with just yourself and two children. According to the Economic Policy Institute (EPI), the real no-frills cost of living for such a family in Chicago, based on what the EPI calls a basic family budget (one that takes into account housing, food, childcare, transportation, healthcare, and other necessities and taxes), was $35,307 in 2001.[42] The federal poverty level is only 41 percent of the real cost of being poor in Chicago.

The second problem is that you need to break down the official poverty population to see who is suffering most. Break that population down by age and you quickly see that kids are significantly poorer than adults. Children make up 26 percent of the total US population but 36 percent of the nation's poverty population. Here in Chicago, 19.6 percent of the overall population but 28 percent of the city's children were officially poor at the end of the twentieth century.

Break it down by race and you find that the poverty population is very disproportionately African American. In 2000, the poverty rate for African Americans was 22 percent, basically double the rate for the entire nation. Here in Chicago, the poverty rate for blacks is 29.4 percent and only 8.2 percent for whites. The poverty rate for black children in Chicago is 40 percent, compared to 8 percent for white kids. African Americans from Chicago alone account for 23.4 percent of all the officially poor people in the state of Illinois. African American kids from Chicago account for 29.4 percent of the state's poor kids.

Break it down by levels of misery and you find that a fair percentage of the official poverty population is *extremely poor.* More than 40 percent of the nation's 12 million poor children live in what researchers call "deep poverty," meaning that 5 million of those kids are actually living at *less than 50 percent* of the US poverty level.[43] Put differently, 7 percent of the nation's children live at less than one-fourth of the EPI's basic family budget level.

Combine the factors of age, race, and poverty level and you uncover some truly horrific facts. In a story that ought to have created a national sensation but quickly passed off the radar screen of public attention, researchers with the Children's Defense Fund (CDF) found that 1 million black children were living in deep poverty in 2001, up from "only" 686,000 in 2000—an accomplishment certain to be deleted from George W. Bush's reelection résumé in 2004.

The CDF report sent me running to the US Census in search of the detailed data that would help us get a handle on the extent, depth, and shape of poverty in Chicago. Let's look at some unpleasant facts of life, facts that ought to matter, in some of the neighborhoods that have recently been passed over by an openly imperialist president's helicopter team twice in the last six months.

While 19.6 percent of Chicago's population lived in poverty at the turn of the millennium, I learned, more than half of that population, 10 percent of the city's population, lived in deep poverty.

In Chicago, as throughout the country, there's a strong racial dimension to this poverty. In Chicago zip codes that have an above-average black population for the city, I found, 15 percent of the population lives in deep poverty. In the city's ten most African American zip codes, each more than 90 percent black, 17 percent—more than one in six people—lives in deep poverty.

Our most disturbing findings relate to children. Overall, I learned, at the time of the last census 103,212 Chicago kids lived in deep poverty. In fifteen of the city's seventy-seven officially designated Community Areas, moreover, more than 25 percent of the kids are growing up in deep poverty. There are six neighborhoods—Oakland, North Lawndale, Washington Park, Grand Boulevard, Douglass, and Riverdale—where more than 40 percent of the children are deeply poor and in the last one (Riverdale) it's actually more than half.

All but one of these fifteen neighborhoods are located in predominantly black stretches of Chicago's South and West Sides. The only exception is the Near North Side, which has the tenth-highest percentage of deep poverty kids—and anyone who knows the city can tell you that's because of the presence there of the Cabrini Green housing project. All but one of these community areas have a black population percentage that is considerably higher than the city average. All but three of them are at least 94 percent black.

There are eleven neighborhoods in Chicago with more than 3,000 deeply poor kids and two with more than 5,500 such kids. Forty-three percent of the city's deeply poor kids are found in those eleven neighborhoods.

It should be remembered, of course, that these numbers come from 2000, at the peak of the longest period of continuous American economic expansion since the 1960s. Things have certainly gotten considerably worse—poverty and child poverty have certainly widened and deepened in Chicago—during the last two and a half years.

Bush didn't lie when he said that there are people in our society who hurt. He was right when he cited Martin Luther King to advocate extending hope to all the nation's neighborhoods. But these sentiments are meaningless and disingenuous when they come from the White House. There isn't a single policy initiative emerging from the current party in federal power that is seriously or sincerely designed to alleviate the enormous, racially disparate "hurt" that is deepening in the American inner city beneath the fleeting shadows of the president's imperial helicopters. When we look honestly, in fact, we see that the trend of policy and politics is moving in precisely the opposite direction. We see a radically regressive right-wing political and policy juggernaut, falsely labeled "conservative," that is boldly determined to shift society and government once and for all away from expanding the public good, away from protecting children, and away from providing for the welfare of any but the privileged few.

The disturbing facts of neighborhood poverty that I just presented matter quite a great deal to most, probably all, of us here today. But to the key players in the current right-wing Beltway regime and their allies, they are irrelevant or at best a nuisance. The basic worldview driving this attitude is summarized quite well in a recent comment of Debbie Riddle, a Texas Republican state representative, who can't shake the lingering specter of Communism more than a decade after the end of the Cold War. "Where," asks Riddle, "did this idea come from that everybody deserves free education? Free medical care? Free whatever? It comes from Moscow. From Russia. It comes from the pit of hell." Also relevant is the recent remark of Grover Norquist, a leading right-wing political strategist in Washington, DC. "My goal," says Norquist, "is to cut government in half in twenty-five years, to get it down to the size where we can drown it in the bathtub."[44]

Of course, Norquist's followers target some parts of "government" for downsizing a little more energetically than others. They are most concerned with dismantling the parts of the public sector that serve the social and democratic needs of the nonaffluent majority of the American populace. The parts that provide "free" service and welfare to the privileged and opulent minority and dole out punishment to the poor are reserved from the budgetary ax.

The juggernaut's notion of a noble public work is to build yet another prison (there are many of these in America, the world's leading incarceration state), to attack and occupy a harmless but oil-rich nation halfway across the world, to build another expensive military base in yet another distant corner of the planet. Its core mission, its very raison d'être, is to concentrate wealth and power yet further upward, not to alleviate poverty and other and related forms of misery among the people. Its pretend idea of a meaningful response to Martin Luther King's clarion call to extend hope is yet more regressive tax relief for the wealthy few, yet harsher work requirements for the nation's deeply poor kids' welfare moms, and the insincere, victim-blaming insistence that marriage is the solution to poverty.

This political and policy regime is all about destroying hope and deepening despair among the people we care about in the social service and advocacy community. Under its rule we are witnessing a government that is nullifying its own charter social contract, poisoning democracy, and criminalizing and militarizing social problems at home and abroad.

We will never make serious progress against the problems that activate us without directly engaging this regime and the overall system of inequality and power that gave rise to it.

24
Forbidden Connections:
Class, Cowardice, and War
July 24, 2003

No Class Analysis

Beneath myths of equal opportunity and rampant upward mobility, the United States is a savagely unequal society with a rigidly hierarchical and authoritarian class structure. As a reflection of that harsh structural reality, it is nearly taboo to speak or write in any engaged and meaningful way about class inequality in the nation's "mainstream" (corporate-dominated) media and politics.

That mainstream can host a public debate over the use of race as a preferential factor in college and graduate and professional school admissions. Meanwhile, the richly aristocratic "legacy" system, whereby the affluent children of elite-school graduates receive a significant admissions boost at places like Harvard and Princeton, is beyond the pale of polite discussion and acceptable debate.

How interesting during the last year to watch one legacy product—the dull-witted Yale and Harvard graduate George W. Bush—order his Justice Department to intervene against the use of race as a factor in admissions to the University of Michigan. Bush then claimed to embrace affirmative action when the Supreme Court (unanimously filled by graduates of schools tainted by the legacy system), to which (along with the massive disenfranchisement of black voters in Florida) he owes his office, upheld affirmative action.

The mainstream gives vent to disgust over the revelation that America's great reactionary virtue magnate William J. Bennett hypocritically "lost more than $8 million" to the gambling industry during the last ten years. It says nothing about the higher immorality involved in the maintenance of a social structure wherein one man affordably entertains himself by cycling a sum of money greater than six times the *lifetime* earnings of most of his fellow citizens through slot machines.[45]

"Bring-'Em-On Bush"

An excellent example of class's marginalization in mainstream discourse is found in the short-lived brouhaha that emerged when Bush taunted Iraqi guerillas to attack American soldiers earlier this month. "There are some," an angry Bush told reporters on July 2, "that feel like if they attack us we may decide to leave prematurely. They don't understand what they are talking about if that is the case. . . . There are some who feel like the conditions are such that they can attack us there. My answer is, bring 'em on."[46]

It was a hell of a thing to say. On the same day that Bush blustered, Edward L. Andrews, a reporter for the *New York Times,* noted that "Iraq's plague of violence shows no signs of abating, as US soldiers face angry and vengeful Iraqis and unpredictable attacks in sweltering heat. The gunfire and bombing seemed to come from all directions today, leaving a trail of bitterness, confusion, and hunger for revenge."[47]

The next day, two months after Bush declared American "victory" in Iraq, eleven Iraqis ambushed a US convoy on a highway north of Baghdad and eighteen US soldiers were injured in a mortar attack in the same area. Another American soldier was shot to death guarding the Baghdad Museum.[48] The commander of allied forces in Iraq, Lt. General Ricardo S. Sanchez, acknowledged that "we're still at war" and offered a reward of up to $25 million for the capture of Saddam Hussein. Meanwhile, the US was begging other nations to help them more effectively contain the people of Iraq, an expensive and dangerous operation that the Bush administration never quite factored into its plan for world domination.

On July 10, the *New York Times* reported that 31 US soldiers had been killed since Bush declared the end of major combat, and CNN noted that 1,000 American troops had been injured since the US launched its war on March 20.[49] More have perished since, and, yes, more will die. More are going to perish, as the multimillionaire and former corporate CEO Donald Rumsfeld recently acknowledged.

Shocked and Appalled, to a Point

To their credit, mainstream voices responded quickly with criticism of the provocative "bring 'em on" comment, uttered in the elegant, air-conditioned confines of the White House's Roosevelt Room. We heard from Representative Richard A. Gephardt, who said he'd had "enough" of the president's "phony, macho rhetoric. I have a message for the president,"

Gephardt added, echoing the comments of many Democrats. "We need a clear plan to bring stability to Iraq and an honest discussion with the American people about the cost of that endeavor. We need a serious attempt to develop a postwar plan for Iraq and not more shoot-from-the-hip one-liners."[50] "When I served in Europe during World War II," said the incredulous Senator Frank Lautenberg, "I never heard any military commander—let alone the commander in chief—invite enemies to attack U.S. troops."[51] Leading Democratic presidential candidate Howard Dean weighed in, criticizing Bush for showing "insensitivity to the dangers" American GIs face.[52]

These basic sentiments seemed to have been shared by *Newsweek* reporter and commentator Howard Fineman. Fineman told MSNBC's Chris Matthews that Bush "tripped up" by "talking tough" when "over in Iraq our troops know that they are in trouble." "The president," Fineman added, "hasn't really explained" the US "plan" in Iraq, "and he doesn't help himself with that kind of thing." Fineman quoted from a postcard he recently received from "a friend who's a high-ranking officer in Iraq." "Have I got some news for you," the postcard read. "The reporters have just fled and the real stories have just begun. Iraq is a mess." Bush "didn't have a plan," Fineman notes, and "we don't have enough troops."

ABC's Diane Sawyer seemed appalled by Bush's comment. On July 7, she was astounded when General Tommy Franks told her that he "absolutely" agreed with Bush's "bring 'em on remark." "You do?!" Sawyer responded, with a look of disbelief on her face. White House reporter Terry Moran, hosting ABC News for the night, was also blown away. "Very interesting, Diane. The commanding general echoing the chief there, 'bring 'em on.'"[53]

Fortunate Son(s)

Yet while the mainstream expressed the legitimate sense that Bush's comment was "irresponsible," "insensitive," reflective of poor planning, and even unpatriotic, it could not note the cowardice and related rich class content of both the president's remark and American militarism. How "macho" is it, really, to dare Iraqis to attack not you but your distant (both spatially and socially), vulnerable, and exposed subordinates, stuck in the streets and sands of an ill-advised, unplanned occupation, opposed, we might add, from the beginning by the preponderant majority of politically conscious humanity?

Like many of fighting age from his privileged, super-wealthy circle, "bring-'em-on Bush" avoided real military service during the Vietnam War. He dodged the central military engagement of his time by "making occasional appearances at the Texas National Guard."[54] Given the opportunity to express his rugged, West Texas sentiments against the "Communist" enemies of American "freedom" in the jungles of Southeast Asia, he was content to leave the bloody and dirty work to the sons of the American working class. He recoiled in horror at the supposedly elitist antiwar movement but was pleased to egg on America's predominantly poor and working-class soldiers to murder and death from the sheltered sidelines of aristocratic advantage. His basic attitude and related position were perfectly captured and savagely ridiculed in the populist Vietnam-era antiwar rock anthem "Fortunate Son" (written by J. C. Fogarty of Credence Clear Water Revival in 1969), which railed against pampered aristocrats who were "born silver spoon in hand" and "made to wave the flag" and who sent less fortunate sons "down to war" while cheating on their taxes.

Now, Bush, truly the ultimate "Fortunate Son," has graduated—thanks to interrelated accidents of birth, campaign finance, electoral racism, oil, and Osama (a class brother)—to a higher role in the sociology of war, captured in Bob Dylan's "Masters of War" (1963), which savagely denounced those who "fasten the triggers, for the others to fire" and "sit back and watch while the death count gets higher. You hide in your mansions," Dylan added, "while young people's blood flows out of their bodies and gets buried in the mud."

It is essential, however, to note that Bush, Rumsfeld, and the rest of their super-affluent war party received carte blanche from the US Congress to pursue illegitimate war and imperial occupation in Iraq. Equally significant, the neo-imperial campaign has been consistently enabled, encouraged, and even largely driven by the corporate-state US media.

Among the children of the 435 members of the House of Representatives and of the 100 Senators (at least 90 percent of the latter are millionaires), it is worth noting, just one—a single, solitary Senator's son—has served in Operation Iraqi Freedom.

There is no available comparative data on the sons and daughters of war-profiteering media and "defense" company executives. Still, the existing data suggest that we will not find many of them among those who served in the supposed great struggle to save America and the world from Saddam Hussein.

"The Military Mirrors Working-Class America" and "Our Upper Class No Longer Serves"

Who exactly is stewing, dodging and taking bullets, dying, and killing in Iraq? According to the *New York Times,* in an important study released as the invasion moved into full swing, "a survey of the American military's endlessly compiled and analyzed demographics paints a picture of a fighting force that is anything but a cross section of America." The military, the *Times* found, "mirrors Working-Class America," resembling "the make-up of a two-year commuter or trade school outside Birmingham or Biloxi far more than that of a ghetto or barrio or four-year university in Boston." It is, "in essence, a working-class military," one that is "require[d] to fight and die for an affluent America."

Even among the officer ranks, notes Northwestern University sociologist Charles C. Moskos, affluent Americans are essentially missing. "The officer corps today," Moskos told the *Times*, "does not represent nobility. These are not people who are going to be future congressmen or senators. The number of veterans in the Senate and the House," he added, "is dropping every year. It shows you that our upper class no longer serves."

There is no draft, to be sure, but the "volunteer" military is full of people who enter because they lack, by accident of birth, access to America's standard middle-class pathway to career success. A key motive is the opportunity to learn a skill and to receive college tuition assistance, something the military offers as a bribe to lure recruits. "It's not fair," noted one young Army private quoted by the *Times*, "that some poor kids don't have much of a choice but to join if they want to be productive because they didn't go to a good school, or they had family problems that prevented them from doing well, so they join up and they're the ones that die for our country while the rich kids can avoid it."[55]

The formerly expendable and now officially celebrated Jessica Lynch provides a perfect example. Still severely injured due to her service in Bush's war, Lynch is the daughter of a truck driver from coal-mining territory in West Virginia's Wirt County. A fifth of that county's population, including more than a fourth of its children, lived beneath the federal government's notoriously inadequate poverty level at the peak of the 1990s economic boom.[56] Like numerous other young Americans from her socioeconomic cohort, Lynch joined the predominantly working-class ranks of the armed forces looking for more than immediate employment. She was also pursuing college tuition assistance to attain the educational certification so essential to making a decent living in the United States, the most unequal nation in the industrialized world. Military service is the price she and many other Americans pay for being born into the lower ranks of the American hierarchy. As one iconoclastic West Virginian puts it, "here in West Virginia, we have the highest enlistment per capita of any state. I suppose that speaks volumes about the opportunities this economy offers the young in these parts. Jobs in the coal mines aren't even very plentiful anymore. Jessica was one of the hopeful, looking for a way to get the skills and education she needed and eventually to return to her beloved mountain home. She sure got more than she bargained for in more ways than one."[57]

Armchair Cowboy

George W. Bush, who has led a life of privilege, far-removed from the US mainstream, likes to cultivate a folksy, faux-populist familiarity with

America's working class. Curiously enough, he and his handlers regularly screw that class over with a domestic policy that includes regressive taxes that play like something out of "Fortunate Son." And the closest Bush wants to come to hazardous military action is to sit in front of a television, to watch cruise missiles blow up in Baghdad, or to enjoy the thespian brilliance of his favorite action actor—the one-dimensional Cold War action hero Chuck Norris. Bush imagines himself, perhaps, a real-life Norris, striking fear into the hearts of those "evil" Arabs, who dared to attack God and History's chosen state, the center of "goodness" on earth, on September 11, 2001. In reality, he's an armchair cowboy from the effete circles of privilege, where supposed great men of power are happy to send young men and now young women of inferior social status to the military hospitals or to an early grave in the pursuit of imperial dreams that profit the privileged few. No, everything did not change on 9/11.

Notes for Part III

1. Noam Chomsky, *American Power and the New Mandarins* (New York: Pantheon, 2002 [reprint of 1966 edition]), p. 313.

2. Quoted in *New York Times*, June 22, 2003, sec. 4, p. 1.

3. US Senator Kay Bailey Hutchison, Senate Floor Speech, *Congressional Record, Proceedings and Records of the 107th Congress, Second Session* (October 9, 2002), p. S10149, available online at http://hutchison.senate.gov/speec274.htm.

4. To cringe at hundreds of statements that rival and even go beyond Hutchison's, see Marc Crispin Miller's *The Bush Dyslexicon: Reflections on a National Disorder* (New York: W. W. Norton, 2002).

5. Albright is quoted in William Pfaff, "Thinking with a Manichean Bent," *International Herald Tribune* (November 28, 2002).

6. Dobbins is quoted in Council on Foreign Relations, *Iraq: The Day After* (2002), which, in turn, is quoted in John Bellamy Foster, "The New Age of Imperialism," *Monthly Review* (July–August 2003), p. 12.

7. "The Repair of 'Broken Societies' Begins at Home," *ZNet Magazine* (July 18, 2003), available online at http://www.zmag.org/content/showarticle.cfm?SectionID=40&ItemID=3928.

8. David E. Sanger, "US Is Completing a Plan to Promote a Democratic Iraq," *New York Times* (January 6, 2003), p. A1.

9. Edmund Andrews, "Bush Budget Plan Would Eliminate Taxes on Dividends," *New York Times* (January 6, 2003), p. A1.

10. John Tierney, "Business Sees Its Chance to Be Heard," *New York Times* (January 6, 2003), p. A15; emphasis added.

11. Noam Chomsky, *What Uncle Sam Really Wants* (Berkeley, CA: Odonian, 1993), pp. 86–87, 94–95.

12. William D. Nordhaus, "Iraq: The Economic Consequences of War," *New York Review of Books* (December 5, 2002).

13. John J. Mearsheimer and Stephen M. Walt, "An Unnecessary War," *Foreign Policy* (January–February 2003).

14. Paul Krugman, "An Irrelevant Proposal," *New York Times* (January 7, 2003).

15. R. C. Longworth, "Ultimately, an Attempt at Major Tax Reform," *Chicago Tribune* (January 8, 2003), sec. 1, p. 1.

16. Scott Fornek and Curtis Lawrence, "President Unveils Economic Stimulus in Chicago," *Chicago Sun Times* (January 8, 2003), p. 1.

17. Bob Kemper, "Bush Touts 'Bold Plan' for the Economy," *Chicago Tribune* (January 8, 2003), sec. 1, p. 1.

18. Elizabeth Bubmiller, "A Bold Plan with a Risk," *New York Times* (January 8, 2003), p. A1; Richard Stevenson, "Bush Unveils Plan to Cut Taxes and Spur Economy," *New York Times* (January 8, 2003), p. A1; Edmund Andrews, "Plan Gives Most Benefits to Wealthy and Families," *New York Times* (January 8, 2003), p. A15.

19. Andrews, "Plan Gives Most Benefits to Wealthy." For an excellent graphic representation of the projected regressive outcomes, see the accompanying chart, provided to the *New York Times* by the noted Marxist research agency Deloitte and Touche.

20. Kemper, "Bush Touts 'Bold Plan.'"

21. Krugman, "An Irrelevant Proposal."

22. Longworth, "Ultimately, an Attempt at Major Tax Reform."

23. Paul Street, "Marriage as the Solution to Poverty: Bush's Proposal for Welfare Moms and the Real White House Agenda," *Z Magazine* (April 2002), pp. 33–39.

24. Calculations from 2000 US Census by the Chicago Urban League, Department of Research and Planning (January 2003).

25. An issue of the *Red Eye*, the *Chicago Tribune*'s silly effort to compete with "alternative" Chicago weekly papers like *The Reader* and *New City*, presented a picture of Hussein alongside the question "Nuke Him?" Readers were left to wonder how America might launch an atomic war directed at one man, even less plausible than Bush's claim last October that Iraq could *attack United States territory* with unmanned airplanes fitted to distribute chemical and biological weapons.

26. "Bush: Saddam Throwing Last Chance Away," *CNN.COM.US* (February 20, 2003), available online at http://www.cnn.com/2003/US/02/20/sprj.irq.bush.

27. Quoted in Eric Schmitt and Elizabeth Bubmiller, "Top General Sees Plan to Shock Iraq into Surrendering," *New York Times*, March 5, 2003, p. A1; Lynn Sweet, "U.S. Will 'Shock and Awe' Iraq," *Chicago Sun Times*, March 5, 2003, p. 6.

28. Text of Bush News Conference, *CBSNews.com* (March 7, 2003), available online at http://www.cbsnews.com/stories/2003/03/07/iraq/main543108.shtml.

29. George W. Bush, preface to *The National Security Strategy of the United States*, available online at http://usinfo.state.gov/journals/itps/1202/ijpe1202.pdf.

30. J. A. Hobson, *Imperialism: A Study* (Ann Arbor: University of Michigan Press, 1971 [1902]).

31. See William Appleman Williams, *The Great Evasion* (Chicago: Quadrangle, 1964).

32. *USA Today*, February 28, 2003.

33. The information presented below was found in a voluminous number of Internet websites, including www.penpress.org; www.centeronhunger.org/fsifacts.html; www.bread.org/hungerbasics/domestic.html; http://www.elca.org/

hunger/facts.html; http//:cpmcnet.columbia.edu/dept/nccp/ycpf-01.html; www.chausa.org/PUBLICPO/FOR ALL.ASP; www.fathom.com/course/56756004; www.coveringkids.org; www.cmwf.org; www.acde.org/common/Alcohol.htm; www.drugabuse.gov/NIDA_Notes/NNVol13N3/tearoff.html; www.infoplease.com/ce6/sci/A0816135.html; http://jama.ama-assn.org/issues/v284n13/ffull/jlt1004-4/html; and "Obesity Trends" at www.cdc.gov/nccdphp/dnpa/obesity/trend/prev_reg.htm; www.surgeongeneral.gov/topics/obesity/calltoaction/fact_glance.htm; www.americandrivingacademy.com/facts.html; http://wheres-daddy.com.fatherhood/divorce.htm; www.gun-control-network.org/facts.htm; www.ems.org/cleanwater/sub2_cleanwater.html; www.cdc.gov/ncipc/factsheets/yvfacts.htm; www.cdfactioncouncil.org/americayc.htm; www.wshe.org/facts.html; www.ncpc.org/11stat.htm; www.soparents.org/facts.html; www.ojp.usdoj.gov/bjs/cvictgen.htm; www.ichv.org/Statistics.htm; www.effexor.com/resources/media/fact_depression.jhtml; http://ethos4.wustl.edu/DepressionFacts.html; www.cdc.gov/nchs/fastats/suicide.htm; www.ndmda.org/DepressionFacts.html; and http:/ /mumford1.dyndns.org/cen2000/wholePop/WPreport/. For race statistics, see especially the National Urban League's latest annual report *State of Black America*. For incarceration stats, see Paul Street, *The Vicious Circle*, available online at www.cul-chicago.org. See also the special appendix following this chapter.

34. Greg Palast, *The Best Democracy That Money Can Buy* (London: Pluto Press, 2002).

35. Street, *The Vicious Circle*.

36. US Senator Kay Bailey Hutchison, Senate Floor Speech, *Congressional Record, Proceedings and Records of the 107th Congress, Second Session* (October 9, 2002), p. S10149, available online at http://hutchison.senate.gov/speec274.htm.

37. George W. Bush, "Remarks to the Illinois Sate Medical Society" (June 11, 2003), available online at http://www.whitehouse.gov/news/releases/2003/06/20030611-4.html.

38. George W. Bush, "Remarks to the Economic Club of Chicago" (January 7, 2003), available online at http://www.whitehouse.gov/news/releases/2003/01/20030107-5.html.

39. Quoted in Sean Loughlin, "Bush Honors King: Tribute Comes Amid Renewed Debate on Affirmative Action," *CNN.com/Inside Politics* (January 21, 2003), available online at http://www.cnn.com/2003/ALLPOLITICS/01/20/politics.mlk/.

40. Quoted in Arundhati Roy, "Instant Mix Imperial Democracy (Buy One, Get One Free)," speech delivered to the Riverside Church, New York City (May 13, 2003), available online at http://www.commondreams.org/views03/0518-01.htm.

41. Robert Pear, "Number of People Living in Poverty Increases in US," *New York Times* (September 25, 2002); Food Research and Action Council, *State of the States* (2001), available online at http://www.frac.org/html/federal_food_programs/states.us.pdf.

42. Economic Policy Institute, *Hardships in America: The Real Story of Working Families* (Washington, DC: Economic Policy Institute, 2001), pp. 1–43, Table A4.2.

43. Robert Rector, "Despite Recession, Black Child Poverty Plunges to All Time Historic Low," Heritage Foundation (September 27, 2002), p. 5, available online at http:www.heritage.org/Research/Welfare/BG1595.cfm.

44. Both Riddle and Norquist are quoted in Henry Giroux, "War Talk, the Death of the Social, and Disappearing Children: Remembering the Other War,"

Cultural Studies Conference, Pittsburgh, PA (June 5, 2003), in the author's possession.

45. US Census Bureau, *The Big Payoff: Educational Attainment and Synthetic Estimates of Work-Life Earnings* (July 2002).

46. Quoted in Sean Loughlin, Bush Warns Militants Who Attack U.S. Troops in Iraq," *CCN.Com/INSIDEPOLITICS* (July 3, 2003), available online at http://www.cnn.com/2003/ALLPOLITICS/07/02/sprj.nitop.bush/index.html.

47. Edward L. Andrews, "In Day of Violence, Attacks from All Directions," *New York Times* (July 2, 2003), p. A16.

48. "Attack Leaves US Soldier Dead, 18 Hurt," *USA Today* (July 4, 2003).

49. This CNN report is available online at http://truthout.org/docs_03/071103C.shtml.

50. Quoted in Loughlin, "Bush Warns Militants Who Attack U.S. Troops in Iraq."

51. Quoted in "White House Defends Bush Remarks on Iraq Attacks: Democrats Slam President for 'Bring 'Em On' Challenge," *CNN.Com/INSIDEPOLITICS* (July 3, 2003), available online at http://www.cnn.com/2003/ALLPOLITICS/07/02/sprj.nitop.bush/index.html.

52. Quoted in James W. Pindell, "In New Hampshire, Democrats Criticize Bush's Language over Iraq," *PoliticsNH.COM* (July 4, 2003), available online at http://www.politicsnh.com/archives/pindell/2003/July/7_4.shtml.

53. Quoted in "Franks Defending Bush's 'Bring 'Em On' Comments Astounds ABCers," *Media Research Center* (July 8, 2003), available online at http://www.mediaresearch.org/cyberalerts/2003/cyb20030708.asp#1.

54. Eric Margolis, "Bring 'Em On, Bush," *Toronto Star* (July 3, 2003).

55. David M. Halbfinger and Steven A. Holmes, "Military Mirrors Working-Class America," *New York Times,* March 30, 2003.

56. US Census, *Census 2000 Summary File 3—Wirt Country, West Virginia.*

57. Anne Tatelin, "The Gospel According to Jessica Lynch," at http://wheresmypants.net/jessica.htm.

Appendix for
"Mirror, Mirror on the Wall..."

On race statistics, see the National Urban League's latest annual report *State of Black America*. See also the studies cited on the website of the Lewis Mumford Center as well as perhaps the Harvard Civil Rights Project.

On the Hutchison speech, see http://hutchison.senate.gov/speec274.htm.

On trust in the US Congress, see Gallup News Services (1997), cited on the website of the Public Education Network at www.penpress.org.

On the fact that the average American watches 3 hours and 46 minutes of TV each day, see Nielsen Media Research (1999), cited on the website of the Public Education Network at www.penpress.org.

On the fact that white men comprise 43 percent of the Fortune 2000 workforce but hold 95 percent of senior management jobs there, see US Department of Labor, *Glass Ceiling Commission Report*, cited on the website of the Public Education Network at www.penpress.org.

On hunger and food insecurity, see Center on Hunger and Poverty, "National Facts and Figures on Hunger and Food Insecurity in the U.S.," at www.centeronhunger.org/fsifacts.html; Bread for the World, "Hunger Basics," at www.bread.org/hungerbasics/domestic.html; and ELCA, "Facts About Hunger and Poverty" at http://www.elca.org/hunger/facts.html.

On child poverty, see National Center for Children in Poverty, "Child Poverty Fact Sheet" (June 2001), at http://cpmcnet.columbia.edu/dept/nccp/ycpf-01.html.

On food that goes to waste in the US, see U.S. Department of Agriculture, "A Citizen's Guide to Food Recovery" (1999), cited on the website of the Public Education Network at www.penpress.org.

On petfood and world hunger, see United Nations Development Programme, Human Redevelopment Report (1998), cited on the website of the Public Education Network at www.penpress.org.

On the uninsured in the US, see Phyllis Baxandall, "How U.S. Health Care Stacks Up Internationally," *Dollars and Sense Magazine* (May/June 2001); The Catholic Health Association of the United States at www.chausa.org/PUBLICPO/FORALL.ASP; and FATHOM, the source for online learnings at www.fathom.com/course/56756004. On uninsured kids in the US, see www.coveringkids.org.

On alienation from the US healthcare system, see "United States Adults' Health Care System: Views and Experiences, 2001" at www.cmwf.org.

On alcoholism, see American Council for Drug Education, Basic Facts About Drugs and Alcohol at www.acde.org/common/Alcohol.htm.

On cigarette addiction, see NIDA Notes, "Facts About Nicotine and Tobacco Products," at www.drugabuse.gov/NIDA_Notes/NNVol13N3/tearoff.html.

On the fact that the US has the highest substance-abuse rate of any industrialized nation, see www.infoplease.com/ce6/sci/A0816135.html.

On obesity, see "The Continuing Epidemic of Obesity in the US" at http://jama.ama-assn.org/issues/v284n13/ffull/jlt1004–4/html; "Obesity Trends" at www.cdc.gov/nccdphp/dnpa/obesity/trend/prev_reg.htm; and www.surgeongeneral.gov/topics/obesity/calltoaction/fact_glance.htm.

On car accidents and alcohol-driving deaths, see American Driving Academy, "The Facts," at www.americandrivingacademcy.com/facts.html.

On the death-row population and racial disparities in capital crimes and executions, see the US Department of Justice's Bureau of Justice Statistics and Amnesty International's 1998 "USA Human Rights Report," both cited on the website of the Public Education Network at www.penpress.org.

On divorce, see *Demography*, Vol. 27.4 (1990), at http://wheres-daddy.com.fatherhood/divorce.htm.

On auto fatalities, see US Department of Transportation (1999), cited on the website of the Public Education Network at www.penpress.org.

On gun-related deaths/suicides, including international comparison data, see the facts and sources cited by "USA Statistics" at www.gun-control-network.org/facts.htm.

On pollution, see Environmental Media Services, "Fast Facts," at www.ems.org/cleanwater/sub2_cleanwater.html.

On youth violence/homicide, see Center for Disease Control, "Youth Violence in the US," at www.cdc.gov/ncipc/factsheets/yvfacts.htm, and "Facts on Youth Violence and Crime" at www.cdfactioncouncil.org/americayvc.htm.

On domestic violence and violence against women and girls, see Women's

Supported Housing and Empowerment at www.wshe.org/facts.html and "Fast Crime Facts" at www.ncpc.org/11stat.htm.

On televised violence and the fact that kids are spending lots of time watching TV (more than the hours they spend in school), see Center for Successful Parenting at www.soparents.org/facts.html.

On violent crime rates, see www.ojp.usdoj.gov/bjs/cvictgen.htm.

On kids killed by guns, the number of guns owned and manufactured, and the number of firearm suicides in the US, see Illinois Council Against Handgun Violence at www.ichv.org/Statistics.htm.

On mental illness, depression, and suicide, see www.effexor.com/resources/media/fact_depression.jhtml; http://ethos4.wustl.edu/DepressionFacts.html; www.cdc.gov/nchs/fastats/suicide.htm; and www.ndmda.org/DepressionFacts.html.

On racial segregation, see Lewis Mumford Center, "Ethnic Diversity Grows, Neighborhood Diversity Lags Behind" at http://mumford1.dyndns.org/cen2000/wholePop/WPreport/.

On rates of incarceration, see Paul Street, *The Vicious Circle: Race, Prison, Jobs and Community in Chicago, Illinois, and the Nation* (Chicago: Chicago Urban League, 2002). See also Street, "Color Bind...," *Dissent Magazine* (2001), which can be viewed at www.cul-chicago.org (click on "Research Reports Now Available Online").

On inequalities in wealth and income in the US, just go to www.yahoo.com and plug in "wealth" and "inequality" and "United States" (do the same for "income"), and you will find an abundance of material.

Index

Index

Index

Index

About the Author

Paul Street is an urban social policy researcher and teacher in Chicago. He holds a Ph.D. in modern United States history from Binghamton University. He writes regulary for *Z Magazine, Black Commentator,* and *ZNet Magazine.*